Routledge Revivals
I0113007

Organisation Theory and Local Government

Originally published in 1980, this book provides an analysis and assessment of events in local government management during the late 20th Century set within an overall conceptual framework of organisation theory. The book fills the gap between theoretical prescription and practical management application. The analysis focuses on three areas of organisation design and functioning – the structural, the procedural and the cultural. In each of these areas the interrelationship between broad theoretical prescriptions and the actual management innovations introduced in local authorities is examined. A major portion of the book is devoted to an assessment of the importance of behavioural/cultural factors in the introduction and assimilation (or rejection) of managerial change, an aspect of organisational functioning which was neglected in the literature on local government management.

Organisation Theory and Local Government

Robert J. Haynes

Routledge
Taylor & Francis Group

First published in 1980 by George Allen & Unwin Ltd

This edition first published in 2024 by Routledge
4 Park Square, Milton Park, Abingdon, Oxon, OX14 4RN
and by Routledge
605 Third Avenue, New York, NY 10158.

Routledge is an imprint of the Taylor & Francis Group, an informa business

ISBN 13: 978-1-032-95006-8 (hbk)
ISBN 13: 978-1-003-58281-6 (ebk)
ISBN 13: 978-1-032-95023-5 (pbk)
Book DOI 10.4324/ 9781003582816

ORGANISATION THEORY AND LOCAL GOVERNMENT

ROBERT J. HAYNES
Senior Lecturer in Public Administration,
Wolverhampton Polytechnic

London
GEORGE ALLEN & UNWIN
Boston   Sydney

First published in 1980

GEORGE ALLEN & UNWIN LTD
40 Museum Street, London WC1A 1LU

© Robert J. Haynes, 1980

British Library Cataloguing in Publication Data

Haynes, Robert J
    Organisation theory and local government. – (New local government series; no. 19).
    1. Organizational change – Great Britain
    2. Local government – Great Britain
    I. Title   II. Series
    352.041   JS3512.0/   80–40333

    ISBN 0–04–352088–X
    ISBN 0–04–352089–8 Pbk

Set in 10 on 11 point Times by Trade Linotype Ltd, Birmingham and printed in Great Britain
by Billing and Sons Ltd, Guildford, London and Worcester

CONTENTS

To Wilfred Austin Latham

PREFACE

The purpose of this book is to provide an analysis of recent innovations in local government management within an overall conceptual framework of organisation theory. The particular relevance of such an approach has been re-emphasised by the need to analyse and interpret the fairly traumatic events of the 1970s, especially the advent of the corporate management revolution and the subsequent problems of its assimilation in local authorities.

A tripartite framework of organisational design and functioning is used as an aid to analysis and assessment. Within this framework the structural, procedural and cultural aspects of the innovations introduced in local authorities are each shown to draw on specific areas of organisation theory. However, it is the close interrelationship and interdependence which exists between these three aspects which forms the central theme of the book. Case study material is used to emphasise that a lack of correlation and adjustment between the three aspects, caused by the lack of a comprehensive and fully integrated approach to the initiation and introduction of change, can have serious consequences in terms of internal conflict and, in extreme cases, a complete negation of a reform strategy.

The work does not set out to provide an exhaustive survey of the literature of organisation theory. Rather, it takes as its overall objective an analysis of theory in action in the context of local government management. It is hoped that this treatment will assist both students and practitioners to relate broad theoretical prescriptions to practical management situations in local authorities.

The book has been designed to meet the needs of students studying local government and public sector management on degree courses and professional courses such as those sponsored by the Local Government Training Board (CMA/DMA) and the Chartered Institute of Public Finance and Accountancy. It is hoped that the book will also prove useful for students studying for the new BEC Higher National awards in public administration.

Many people have contributed to the completion of this project. In particular I wish to express my sincere gratitude to all those officers and members of Birmingham Metropolitan District Council who gave their time and assistance during the compilation of material for the case study. I also wish to thank Professor Peter Richards of the University of Southampton and Doctor W. P. Grant of the University of Warwick for their helpful comments and suggestions.

Figure 3 appeared originally in an article of mine in *Local Government Studies* and I am grateful to the editor, Alan Norton, and the publishers, Charles Knight, for their permission to reproduce it here.

A special vote of thanks must go to my friend and colleague Martin Grocott for the many hours he spent reading through the drafts, making many useful practical suggestions on presentation and providing invaluable assistance by engaging the author in constructive debate and argument. In a very real sense this is as much his book as it is mine.

Last but by no means least I should like to thank my wife Claire for putting up with the many household disruptions suffered whilst the project was in progress and Barbara Abbott who typed the whole manuscript with her usual speed and accuracy.

Wolverhampton 1979   ROBERT J. HAYNES

PART ONE

THEORY AND APPLICATION:
THE STRUCTURAL ASPECT

Chapter 1

THE PRISONER OF CLASSICAL DESIGN

CLASSICAL AND MODERN PERSPECTIVES

A broad classification of organisation and administrative theory into classical and modern branches has little chronological significance. The terminology merely serves to distinguish between two perspectives associated with the body of theoretical knowledge which is concerned with the structure and functioning of human organisations and the interrelationships and behaviour of individuals and groups within them.

The classical perspective is characterised by a preoccupation with the achievement of internal, machine-like efficiency within an organisation. This objective is sought through the imposition of rigid, hierarchical structures and authoritarian practices and procedures. In contrast the perspective associated with modern organisation theory tends to emphasise the fact that organisations are more like living organisms than machines and that it is important to recognise both the informal relationships which exist within them and the interactions which take place between the organisation and the wider social and technological environment in which it exists.

It would be misleading to represent modern theory as completely supplanting classical concepts and rendering them obsolete. A more accurate assessment of the respective positions of the two branches of theory must involve recognition of the fact that classical principles can still be usefully applied and indeed make a meaningful and legitimate contribution to the development of ideas about how organisations should be structured and managed. Modern organisation theory merely calls for the recognition of classical theory's limitations. More specifically it calls for realisation of the fact that classical theory is based on a unidimensional and therefore oversimplified perception of the multidimensional and highly complex phenomenon which is the human organisation. Once their limitations are recognised and the need for substantial augmentation is accepted then classical principles and concepts can still provide a useful analytical framework, a backcloth against which the other dimensions of organisational dynamics can be placed.

Within the area of local government organisation the limitations of classical prescriptions have only recently been given tangible recognition. In this sense, local government organisation has been out of step with theoretical developments. This has been true within the field of public administration in general as Garrett observes:

> Though the focus of present day organisation theory is on the construction and evaluation of models of the sub-structures and integrating mechanisms of complex organisations . . . the principles of the classicists still determine the form of most organisations in public administration. (Garrett, 1972, p. 82)

In the particular context of local government organisation Baker has noted that:

> until very recently all discussion of management and organisation in local government . . . implicitly assumed frameworks of thinking which were identical with those of the earliest classical management theorists. (Baker, 1975, pp. 21–2)

Why has there been this preoccupation with classical theory in the public sector? In this chapter we will examine the special utility or usefulness of classical principles for local government organisation. This will be explained by reference to the apparent relevance and appropriateness of classical design, given the special operational requirements experienced by local authorities operating within the framework of a democratic political system.

HENRI FAYOL AND MAX WEBER – FOUNDING FATHERS OF CLASSICAL THEORY

The consequence of a preoccupation with classical prescriptions has been a long-term adherence to what such leading advocates of classical theory as Henri Fayol (1916), L. F. Urwick (1943) and J. D. Mooney (1954) deemed to be universally applicable principles of management and administration. The universalist assumption is that, despite all the functional and environmental variations which serve to differentiate individual organisations, it is still possible to identify certain basic administrative principles which can be applied generally.

Fayol's exposition of the general principles of administrative organisation, contained in his definitive work 'Administration industrielle et generale', asserts his belief in the value of strong centralised authority, discipline and obedience. He was essentially concerned with the advocacy of the precise definition and rational division of functions in orderly hierarchical structures where authority is concentrated and clearly identified and where the emphasis is on order, clarity and simplicity.

Fayol includes the following among his general principles:

1 Division of work
2 Authority
3 Discipline
4 Unity of command
5 Unity of direction
6 Subordination of individual interests to the general interest
7 Centralisation
8 Scalar chain of authoritative communication
9 Order
10 Initiative

Fayol sees specialisation of function and division of work as part of the natural order of things, a principle which can be seen in operation at any time in nature and biology. The object of the principle is to increase ability by repetition and avoid the waste of productive capacity inherent in the process of continual adjustment made necessary by task and skill variation: 'The worker always on the same part, the manager concerned always with the same matters, acquire an ability, sureness and accuracy which increase their output' (Fayol, 1971 translation, p. 20).

Authority is defined by Fayol as the right to give orders and the power to exact obedience. The need for the existence of authority and the presence of suitable sanctions (penalties) arises from the need to encourage useful actions, that is, those which are generally beneficial to the interest of the organisation, and to discourage disruptive or harmful actions. Outward respect for authority is one manifestation of discipline within an organisation. According to Fayol discipline (as essential to the effective organisation as to an army during wartime) is best established and maintained by ensuring a high quality of leadership and a judicious application of sanctions.

Fayol places great emphasis on the importance of the principle of unity of command, the infringement of which can undermine authority, put discipline in jeopardy and seriously threaten order and stability. Unity of command exists within an organisation when, for any action, an employee receives orders from one superior only. The principle is infringed when dual command exists, that is, where an employee is subjected to the commands of two or more superiors. Such dual command can be the source of irritation and dissatisfaction among superiors and confusion, hesitation and consequent inefficiency on the part of employees. Fayol points out that dual command often arises from a failure to make explicit the demarcation of responsibility as between departments or the failure to describe accurately and precisely an individual's duties and area of functional competence.

Closely linked to the principle of unity of command is the principle of unity of direction. The latter is defined by Fayol as simply meaning 'one head and one plan for a group of activities having the same objective'. Fayol expresses the principle in a rather more dramatic way when he points out that: 'A body with two heads is in the social, as in the animal sphere, a monster, and has difficulty in surviving' (1971, p. 25). The principle of unity of direction reinforces the need for unity of action, and for focusing and concentrating effort if objectives are to be achieved efficiently and effectively.

Fayol points to the perpetual war which rages between the selfish interest of the individual and the general interest of the organisation. The need somehow to reconcile these two spheres of interest is presented as one of the great difficulties of management. It also represents one of the most basic underlying themes of the human relations school of thought which will be discussed more fully later. At this point, however, it is useful to note that whereas the human relations theorists such as Mayo, Argyris and McGregor put forward fairly complex solutions to this problem, for example, by advocating sophisticated methods and psychological approaches to management which would result in the individual's equation of his own selfish interest with the best interests of his organisation, Fayol's solution is more direct and straightforward. He advocates a reliance upon firmness and good example on the part of superiors and, in a rather more authoritarian vein, constant supervision. This serves to highlight a basic difference between the somewhat simplistic, authoritarian approach adopted by the classical theorists, and that associated with modern theories which tend to place the emphasis on the need to understand and interpret the complex social interactions which take place between the individual, the work group, and the total organisation.

For Fayol, centralisation is as natural as the specialisation of function and division of work, although he does emphasise that as a principle of management it needs to be applied with some flexibility. Its appropriateness is normally a diminishing function of scale in that the need for delegation to sub-groups and sub-units of the organisation increases with the size and complexity of the organisational task.

Scalar chain is the term used by Fayol to describe the critical path of authority communications from the lowest ranks through a

```
                    A
                 B     L
               C         M
             D             N
           E     Gang-plank   O
         F ◄ ─ ─ ─ ─ ─ ─ ► P
         G                   Q
```

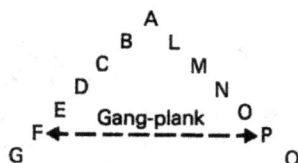

Figure 1 The scalar chain of command

chain of superiors to the highest levels of authority and responsibility in the organisation. This line of authority communications must be clearly laid down and must follow as closely as possible the principle of unity of command. The diagram in Figure 1 is used by Fayol to represent the scalar chain of authority in a fictitious organisation (1971, p. 34). If the scalar principle is followed F's line of communication with P must pass through E–D–C–B–A–L–M–N–O. Clearly, regard for the scalar principle must somehow be reconciled with the need for speedy communication and action. Fayol recognised this problem and introduced the concept of the gang-plank, a device whereby F can contact P directly by short-circuiting the scalar chain. It would appear that by doing this Fayol is establishing a principle of management and then destroying its validity. However, he emphasises that the scalar principle is still important and is not invalidated by the introduction of more direct avenues of communication. The principle is protected so long as the immediate superiors of the two subordinate communicators have specifically authorised direct communication and so long as they are kept informed of the outcomes of such communication. In summary, Fayol thought it an error to depart needlessly from the agreed line of authority communication within an organisation but saw as an even greater error blind adherence, when this could be to the detriment of efficient operation.

Fayol's belief in material and social order within an organisation, 'a place for everyone and everyone in his place', leads logically to his advocacy of the organisation chart as a means of establishing and controlling human arrangement. Slightly less logical, however, is his encouragement of the development and use of initiative on the part of employees, a quality which, as we shall see later, is generally observed to be effectively stifled within the rigidly ordered, hierarchical type of organisation which is the structural outcome of the application of his major principles. However, Fayol's call for the encouragement of initiative must be seen against his simultaneous emphasis on the need to keep such development 'within the limits imposed by respect for authority and for discipline'.

For Fayol and other classical theorists the forecast result of adherence to these principles was optimal task performance and maximum goal achievement, the continued attainment of which would be aided by the continuity and precision associated with the formal disciplined organisation.

This reliance on formal structure and authoritarian assumptions as a means of achieving and maintaining efficiency in management is the principal characteristic of the classical perspective. It takes as its foundation a Weberian belief in the technical superiority of the bureaucratic organisational form and the rational/legal authority system which it sustains.

Max Weber (1864–1920) was a German sociologist whose main contribution to organisation theory was a classification of organisations by reference to their type of internal authority system and in particular the basis upon which authority within an organisation establishes a claim to legitimacy. Weber (1947 translation, p. 328) distinguished between three types of authority system:

1 The charismatic
2 The traditional
3 The rational/legal

The charismatic authority system is founded simply upon the personal qualities and character of an individual leader. Obedience is demanded through the leader's own claim to moral authority. The system is clearly unstable over time given the relative fragility of such an individual's position.

The second type of authority system rests purely on the strength of custom with the location of authority being determined by tradition, as, for example, with the passing of authority from father to son in a family business. In this system rationality gives way to a blind acceptance of historical precedent.

The third type of authority system is, for Weber, far superior to the other two. In the rational/legal system authority is vested in an impersonal order, or body of impersonal rules, to which all who fall within its sphere of jurisdiction are equally subject. Weber demonstrated that this type of authority system forms the basis of the bureaucratic organisational form.

For Weber the ideal bureaucratic organisation was essentially the well-designed machine within which all the component parts work efficiently and without distraction towards the maximum attainment of some clearly defined goal or goals. Structurally the emphasis is on:

1 A functionally specialised and firmly ordered hierarchy with each level of authority subject to supervision and control by the level immediately above it.

2   The presence of a comprehensive impersonal body of rules and standardised procedures.
3   The clear, precise definition of the rights, duties and scope of authority for each and every office within the hierarchy.
4   Fitness for any office within the hierarchy being determined by objective assessment of technical competence, for example, by means of prescribed examination and qualification.

The structure is presented as imparting rationality and efficiency in the attainment of organisational objectives through the means of effective co-ordination and control, consistency and predictability, and an emphasis on the depersonalisation of all administrative matters.

Consistency and predictability are assured because of the preponderance of rules and routine procedures theoretically designed to meet every possible contingency. Control is assured because of the existence within the organisation of legitimate authority based on rational grounds. This means that the exercise of authority does not depend upon the strength of traditional association, or on the charismatic qualities of an individual, but rests instead upon the general recognition of the legitimate right of a particular office within the hierarchy to exercise such authority. This right is automatically attributed to an office by virtue of its status position within the organisation and because of its technical competence (only those with appropriate qualifications are allowed to hold a particular office). Thus commands issued within the organisation, so long as they fall within the prescribed area of competence of the issuing office, are underpinned by legitimate authority or legal authority and are therefore obeyed voluntarily by subordinates.

The rationality of the bureaucratic form is further advanced by the emphasis placed on what Weber calls the 'spirit of formalistic impersonality'. By this is meant administration without hatred or passion, without affection or enthusiasm:

> The dominant norms are concepts of straightforward duty without regard to personal considerations. Everyone is subject to formal equality of treatment; that is, everyone in the same empirical situation. This is the spirit in which the ideal official conducts his office. (Weber, 1947, p. 340)

The classical perspective has been examined here by reference to the work of its two principal founding fathers. It has been presented as being characterised by a mechanistic view of organisation which places great reliance on formal structure and authoritarian assumptions. For the classicists all organisational ills must be the result of some form of structural inadequacy or some weakness in the formalisation of rules and procedures. To take a biological analogy, the classical approach is preoccupied with skeletal and muscular design and tends to ignore the nervous systems of organisations and the subtle environmental, social and psychological factors which invariably exert such a great influence upon their functioning.

However, despite their limitations classical design principles, with their concentration on the logical ordering of complex organisations involving large labour forces, still have a great deal of practical relevance for managers in large organisations. It is the relevance of classical theory to the operational practicalities of organisational life which, as we shall see, goes far to explain the long-term utilisation of its principles, particularly within the field of local public administration.

TRADITIONAL LOCAL GOVERNMENT ORGANISATION – THE PRISONER OF OPERATIONAL REQUIREMENT

In the field of local government administration prolonged adherence to classical principles can be explained by reference to certain operational requirements which gradually assumed crucial importance as the work of local authorities developed. These operational requirements were:

1 The need to cope with the logistical problems which accompanied the growth in the scale and complexity of administrative tasks.
2 The need to provide impartial and accountable administration.

The growth in the size and complexity of the administrative task facing local authorities was due primarily to the assumption of responsibility by government for a whole range of social, environmental and economic functions which it had not discharged before. Most of the functions carried out by local authorities today can be seen as having their roots in the Industrial Revolution and the demands of a new, urbanised industrial society. More recently, the development of local services can be seen as forming part of the larger national movement towards the creation of a welfare state, a movement which was based on the general acceptance in the present century of the principle that, in the last resort, national resources can and must be used for the promotion of the common good. It is not the place here to enter into a detailed description of the historical sequences involved in these national developments. However, the connection between the historical development of services and administrative organisation is well illustrated by a brief reference to the formative years of Birmingham Corporation which provided a model for local government organisation both in this country and abroad (Briggs, 1952).

The embryonic corporation formed in December 1838 initially shared the government of the borough with several other local bodies which had been created by previous Acts of Parliament. Notable amongst these bodies were the Birmingham Commissioners of Street Acts, with powers of paving, lighting and cleaning streets, markets, and so on, and the Guardians of the Poor of Birmingham, which had the power to appoint officers and raise revenue for the purpose of improving the administration of the poor law. Such bodies levied rates, exercised authority, and absorbed important departments of administration. The new corporation had to content itself with a limited range of functions which included providing and maintaining a police force and goal, a lunatic asylum and baths and wash-houses. It also had responsibility for administering the control of weights and measures. It was not until the passing of the Birmingham Improvement Act in 1851 that the municipal corporation was established as the principal local authority for the area. This act endowed the corporation with all the powers of control over the local environment and provision of civic amenities.

The drive, energy and foresight of Joseph Chamberlain during his period of mayoral office in Birmingham between 1873 and 1876 led to Birmingham's emergence as a pioneer of municipal enterprise and organisation. Chamberlain, a successful local industrialist, was ashamed and horrified by the existence of the conditions which had produced a death rate of fifty-three per thousand in Birmingham in the late 1860s. He was determined to put an end to neglect and misgovernment. To this end he embarked upon the methodical destruction of slums and the adoption of great housing schemes, the acquisition and development of gas and water undertakings and the provision of parks and recreation grounds. Such developments had a dramatic effect on the council's administrative organisation and led to the establishment of a structural pattern which is now identified with the Chamberlain tradition. Chamberlain believed that the technical preparation of plans directed towards the achievement of his objectives was rightly a matter for his trained and expert officials. Accordingly he left the work of detail to them. He had a great capacity for understanding the official's point of view and vigorously protected his officials from attack. Thus, under Chamberlain, the pattern was established of powerful departmental heads serving autonomous committees, with committee chairmen and chief officers becoming very influential in their respective fields. Strong functional specialisation – the departmentalism of local government – was further reinforced by professionalism, since the wide range of services and functions which the authority was providing called for high levels of professional and technical skill, training and experience.

Commitment to the principles of vertical hierarchy for purposes of control, authority and communication was clearly in evidence within individual departments. A rigid hierarchy of command was established, moving down from chief officers through deputies and broad bands of lower tier officers. This was the pattern in Birmingham and in all other local authorities. A rigid internal framework emerged, into which any new local functions and services had to be fitted.

Rigid hierarchy was accompanied by the precise definition of the rights, duties, technical qualifications and *modus operandi* attaching to every functional role. The presence of rigid grading structures and an emphasis on standardised procedures and the maintenance of discipline through the application of impersonal rules added to the catalogue of classical organisational characteristics gradually assumed by local government units.

As well as handling greater quantities of work over a growing range of functions and services local authorities also had to meet the requirements of impartiality and accountability in administration. The demand for both qualities has been the result of the political and moral reaction against fraud, corruption and the blatant use of sinecures in the public service (a prominent feature of local administration in the eighteenth and early nineteenth centuries), and also the theoretical and practical prerequisites for the democratic control of organisations operating for the public good and financed by public funds.

Citizens, in their dealings with public organisations, have a right to expect their claims to be dealt with in an impartial and unbiased fashion. For example, we know that the award of a specific social service or benefit will depend upon whether or not our particular circumstances meet the requirements laid down in the rules and not upon how well we can convince the public servant charged with the administration of that social service that we are a deserving case. The guarantee of such impartial administration assumed crucial importance with the coming of the welfare state and is indeed essential if the benefits of the welfare state are to be equitably and rationally distributed.

Clearly the attitudes and values inherent in Weber's depersonalised bureaucratic model are particularly appropriate to the attainment of such impartiality in administration. This is what Weber meant when he referred to 'formal equality of treatment' for everyone in the same empirical situation. Weberian bureaucracy produces the personally detached and strictly objective expert. The utility of a classical administrative environment in this context is further advanced by R. G. S. Brown when he observes that: 'The clients of large (and particularly public) organisations expect fair and uniform treatment which can best be secured by a system of centralised authority implemented according to rules' (Brown, 1971, p. 125).

Accountability is associated with democratic control. Control by locally elected representatives is central to the concept of local self-government. The term 'local government' describes the division of central government into smaller territorial units for purposes of administration. Local self-government, on the other hand, implies some degree of local autonomy and local responsibility. Accountable administration in local government refers here to the ability of councillors to make local administrators accountable to them for their administrative actions and to ensure that policies which represent the outcome of the democratic decision-making process are implemented as efficiently as possible. The exact extent of the democratic accountability of officials in local government and the question of administrative discretion has been the source of protracted debate in recent years. The central theme of this debate has focused on the practicality of distinguishing between areas of a local authority's work which are political and thus demand the more generalised judgement of the elected public representative, and those which can be regarded as purely administrative and which can safely be left in the hands of suitably qualified professional administrators. The Maud Committee on the Management of Local Government expressed the difficulties involved in attempting to draw such lines of demarcation:

> We do not believe that it is impossible to lay down what is policy and what is administrative detail; some issues stand out patently as important and can be regarded as 'policy'; other matters, seemingly trivial, may involve political or social reaction of such significance that deciding them becomes a matter of policy and members feel that they must reserve to themselves consideration and decision on them. A succession of detailed decisions may contribute, eventually, to the formulation of a policy . . . policy-making can arise out of particular problems when consideration of a new case leads to the determination of general guides to action which have a general application. (Report of the Maud Committee, 1967, Vol. 1, p. 30)

It is, therefore, difficult to argue against the proposition that the councillor has a right to ask questions about, and if necessary challenge, any administrative action taken by officers, since all such actions can be viewed as manifestations of policy. Of course the highly technical nature of many local government services makes such all-pervasive accountability difficult to achieve in practice. Moreover, it is a well-recognised fact that experienced and often highly qualified senior officers are in a potentially powerful position with regard to policy formulation. In fact it has been advanced that the traditionally ascribed functions of policy formulation and administration have been reversed, with the officer formulating policy and the councillor working out administrative detail in committee (Heclo, 1969). However, Newton (1976) has more recently produced evidence which casts doubts on the validity of this traditional 'dictatorship of the official' thesis.

In his study of Birmingham, Newton shows that the weakness of the councillor's position *vis-à-vis* the official can be overstated. Traditionally the councillor is shown to be put at a disadvantage because of the impermanent nature of his position and his lack of expertise. Newton, however, points to the longevity of service of many Birmingham representatives and the fact that many had specialised in the work of one committee for many years. These people had certainly gained an expertise equivalent to and even arguably superior to that of their official advisers. Newton's analysis also undermines the assumption, implicit in the traditional view, that local politicians will always submit their own judgements to the technical superiority of the official's arguments. He points out that there are many examples in Birmingham alone of politicians following their own policies in the teeth of all professional advice.

It would be naive to assume that the most politically prominent and senior councillors are not well aware of the official's potential for influence. Again, Newton's research has shown that they are well aware of the tricks of drafting and presentation of reports which may be used to disguise the application of such influence. In addition, the development of disciplined party organisation at local level has tended to shift the balance of power and influence in favour of the elected representative. Officers find it difficult to manipulate councillors who are embarked upon the pursuit of politically defined objectives and who are following carefully formulated and monitored political programmes.

In the final analysis the councillor still has overall and ultimate responsibility for the running of the local authority. As the elected representative of the public he must be allowed active democratic control. This means that administrators must be prepared to account for their actions if required to do so.

In organisational terms the significance of the requirement of administrative accountability lies in the fact that the presence of well-documented rules and standardised procedures offers safeguards to officials who must constantly stand ready to justify their actions retrospectively. In this context the bureaucratic preoccupation with the keeping of written records of all administrative acts and decisions is of particular value as are its more general attributes of precision, consistency and an exaggerated respect for precedent.

It would be wrong to suggest that local government consciously paid heed to the prescriptions of classical theorists in some once-and-for-all design exercise. Clearly the classical pattern of local government's administrative organisation has been the result of an evolutionary process, in many ways an automatic response to operational circumstance. For example, functional specialisation and departmentalism, which has formed the most prominent structural characteristic of local government organisation and which forms a principal design trait of classical theory, was to a large extent the inevitable result of the *ad hoc* way in which local authority services had been established and developed. Often this development followed a tortuous route of numerous Acts of Parliament passed during different periods of social history, dealing with what appeared to be totally separate social problems. The highly structured, rule-bound, and functionally specialised organisational form provided a particularly suitable administrative environment for the methodical assimilation and execution of a rapidly expanding body of work within local authorities. It is the argument here, however, that once this structural pattern had been established the weight of operational requirement acted to prevent its further development. The writings of the classical theorists served to reinforce and lend theoretical legitimacy to principles of organisation which had already evolved and been applied as the logical solutions to problems of local government organisation. The legacy of classical theory was essentially a blueprint for the attainment of internal efficiency of operation, a means of imposing order and logic upon potential chaos. In local government throughout the crucial years of its development the emphasis was on the efficient performance of the daily administrative requirements associated with the provision of a growing range of democratically controlled public services. In this situation effort had to be concentrated on organising internal functioning in the most efficient way. In this sense operational practicalities rendered local government organisation the prisoner of classical prescriptions.

As organisation theory developed so too did the constraints acting upon local authorities. The structural qualities which classical design promoted were in even greater demand as the size of the local government undertakings grew and administrative problems increased in complexity. As an administrative environment local government was rendered less amenable to experimentation in organisational forms and management styles by the sheer weight of operational requirement. It is not really surprising that the continued validity of classical assumptions and structural prescriptions has only recently been challenged and reforms and innovations attempted.

In the next chapter we turn to an examination of the theoretical grounds for this challenge and trace the gradual emergence of a new and different conception of local government management organisation.

Chapter II

THE EMERGENCE OF AN
ENVIRONMENTAL ORIENTATION

DYSFUNCTIONS AND VICIOUS CIRCLES

Critical assessments of Weber's bureaucratic model and of the classical universalist approach to organisational design and administrative theory are plentiful and well documented. It is not intended in this chapter to embark upon an exhaustive survey of this literature but rather to identify those dysfunctional qualities of classical design which can be seen as having had particular causal significance in the recent reform of organisational structures within local government. It will be shown that this causal significance is to be found in the cumulative effect of the complex interrelationships which exist between these dysfunctional qualities and in the fact that they tend to be self-perpetuating through a series of vicious circles which can only be broken by a radical and comprehensive reform strategy.

For ease of description the dysfunctions of bureaucracy which concern us here can be grouped into five categories:

1 Inflexible behaviour
2 Reduced incentive for high personal achievement
3 Goal displacement
4 Poor internal and external communications
5 Lack of adaptive capacity

Robert Merton (1952) emphasises that close control by rule and conformity to standardised procedures, although being undoubtedly conducive to reliability, predictability and a safeguard against arbitrariness, can also produce the dysfunctional quality of inflexible behaviour, 'the familiar phenomenon of the technicism or red tape of the official'. The rules become absolutes and cease to be the utilitarian means to attaining overall organisational goals. Predetermined rules and procedures necessitate the broad categorisation of the infinite variety of cases which can never be clearly envisaged by those with responsibility for drawing up the general rules. As a consequence, 'the very elements which conduce toward efficiency in general produce inefficiency in specific instances'. This in turn can be the cause of strained or even hostile relationships between administrators and clients. The client interprets the administrator's insistence on the application of general criteria and rules, which may appear to have little bearing on the merits of his particular case, as deliberate obstructiveness. Such conflict can cause the administrator to retreat even further behind the barricade of the rule book and to adopt an even more formalised approach in an effort to defend his position. Hence a vicious circle is established.

Concentration within the organisation on achieving conformity to rules and the strict observance of set procedures can actually displace the goal of good service provision to clients. There is a tendency for the means, in the form of adherence to the rules and procedural regulations, to become ends in themselves. In this particular variation of goal displacement operational goals are replaced by the goal of administrative expediency with the result that:

> Discipline, readily interpreted as conformance with regulations, whatever the situation, is seen not as a measure designed for specific purposes but becomes an immediate value in the life-organisation of the bureaucrat . . . Formalism, even ritualism, ensues with an unchallenged insistence upon punctilious adherence to formalised procedures. (Merton, 1952, pp. 365–6)

Crozier (1964) identifies a further potential vicious circle associated with the proliferation of impersonal rules. He sees it as producing a system of human relations within the organisation which effectively 'devaluates superior–subordinate relations'. Superiors are concerned only with applying the rules, subordinates are concerned with staying within the limits prescribed in the rules. There is little emotional commitment on either side. If all subordinates have to be treated in the same way and enjoy predetermined career expectations then much of the superior's potential power is removed. Also, it is pointless for subordinates to attempt to influence or apply pressure to superiors whose actions are entirely controlled by rules. Such a system can result in a reduction in performance levels since it incites participants to accomplish the minimum standards required. There is little incentive or opportunity for the use of initiative and the achievement of high performance levels and standards since the administrator's reward is likely to be the same if he achieves the minimum necessary or displays administrative flair and excellence. Satisfaction with minimum standards reduces the effectiveness of the organisation and, in line with the classicist belief that any organisational malfunction must have its roots in the organisation's structure or reflect a weakness in the formal procedure and rule system, this leads to pressure for more control and more rules. In this way another vicious circle is established.

It is possible to identify other administrative conditions inherent in the public bureaucracy which act to discourage high levels of personal endeavour. For example, the nature of the public administrator's work makes it difficult to identify, for purposes of blame or praise, the individual administrator's personal contribution to an end product. The administrator's individual actions are usually screened or absorbed by the corporate identity of the authority or the department. Also, objective evaluation of an administrator's work is made difficult in a party political setting since, as Peter Self has observed, 'political recognition of administrative worth is uncertain and erratic' (1972, p. 225). Of course, even if one could easily identify the portion of administrative effort attributable to the individual and overcome the problem of the subjective value judgements of the party politicians, one would still be left with the problem of evaluating administrative output. Clearly the outputs of public administrative organisations are not suited to the conventional profit and loss computations used as the normal test of efficiency in the private sector. Thus, as far as the individual is concerned, the only objective measure of fitness for promotion is seniority, a criterion which provides little incentive for exceptional effort.

One example of the dysfunction of goal displacement has already been noted, namely, the supplanting of general organisational goals with the goal of administrative expediency (rigid conformity to rules and procedures). However, goal displacement can also occur between general organisational goals and the more parochial and partial goals of organisational sub-units. This sort of goal displacement is, in a sense, the inevitable result of functional and hierarchical differentiation within the bureaucratic organisation. The dysfunction has two dimensions – the vertical and the lateral (see Figure 2).

Goal displacement in the vertical dimension is associated with hierarchical differentiation and involves the displacement of goals between the organisation and the various peer groups which form lateral strata within the hierarchical pyramid. The lateral dimension of goal displacement is the outcome of functional differentiation, the dividing of the organisation into functionally specialised sub-units or departments.

The nature of the workload makes some delegation of power to sub-units inevitable and indeed essential. They are thus given some power of self-determination. The potential for conflict between overall organisation goals and the goals of specific sub-units is great, since it is feasible that what is in the best interests of the

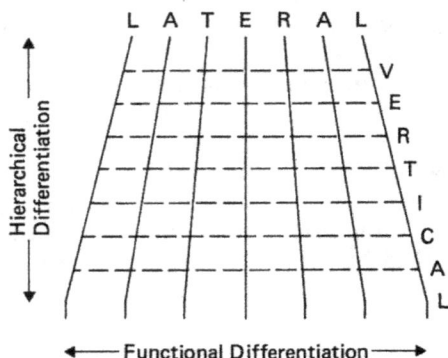

Figure 2   The dimensions of goal displacement

organisation as a whole may be to the detriment of a specific department. Thus not only do organisational sub-units have the capability for pursuing their own goals but they often have the incentive for so doing. The pursuance of parochial goals is the more likely the more self-identification exists within the departments of sub-units. In traditional local government structures, for instance, the professional identification which often coincided with departmental boundaries encouraged separatism and goal displacement.

In the vertical dimension Crozier points to the isolation of different strata which occurs as a direct result of hierarchical differentiation within the organisation and the lack of communication between different levels. In the context of local government organisation, Crozier is pointing out the possibility of goal displacement occurring between different grades of officer. Experience has shown, however, that in local government the forces of departmentalism, and therefore lateral goal displacement, are far stronger than those of vertical differentiation. If goal displacement occurs in the vertical dimension it is most likely to occur between the top decision-making echelons and the middle management grades who bear the brunt of policy implementation.

The lack of correlation between the goals of organisational sub-units and major organisation-wide objectives can lead to organisational ineffectiveness and this, again following the diagnostic pattern associated with the classical perspective, increases the pressure for greater rationalisation and task diversification thus creating yet another vicious circle.

Blau and Scott (1963), when discussing the dilemmas of formal organisations, point to the dysfunctional effect on an organisation's decision-making capacity of strictly enforced hierarchy, since this type of organisational design interferes with the free flow of communication within the organisation:

Status differences restrict the participation of low status members, channel a disproportionate amount of communication to high status members, discourage criticism . . . encourage rejecting correct suggestions . . . and reduce work satisfaction and motivation to make contributions. (Blau and Scott, 1963, p. 243)

Blau and Scott go on to outline a principal dilemma caused by the conflicting organisational requirements of effective co-ordination, which is assisted by restricting and directing the flow of communication, and effective problem-solving, which is best achieved through allowing the free play of ideas and their communication. The conclusion is reached that 'the dilemma imposed by the conflicting needs of restricted and unrestricted communication cannot be resolved but must be endured'. This fact was also recognised by Fayol when discussing the apparently conflicting requirements of the scalar chain and the need for speedy and efficient communications.

The absence of a free flow of communication can be identified as an important contributory factor in explaining the difficulties encountered by bureaucratic organisations when they are confronted with the need to cope with the problem of change and the need for organisational adaptation. In a fully efficient and effective organisation adjustment to change, whether internal or external, is a gradual and more or less constant manoeuvre. However, any such relatively smooth and incremental process must rely upon the sensory capacity and innovatory activities of those members of the organisation who are positioned at a level where the need for change is most easy to detect. By this one generally means the lower echelons, who are normally in closest proximity to the client environment where organisational services and activities have, or fail to have, their impact. However, in a bureaucratic organisation the exercise of such reflex initiative at lower levels in the hierarchy is traditionally discouraged. The identification of the need for change and the initiation of measures to achieve it must be the functional prerogative of the top ranks who, because of their remoteness from the client environment and the failures of the organisational communications system, are least able to exercise it. As a consequence, any environmental or internal pressure which might actually generate organisational response and adjustment will normally be of a magnitude and significance sufficient to present the organisation with a crisis situation, otherwise it would go unrecognised. Thus, as Crozier observes: 'the essential rhythm prevalent in such organisations is an alternation of long periods of stability with very short periods of crisis and change' (Crozier, 1964, p. 196).

This description of the bureaucratic adjustment rhythm indicates the absence of planning as far as the management of change is concerned. The function of the modern planning process is by definition to equip the organisation with an adjustment mechanism which will enable it to accomplish more than a mere lurching from crisis to crisis. Any such adjustment mechanism must, however, be based on information and a well-developed communications system both within the organisation and, even more important, between the organisation and its environment. As will be shown later, the classical perspective fails to recognise the need for such an open exchange of information across organisational/environmental boundaries. The approach is insular to the extent that the environmental setting is taken as a constant, as a known and unchanging quantity. With such an assumption organisational design and the process of management itself becomes focused exclusively on achieving internal efficiency. Thus the organisation is deprived of the intelligence necessary for it to identify the need for change well in advance and establish a much less violent adjustment rhythm.

Peter Self (1972) notes the ease with which one can make intellectual mincemeat of classical assumptions and principles. He highlights specifically the classicists' 'naive view of individual motivation' displayed in their reliance upon discipline and formal structure and the lack of consideration given to the need for an organisation to adjust to important social and psychological factors critical to its operation (though he does concede that the subtle nature of such factors has only recently been appreciated). In fact Self follows a fairly well-established pattern for critiques of the classical school. This focuses in part on what classical theory excludes – most obviously the informal human relations aspect of organisation – and partly, following H. A. Simon (1957), on the apparently contradictory character of many of the principles advanced. An example of such apparent contradiction is the maintenance of the principle of unity of command and the simultaneous call for the maximum utilisation of specialist expertise. In this context one can envisage a situation where the authority of knowledge conflicts with the rules of formal hierarchy. This is because there is no guarantee that, with increased specialisation, the most senior officials in terms of hierarchical status will necessarily be the most knowledgeable in a particular situation or when dealing with a specific subject matter. Even if one considers individual principles of classical design in isolation there remains the problem of their generality, many in fact so general 'as to be of little use as guides to concrete situations' (Mouzelis, 1967). For example, the principle of specialisation is not normally subject to any qualification with regard to the extent to which specialisation should be pursued under particular conditions or indeed the need to balance the gains of specialisation with the additional cost of increased co-ordination which it invariably induces within a large organisation.

Such criticisms demonstrate the dangers inherent in attempting definitional exercises in universally applicable principles of management or administration. Nevertheless, it is the partiality and limited nature of the classical approach which condemns it most. The approach ignores the behavioural facts of organisational life by viewing the human members of organisations as automatons who will respond in a predictable and consistent way to well-defined rules and an authoritative atmosphere. It fails to recognise that organisations consist of individuals with personal feelings, private goals and informal social relationships within the work situation. Such factors can collectively render the reality of organisational operation very different from that portrayed in an organisation chart or laid down in elaborate procedure manuals. Of course such considerations by no means eliminate the need for, nor devalue the importance of formal organisational structure. However, there remains a great deal of validity in the question posed by critics concerning the extent to which any theory of organisation and management can remain isolated from the behavioural aspects of organisation about which our understanding has grown and is growing. The criticism of partiality is valid when one applies it to schools of thought which proclaim purely structural, mechanistic principles in prescriptive exercises with the intention of providing a complete blueprint for efficiency and effectiveness in real-life administrative settings.

The causal interrelationships existing between the dysfunctional qualities identified in the foregoing discussion are illustrated in Figure 3. The ultimate and inevitable result of their interaction is presented as conflict and imbalance between the organisation and its client environment. This conflict arises from the classical organisation's inherently rigid, uncommunicative and insular character. As was pointed out earlier, the classical perspective tends to take an organisation's environment as given, as a known and unchanging quantity, and that consequently the primary concern of management and the organisational structure within which it operates can be limited to that of achieving maximum internal efficiency. There are dangers in such an assumption about environmental context, not the least of which is that of achieving internal machine-like efficiency (with its overtones of administrative expediency) at the expense of organisational effectiveness which, as will be shown, implies a healthy and well-understood inter-relationship between the organisation and its wider environment.

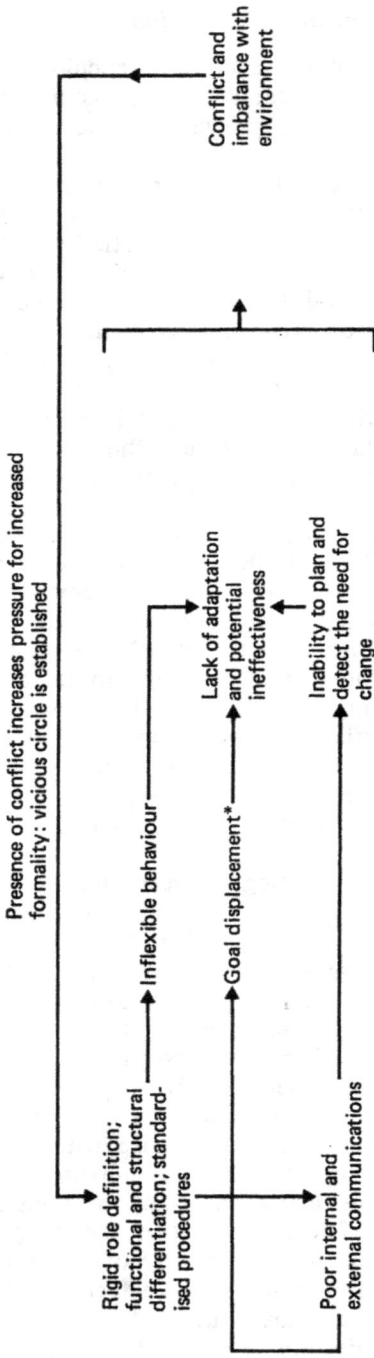

Presence of conflict increases pressure for increased
formality; vicious circle is established

Conflict and
imbalance with
environment

Rigid role definition;
functional and structural
differentiation; standardised procedures

Inflexible behaviour

Lack of adaptation
and potential
ineffectiveness

Goal displacement*

Inability to plan and
detect the need for
change

Poor internal and
external communications

*Displacement of overall organisational goals with partial departmental
or sectional goals, or the goal of administrative expediency.

Figure 3 Causal inter-relationships of major dysfunctional areas of
classical design

THE SYSTEMS PERSPECTIVE

The need to recognise and fully understand the interdependence which exists between an organisation and its environment is emphasised by the systems approach to organisational analysis. More specifically it has been strengthened by the conceptualisation of the organisation as a dynamic open system. By this is meant an entity consisting of a set of elements in interaction which maintains itself in a state of relatively stable equilibrium by experiencing a dynamic and constant interchange of energy and information with its environment.

The intellectual origins of the systems approach are difficult to trace with any degree of certainty. Baker (1975), for example, presents the philosophy of organism expounded by A. N. Whitehead (1929) as an exploration in the field of systems theory. However, it seems that Whitehead himself acknowledges some debt to Locke and even to Plato as his intellectual forebears. Sociologists see the roots of the systems perspective in the work of Comte and Durkheim and their ideal of a social system held together by shared values and goals. Later the structural/functional model of society expounded by Talcott Parsons (1951) rested upon similar system assumptions. However, it is from the natural sciences that the most specific theories have been forthcoming. It is from this area that the concept of a general systems theory has emerged with the writings of Ludwig von Berthalanffy (1950 and 1968).

Basically, the systems approach focuses on the whole rather than the parts. Parts, whether of organisms, organisations or societies, are not looked at separately but together in the faith that the functioning of the whole is causally and inescapably tied to the functioning of each individual part. It is also recognised that the system is often very complex – a mixture of sub-systems which interact with each other in various planes and dimensions. Finally, it is recognised that all systems are related to other systems in an almost infinite and multidimensional hierarchy.

The fact that all this points to alarmingly complex interactions is not considered sufficient reason for avoiding the issue of interdependence. Systems theorists see a futility in hiding behind convenient or manageable fragments of problems or structures. Here, the systems theorists argue, is a structure to make sense of our fragmented and confusing pockets of knowledge so painstakingly assembled, a conception to guide our future searches along more rational pathways.

An important part of Berthalanffy's work on systems theory involves the distinction between open and closed systems and, since the promise of systems thinking in the present context is that it justifies a break with classical organisation theory which tends to view human organisations as exclusively closed systems, we will now concentrate on open systems theory as the relevant aspect of the general systems approach.

From the physical point of view, the characteristic state of the living organism is that of an open system. A system is closed if no material enters or leaves it; it is open if there is import and export and, therefore, change of the components. Living systems are open systems, maintaining themselves in exchange of materials with environment, and in continuous building up and breaking down of their components. (Berthalanffy, 1950)

Thus an open system interacts with its environment, a closed system does not. Moreover, during the process of open interaction a transformation takes place in that supplies of energy and information received from the environment are converted and later exported back into the environment. This process is continuous and cyclical: input is a product (though not always directly) of previous output; output provides a new source of energy for later inputs; output for one system is input for another.

Inputs also represent sources of information about the way in which the environment is changing or reacting to outputs of the system and to the activities of other systems. The simplest type of information input of this nature is that termed 'negative feedback'. This is information which indicates that the system is deviating from a prescribed course and should readjust to a new state of equilibrium. Without this the system would have no direction or real potential for systemic continuance. The closed system loses access to the very mechanism which assists the achievement and maintenance of organisational health and effectiveness, namely, the continual interchange of inputs and outputs across the organisation's boundaries with its environment. It is less able to combat the natural entropic processes by which all organisms move towards deterioration and decay. Open systems utilise the environmental inputs of energy and information to offset this process of decline and decay. They develop adaptive response mechanisms which bring about adjustments in internal structure and processes which facilitate the maintenance of a homeostatic status quo. By this is meant a dynamic equilibrium which, although constantly changing, still allows the organisation to experience a steady state and to perform its functions efficiently and effectively. In this way the system of the organisation is potentially adaptive or responsive to a changing environment whilst maintaining its essential form and purpose. This applies also to the organism's or organisation's sub-systems which need to be in balance if the whole is to perform properly. For example, changes in internal structure or process may well have wide repercussions within the organisation's complex social structure and affect interpersonal relationships at an individual and group level. The systemic character of the organisation dictates that adaptation at one level, whilst ignoring consequences for another level or within another dimension of organisational life, will reduce the organisation's capacity for effective adaptive response.

Finally, there is the tendency to what is termed equifinality in open systems. This concept means that complex social and living systems can reach a steady state by various routes, or by different ways or methods and from different initial conditions, whereas in most inanimate closed systems the final state is determined by the initial conditions. (Berthalanffy gives the example of a chemical equilibrium where the final concentrations depend on the initial ones. If there is a change in either the initial conditions or the process the final state is changed.) The concept of equifinality is important since it means that organisations can adapt different inputs and use different internal activities to reach their objectives regardless of initial conditions. There is, therefore, flexibility and a turning-away from the search for the universally applicable 'one best way' to organise and manage, which is characteristic of the classical approach to organisation theory.

Open systems theory stresses the mutual dependence which exists between an organisation and its environment. It follows that effective management must concentrate on the total organism or system of the organisation and the monitoring of organisational/environmental interchanges rather than be primarily concerned with the internal regulation and control of artificially differentiated segments of it as if they existed within a vacuum. In short, the whole process of management and organisational structuring should have an environmental orientation.

Case studies from the world of business have been used to demonstrate the risks being run by a management which takes its environment as given and concentrates on organising for internal efficiency (Emery and Trist, 1965). A particularly graphic case involved a firm in the British food canning industry which, influenced by its market environment's history of stability and a healthy market share, invested heavily in a new, automated factory. The firm thus incorporated an in-built rigidity, namely, a dependence on long-run full-capacity production. However, even as the new factory was being built the character of the firm's environment wac changing. Competition from unforeseen quarters owing to technological advances and changes in consumer habits brought about by general economic and social trends combined to seriously damage the company's competitive position and consequently reduced its market share. The able but traditional management failed to recognise the changing nature of the environment in time and the rigid production arrangements to which the firm was now fully committed rendered any swift innovation in product range impossible. The result was a seriously reduced market share, a painful process of management upheaval and serious rethinking of objectives and strategies. The case study is presented as a clear indication of the way in which systematically related factors in the environment, usually beyond the control of the organisation, can cause environmental turbulence and uncertainty which may require an organisation to redefine its basic objectives, its market and its outputs, before a new dynamic equilibrium can be reached.

RELATING STRUCTURE TO ENVIRONMENTAL CONTEXT

The systems perspective and, particularly, open systems theory prescribe an organic, environmental orientation for organisational design and functioning. However, such prescriptive statements are in just as much danger of generalisation and oversimplification as were the prescriptions of the classical theorists. As we shall see, the relative appropriateness of the mechanistic and organic models of organisation depends on the nature and characteristics of specific environmental contexts.

Emery and Trist produced a fourfold classification of environmental contexts. According to this classification the simplest form of environment within which an organisation may be set is the *placid, randomised type.* Such an environment displays characteristics of inherent stability and lack of any complex patterns of interdependence between its various elements. Prearranged tactical solutions are suitable for all problems. Objectives, once established, are unlikely to need reassessment and therefore a classical, mechanistic orientation is likely to be effective. The next environmental situation moving up the scale of complexity and turbulence is termed the *placid, clustered type.* This is perhaps best explained by reference to a similar market situation described in economic theory, namely, that of imperfect competition. In this type of market situation the products and services produced by competing organisations are differentiated one from another so that consumers can display a preference. Each organisation must begin to know something about its market and to utilise this knowledge in the design and marketing of its product or service. Knowledge and efficiency vary between organisations and, in consequence, power tends to cluster around the most efficient and adaptive organisations. Survival is linked to knowledge of the environment or market. Strategy becomes important: 'To pursue a goal under its nose may lead it [the organisation] into parts of the field fraught with danger, while avoidance of an immediately difficult issue may lead it away from potentially rewarding areas (Emery and Trist, 1969, p. 247). In this environmental situation organisations tend to grow in size and become hierarchical with a tendency towards central control and co-ordination. The third type of environment is termed the *disturbed, reactive type*, in which a number of similar organisations with similar goals compete for scarce resources. Stability is lost, the environment is dynamic rather than static. The activities of one organisation can have adverse repercussions on the others. Uncertainty increases as organisations respond to competitive values and rivalries develop. Strategy in this situation must allow for the reactions of others, reactions which are difficult to predict. Interdependence is thus now extremely pronounced. The flexibility required encourages decentralisation and 'puts a premium on the quality and speed of decision at various peripheral points'. The fourth and most extreme environmental context identified by Emery and Trist is the *turbulent field type*. This environment experiences an additional dimension of dynamism emanating from changes occurring in the field itself as well as from the interaction of participant organisations. Obvious examples are changes in technology, the strategic repercussions of government legislation and other social and cultural variables. Organisations in such a setting experience a gross increase in the area of relevant uncertainty and experience the need to develop collaborative as well as competitive relationships with similar organisations, especially in order to reduce the area of technological uncertainty. Organisations must devote more resources to research and development activities if they are to increase their capacity for meeting competitive challenge.

Clearly the type of environmental context should prescribe the pattern of organisation structure, and as Emery and Trist point out: 'turbulent fields demand some overall form of organisation that is essentially different from the hierarchically structured forms to which we are accustomed' (Emery and Trist, 1969, p. 253).

The relationship between organisational design and environmental conditions has been further analysed by Tom Burns and G. M. Stalker (1961) who studied the relevance and appropriateness of different organisational forms and systems of management to changing conditions. Studies of the impact of technological innovation in the electronics industry led them to describe two polar extremes of management organisation, namely, the mechanistic and the organic models. These represent the black and white extremes of a continuum which has various shades of grey in between. The mechanistic and organic forms are deemed to be appropriate and potentially most effective in stable and changing conditions respectively.

The mechanistic form closely resembles Weber's model of bureaucracy, having amongst its characteristics a strict hierarchy of control, authority and communication and a high level of task differentiation and specialisation. In contrast the organic form places much less emphasis on formal structure and hierarchical command and communications patterns.

Within the organic form strict hierarchy is supplanted by a more fluid pattern of stratification with focal points of authority varying in accordance with the location of relevant expertise and knowledge, given the particular problem to be solved or project to be administered. There is a lateral rather than a vertical direction of communication within the organisation and communication between participants of different rank is of an informative and consultative rather than a commanding and authoritative nature. There is an 'adjustment and continual re-definition of individual tasks through interaction with others' and a perception of responsibility as something more than a limited field of rights, obligations and methods. Commitment goes beyond any technical definition. It is a far more extensive and internalised commitment to the values, beliefs and goals of the organisation and the assumption of a shared common interest in its survival and development which offsets the loss of formal controls incurred through the abandonment of rigid formal structure and authoritarian procedures.

The organic form is considered to be well adapted to the innovative requirements made necessary by a constant stream of fresh and unforeseen problems which would not readily fit the rigid, precisely defined functional roles within a mechanistic structure. Perhaps the most important characteristic of the organic form is the replacement of formal hierarchy with a pattern of stratification wherein the source of authority is settled by consensus with regard to the location of relevant expertise. This, in theory at any rate, removes the probability of conflict between expertise and status referred to earlier as a dysfunction of excessively rigid hierarchical differentiation. It also increases the problem-solving capacity of the organisation by concentrating its reserves of relevant knowledge for each situation as it arises.

Burns and Stalker take great pains to avoid any suggestion that one form of management organisation is always superior to the other regardless of the circumstances: 'nothing in our experience justifies the assumption that mechanistic systems should be super-seded by organic in conditions of stability' (Burns and Stalker, 1961, p. 125). Moreover, going back to the continuum situation described at the outset, they emphasise that the two extreme forms 'represent a polarity not a dichotomy' and that the relation between the two poles can be elastic in the sense that an organisation which oscillates between conditions of relative stability and relative change may also oscillate between the two forms. However, one would assume that an organisation with such a capability would at any time display a more organic than mechanistic orientation in view of the fundamental nature of the changes required. Burns and Stalker also point out that an organisation may display simultane-ously both organic and mechanistic characteristics within its management system. The emergence of such a situation is easy to understand when one appreciates that the organic approach is as much a state of mind as a structural entity and therefore it is possible to conceive of individual departmental or section heads who may by their own volition impart organic characteristics into their particular domain. However, it is the overall balance of the total management organisation which is important when assessing an organisation's potential for effectiveness in its environmental setting.

In the final analysis it must be the general character and aims of an organisation and the environmental conditions which it experi-ences which must provide the yardstick when deciding upon the most appropriate structural design.

The work of Burns and Stalker takes us further away from the classical belief in a universal 'one best way' to organise and intro-duces part of the basic framework for the approach labelled 'contingency theory' by Paul Lawrence and Jay Lorsch. The con-tingency approach rests on the proposition that organisational performance is dictated by the goodness of fit which exists at any time between the internal attributes of the organisation, that is, its structure and general orientation, and its environmental character-istics (Lawrence and Lorsch, 1967).

Lawrence and Lorsch employ the concepts of differentiation and integration to describe the structural reactions of organisations to environmental conditions.

The concept of differentiation refers to the division of labour within an organisation, the tendency for the organisation to divide up into numerous specialist parts or units. The tendency towards differentiation increases with the complexity of the organisation's environment:

As organisations deal with their external environments, they become segmented into units, each of which has as its major task the problem of dealing with a part of the conditions outside the firm. This is a result of the fact that any one group of managers has a limited span of surveillance. Each one has the capacity to deal with only a portion of the total environment. (Lawrence and Lorsch, 1967, p. 8)

The concept of integration, on the other hand, refers to those structural devices which have as their primary function the co-ordination of the separate parts of the organisation and act to counterbalance the centrifugal forces inherent within the division of labour and specialisation of function. Such integrative devices might include central policy committees and central co-ordinating departments and are essential if one is to achieve a unified pursuance of the organisation's overall goals and objectives.

The competing needs of specialisation and unified effort mean that any organisation will display at any time varying degrees of differentiation and integration. The classical theorists were concerned with both these elements of organisational design. However, what the classicists failed to appreciate was that excessive structural and functional differentiation can actually limit the amount of integration which can subsequently be achieved. This is because the classicists were unaware of the effect which an excessively rigid differentiated structure can have on the attitudes and values of participants. Members of separate departments or units develop their own working styles, their own outlook and departmental orientation. Structural segmentation instils differences in cognitive and emotional orientation on the part of the members of their separate units. This can cause the dysfunctional quality of lateral goal displacement referred to earlier.

Lawrence and Lorsch introduce a broader and more comprehensive definition of differentiation taking it to mean: 'these differences in attitude and behaviour, not just the simple fact of segmentation and specialised knowledge' (Lawrence and Lorsch, 1967, p. 9). In so doing Lawrence and Lorsch extend the concept of differentiation into the behavioural sphere and, as will become apparent later, this behavioural aspect can give rise to a built-in conflict of interests which can seriously hinder attempts to achieve an integrated response to environmental conditions. The point becomes clearer when one examines the definition of integration put forward by Lawrence and Lorsch. They see it as: 'the quality of the state of collaboration that exists among departments that are required to achieve unity of effort by the demands of the environment' (Lawrence and Lorsch, 1967, p. 11).

In summary, contingency theory holds that organisational performance and effectiveness will be a function of the goodness of fit existing between the internal attributes of the organisation, environmental variables (size of environment, its complexity, technological make up, and so on), and the predispositions of the human participants.

REDEFINING THE MANAGEMENT TASK OF THE LOCAL AUTHORITY

So far in this chapter it has been advanced that:

1 A major dysfunctional effect of classical design is poor organisational/environmental relations born out of the mechanistic organisation's rigid, uncommunicative and insular character.

2 This failing is particularly significant in view of the need for an open two-way exchange of inputs and outputs between an organisation and its environment which, as the systems perspective emphasises, is as essential for an organisation to experience as it is for a living organism, if it is to survive and avoid crisis and decline.

3 The organismic analogy is particularly relevant and crucial for an organisation facing unstable environmental conditions under which an organic, relatively unstructured and flexible orientation is likely to prove more appropriate and effective than the classical, mechanistic model.

4 It is important for organisational design and orientation to remain responsive to contingent variables if a high level of organisational performance and effectiveness is to be maintained. In particular, effectiveness will be determined by the degree of correlation which is observed to exist between an organisation's structural and behavioural attributes and its environmental situation.

Therefore it is in this general area of organisational/environmental relations that one discovers a major cumulative dysfunctional quality of classical design. It is in this same area that one finds an important theoretical foundation for many of the recent innovations in internal management structures and processes within English local government. Placed within the context of this theoretical framework the principal management problem facing local authorities prior to reform can be seen as stemming from the presence of a serious incompatibility between the potential functional effectiveness of traditional structures and the environmental conditions experienced.

The conventional mechanistic design and orientation, shown earlier to be particularly characteristic of traditional local government organisation, is compatible with a traditionally held view of local authorities as mechanical producers of a set range of unchanging services designed to meet the needs of an equally static and predictable environment. The organisational structures supportive of such a functional role have often been shielded from pressure for change by the ability of local government to isolate itself from environmental stimuli. Such an ability can largely be attributed to the peculiar market situation with regard to many local government services. For example, there is no accurate way of gauging consumer preference for many public services for which there are few, if any, competitive alternatives. In addition, the demand for particular services may be so great (for example, because consumption is compulsory) as to deter any search for alternatives. The statutory framework within which local authorities must operate also reduces the opportunity and incentive to innovate and show enterprise. The Maud Report on the Management of Local Government, published in 1967, emphasised the restrictive effect of this statutory framework:

> In England and Wales the freedom of local authorities is circumscribed by a strict application of the principle of ultra vires, which means that they must be able to point to specific statutory sanction for every act. It is further limited by ministerial regulations, the need to obtain frequent consents from government departments to proposed courses of action (or even, in some cases, to incidental details), and a rigorous control over capital expenditure. This subordination, reinforced by a central government audit, with power to surcharge members and officers for expenditure incurred without legal authority, hinders internal reorganisation and inhibits enterprise. (Report of the Maud Committee, Vol. 1, para. 45)

In consequence of all these factors local government has been:

> a production-oriented service, devoting little of its resources to research into the social, economic and physical environment of the local authority, or into the demands and preferences of consumers. (Greenwood and Stewart, 1974, p. 5)

The dynamic and systemic character of the complex social conglomerates which make up the environments of most local authorities renders this insular production-oriented outlook particularly inappropriate and harmful. Most of the recent structural and procedural innovations instigated in the area of local government management can be seen as having a common basis in the realisation of the need for local authorities to deliberately expose themselves to environmental pressures for change and to devote a greater proportion of their resources to analysing and interpreting their environments. In 1971 J. D. Stewart published his pathfinding book, *Management in Local Government: A Viewpoint*, advocating the philosophy of general and corporate management for English local government. In this definitive publication the first chapter is devoted to a reinterpretation of the management task of the local authority. Great stress is laid upon the basic underlying need for local authorities to move away from the traditional preoccupation with internal management to the exclusion of external variables (the closed system approach) and instead to 'look outward from the organisation, from the services provided, to the environment on which those services have their impact' (Stewart, 1971, p. 8). Stewart goes on to emphasise the relationship which exists between a local authority and its environment:

> Management in local government . . . must be examined in the environment of the authority. From that environment the authority draws its input – its resources not merely in terms of men and money but of values and ideas. To that environment it gives its output not merely in terms of goods and services but of needs met and problems solved.

However, as we have seen, it is the interdependence which exists between input and output which is important if the organisational system is to avoid ineffectiveness and decline. In traditional local government this relationship has been incomplete in the sense that many important items of input, such as data about how the environment is changing and what form its future demands are likely to take, have not been fully utilised by the authorities. This fact, coupled with the poor quality of environmental intelligence, has meant that outputs have not always represented the product of past inputs and vice versa. In other words, both inputs and outputs have existed but there has been no meaningful conversion process between the two, there has been a failure to identify and respond to negative feedback, to use again the vocabulary of systems theory.

Stewart gives examples of particular service areas where the quality of environmental data has been inadequate. These include the matching of local housing policy with the housing needs of the community (especially certain groups within the community such as the elderly and immigrants) and the provision of services for the elderly. This latter example is seen as raising an important problem,

namely, the futility of attempting to plumb the depth of a bottom-
less pit. Officers quite reasonably shy away from the instigation
of surveys and other exercises designed to identify additional areas
of need when they know that they cannot cope adequately with
existing demands. This represents a stock criticism of the introduction of techniques such as corporate planning in the public
sector – a criticism which challenges the appropriateness of the
market research approach in a situation in which demands will
always outstrip the resources available to meet them. However, the
criticism is only valid if one has as one's overall objective the
satisfaction of all demands identified. The inevitable existence of a
gap between existing needs and available resources calls for the
establishment of priorities and this must be based upon an accurate
assessment of the relative merits of individual claims to resources.
This in turn must be established from as comprehensive a picture
as possible of the needs and demands which exist.

The ability to establish priorities accurately is particularly important in public administration because of the nature of the public
agency's environment. For instance, compare the environmental
situation facing a private firm and that facing a local authority.
The attention of the private firm is focused upon those environmental variables which directly affect its market and it strives to
identify market demands which it is technologically suited to
meet. The local authority, on the other hand, experiences a much
wider, all-embracing environmental situation. The local authority
is not concerned with catering for a narrowly defined market but for
the community as a whole in all its diverse aspects – social,
economic, cultural and political. Its test of success cannot be
reduced to a mere profit and loss computation but must instead
involve the promotion of the far less tangible concept of the
public good. The public good in this context is promoted by the
passing of demands for public resources through the filter of the
democratically elected representative. The establishment of priorities is a political act and as such may not always rest on objective
assessments of relative merit. However, the rationality of any
decision, whether it be tempered by political subjectivity or the
product of the objective calculus of the economic theorist, will be
determined by the quality and completeness of the information
available. In Stewart's opinion, the information available in most
local authorities was far from adequate:

> There is in most authorities no adequate data base for under-
> standing the needs and problems [each one] faces. The needs that
> particular services have to meet are often imperfectly mapped.
> But above all there is no general analysis of the social, economic

and physical environment and of the needs and problems faced by general management of the authority. (Stewart, 1971, p. 38)

Stewart was not alone in his emphasis on the need for local authorities to adopt a more outward environmental orientation. At an official level the Maud Report noted that:

A local authority, in addition to providing a wide range of public services on a scale and to standards prescribed by Parliament, or a minister, must necessarily study the present physical and social environment of the area it serves, and assess its future needs and developments. (Report of the Maud Committee, Vol. 1, para. 144)

Continuing this theme, the Report of the Royal Commission on Local Government in England (1969) drew attention to the way in which demographic, economic and social trends were posing new and formidable problems for local authorities to face, problems which would not be tackled by a blind adherence to traditional patterns of service provision (Vol. 1, ch. 3).

Thus, as a prelude to reform, the management task of local government was interpreted more and more as one of relating the activities of the local authority to the changing needs and problems generated by its essentially dynamic and complex environment. This represented a functional role for local government to which its traditional mechanistic orientation was ill-suited, owing to its preoccupation with internal efficiency and its exclusion of external variables.

The problem facing local government management as it entered the reforming era of the nineteen seventies was one of devising more organic forms and procedures and adapting itself to an innovatory role which would increase its capacity for effectiveness in changing conditions. This represented a reform objective for which the observations and writings of Berthalanffy, Emery and Trist, Burns and Stalker, and Lawrence and Lorsch provided a clear theoretical foundation.

Chapter III

FROM THEORY TO PRACTICE –
THE CORPORATE REVOLUTION AND
STRUCTURAL INTEGRATION

THE CORPORATE APPROACH AND THE NEED FOR INTEGRATION

The corporate approach to the management of local government means the management of the activities of the local authority as a whole when these are seen as activities aimed at the solution or alleviation of social problems which are interrelated and which exist within a common environment which is constantly changing. Thus, by definition at any rate, the corporate approach is associated with the adoption of an environmental orientation for local government organisation and management. The corporate revolution in local government management can be seen as representing a practical response to the theoretical prescriptions analysed in the previous chapter.

The advocacy of corporate management for local government stemmed from a growing appreciation of the dynamic and systemic nature of the environments facing most local authorities. The Seebohm Report on Local Authority and Allied Social Services (1968) was one of a series of official reports published in the late 1960s which highlighted the complex interrelationships which exist between social problems, especially those associated with education, health and housing. The Plowden Report on Children and their Primary Schools (1967) pointed specifically to the interdependence which was observed to exist between educational standards and changes in the wider social environment in which children grow up and live: 'Our argument . . . is that educational policy should explicitly recognise the power of the environment upon the school and of the school upon the environment' (Report of the Plowden Committee, Vol. 1, para. 80). Local authorities needed to adopt a unified view and an integrated approach to the urban systems of which they formed an important part and which they served.

The achievement of such an integrated approach is all the more important in view of the fact that some social problems can only be fully understood when placed within the context of a more general urban problem or at least placed against the background of wider long-term social trends. Thus a policy aimed at improving educational standards or reducing the incidence of truancy or vandalism in a deprived urban area should be formulated against the background of a much wider inner area policy which would, in all probability, involve the housing, public health, social services and engineering functions of the authority as well as the educational department. An integrated approach also assists in the identification of individual departmental policies which, although beneficial within their own sphere, may in fact be giving rise to new problems which will immediately or at some future time affect the activities of other departments. A recent example of this is provided by high-rise residential developments which, although undoubtedly alleviating an immediate problem of housing shortage and pursued with vigour by housing departments all over the country, have since been identified with a whole range of other social problems such as vandalism, child-beating, excessive depression, suicide, and so on.

Clearly, a corporate approach to local government management is difficult to achieve within the highly segmented, strictly departmentalised structure associated with traditional local government organisation. In terms of both management structures and processes the achievement of a corporate approach was essentially about the achievement of organisational integration in the sense used by Lawrence and Lorsch meaning 'the quality of the state of collaboration that exists among departments that are required to achieve unity of effort by the demands of the environment'.

The procedural aspects of corporate management will be discussed in detail later. The present chapter will concentrate on the attempts to achieve structural integration as an initial step towards the adoption of a more complete and general corporate approach to the management task of local government. Three major reports laid the foundations for such a structural response. These were the Maud Report of 1967, the Report of the Royal Commission on Local Government in England of 1969 and the Bains Report of 1972.

THE MAUD REPORT, 1967

The Report of the Committee on the Management of Local Government, chaired by Sir John Maud, is often presented as a fairly ignominious exercise, principally because its main structural recommendations were not accepted by the local government establishment. The Bains Report, on the other hand, is usually cited as the most influential force behind the actual reforms of internal management structures which were adopted by most local authorities in the period of general reorganisation following the Local Government Act of 1972. Such a view, however, seriously underestimates the influence of Maud and, in some ways, overestimates the impact of Bains.

The Committee on the Management of Local Government was set up in March 1964 by Sir Keith Joseph, then Minister of Housing and Local Government, at the request of the four local authority associations. The Committee's terms of reference were: 'to consider in the light of modern conditions how local government might best continue to attract and retain people (both elected representatives and principal officers) of the calibre necessary to ensure its maximum effectiveness.' At first sight the Committee's final report, preoccupied as it is with questions of internal management organisation, appears curious when related to these terms of reference which indicate the need for a primary interest in staffing matters. In fact many critics considered that, in producing the report it did, the Committee was perhaps too liberal in its interpretation of its task. Nevertheless, the argument put forward by the Committee that inefficient and ineffective management structures act as a deterrent to able administrators seems logical enough.

In the report itself the Committee went straight to the heart of the question of structural integration, noting the absence of unity in the work of authorities and the lack of effective co-ordination both at the level of day-to-day administration and at the level of general policy formulation.

> there exists an organisation which is based on separate parts in each of which there is gathered the individual service, with its professional departmental hierarchy led by a principal officer and, supervising it, a committee of members. There may be unity in the parts, but there is disunity in the whole. (Report of the Maud Committee, Vol. 1, para. 97)

The Committee observed that the work of many service departments was obviously closely connected but went on to note that:

> In the wider context individual services, however disparate, are provided for the community as a whole. Planning for the development of the community, the allocation of priorities for finance or for space on the drawing board, the timing of the various schemes all demand a co-ordinated approach. (ibid., Vol. 1, para. 98)

In terms of structure the Committee considered that the establishment of a small managing body could provide the necessary co-ordination at member level, it could provide 'both a unifying element drawing together the disparate parts of the whole and also the impetus for action'. This managing body would be concerned with co-ordination within the local authority both in the sense of overcoming centrifugal forces of the departmental and committee structure and in the sense of co-ordinating policy formulation for the whole authority. In fewer than a third of the authorities which the Committee consulted was there any committee with responsibility for the initiation of policy for the authority as a whole. When such committees were referred to they were usually concerned with central financial control and were consequently dealing with policies which had originated elsewhere within the departmental boundaries of one service. The Committee meant more than this when it referred to the unification of policy, which was defined as: 'the achievement of a coherent set of objectives within the terms of which the different services are to work, and the general integration of development.' The Committee considered that the case for a powerful central policy committee was strong, given the need for a consistent body of policy designed to meet the needs of the authority and the community as a whole. The Committee therefore recommended the establishment of a managing body, to be called the management board, composed of from five to nine senior councillors. This management board was to have the following functions.

1 To formulate the principal objectives of the authority and to present them together with plans to attain them to the council for consideration and decision.
2 To review progress and assess results on behalf of the council.
3 To maintain, on behalf of the council, an overall supervision of the organisation of the authority and of its co-ordination and integration.
4 To take decisions on behalf of the council which exceed the authority of the principal officers, and to recommend decisions to the council where authority has not been delegated to the management board.
5 To be responsible for the presentation of business to the council subject always to the rights of members under standing orders. (ibid., Vol. 1, para. 162)

Since the Committee had identified the multiplicity of committees and subcommittees as a major contributory element in the excessive fragmentation of local government management organisation it was not surprising that it recommended that the number of committees be drastically reduced and, continuing the theme of structural integration, 'that similar or related services should be grouped and allocated to one committee'. The grouping of functions was seen as having obvious advantages in terms of simplifying the co-ordinative process; however, the difficulties involved were also stressed. Not least amongst such difficulties was the presence of certain legal requirements with regard to both committee and departmental structure. The appointment of certain chief officers and the setting-up of certain committees is a statutory obligation upon authorities. Whilst these requirements pose no logistical barrier to the amalgamation of departmental and committee work (for example, the holder of a statutory appointment could still operate under the direction of another officer and a number of statutory committees could have a common membership), they do nevertheless produce a climate of opinion which makes the idea of amalgamation and integration less acceptable and provides a buttress for the idea of separatism. Other difficulties in this area were seen as:

1   The professionalism of chief officers and their tendency to identify themselves with a particular service rather than with the whole field of an authority's activity. An important corollary of this problem was seen as the prejudicial effect on recruitment of any apparent reduction in chief officer status as the result of departmental amalgamation.
2   The more obvious difficulties caused by the physical dispersement of local authority departments often located in different parts of a town or city.
3   The problem of securing officers with sufficient knowledge and breadth of vision to be able to carry responsibility for a large department with a variety of functions.
4   The need to ensure that groupings are based on 'a substantial interrelation of departmental responsibilities' and not on a need to equalise workloads between individual officers. (ibid., Vol. 5, paras 214–20)

The difficulties of amalgamating departments were seen to be matched by those surrounding the amalgamation of committees. Here a major problem concerned the ability of individual councillors to comprehend adequately the workings of a larger grouping of activities even if these activities were fairly closely related. This was in no way casting doubts on the intelligence of councillors but merely a reference to the sheer physical constraints on their ability to assimilate information on a vastly increased scale and covering a much wider area. Evidence presented to the Committee suggested that the existing subdivision of work 'enabled members to familiarise themselves with one or two aspects of the overall problem and to play a part in the development of individual services'. It followed that a widening of committee responsibilities would proportionately reduce the members' ability to make such a contribution to the authority's work and development. However, the major obstacle to the grouping of committee work was seen as lying within the attitudes of committee chairmen, who tend to have a possessive attitude towards what they regard as their committee. The Maud Committee received a great deal of evidence to the effect that many committees which had outlived their usefulness were maintained in order to protect the personal status of their chairman, a situation often further complicated by party political in-fighting.

Despite all these potential problems the Committee considered that the balance of advantage was towards the grouping of functions. It was thought that the reduction in the number of committees might encourage members to dissociate themselves from detail and to concentrate on more fundamental issues and that the grouping of departments would benefit those services which were at the time controlled by officers who suffer from having less power and influence than their colleagues in larger departments.

The Committee's belief in the need for an effective focal point of authority at officer level was reflected in its recommendation for the appointment of a chief administrative officer or chief executive; he would have a status superior to that traditionally held by the clerk of the council who was essentially a *primus inter pares* in his relationship with other chief officers. Many advantages were seen in having a clearly designated chief administrative officer. Notable among these advantages was the better co-ordination of departments; the presentation to the council of integrated views of officers; improvement in the general level of efficiency; and the wide diffusion of the use of modern management techniques. The Committee did not doubt that clerks in many authorities accomplished many of these things working within their traditional roles but pointed out that, in order to do so, they needed to rely on force of personality and ability, and consent. The choice open to authorities was seen as being one between the clerk as a passive leader by consent or as an official with 'responsibility for encouraging new ideas, for active co-ordination of the work of the authority and for drive in the execution of its decisions'. The Committee was in favour of the latter view of a more positive and authoritative role for the clerk. Objections on the grounds that such an official would in some way usurp the decision-making role of the elected council were met with the assertion that councillors would be in a much stronger position to exercise their democratic control if they had integrated and co-ordinated advice and the assistance of an official with the authority to ensure that their decisions were conveyed to the right department and were efficiently carried out. Further objections on the grounds that a chief administrative officer would overrule professionally qualified officers operating within their specialist field were answered with the belief that no efficient chief administrative officer 'would seek to give instructions to professional officers on actions where their professional skills are involved'. The Committee saw principal officers working together, under the leadership of the clerk, on those matters which transcend purely professional and departmental considerations and so producing agreed and co-ordinated advice.

The Committee made the following recommendations with regard to the formal reassessment of the clerk's role.

1   That the Clerk be recognised as head of the authority's paid service, and have authority over other principal officers in so far as this is necessary for the efficient management and execution of the authority's functions.
2   That the Clerk be responsible to the management board and through it to the council.
3   That the principal officers be responsible to the council through the Clerk.

Among the recommended duties of the clerk were included:

1   Ensuring the effectiveness and efficiency of the organisation and the co-ordination (and integration where necessary) of its activities.
2   To see that the management board is adequately serviced by providing co-ordinated and integrated staff work and seeing that its decisions and those of the council are implemented. (ibid., Vol. 1, paras 179–80)

As far as an appropriate background for the new-style clerk was concerned, the Maud Committee recommended that clerkships should be open to people of all professions and occupations, thus breaking away from the traditional domination of the post by members of the legal profession.

One of the most controversial aspects of the Maud Report concerned its recommendations for the future role of committees. We have already noted that one effect of its proposals for structural integration was to be a reduction in the number of committees and a widening of the range of work for those that remained. This of course had vast implications for the degree of participation allowed to councillors since there would be fewer committees on which they could serve and these would not necessarily be any larger. Objections that this would be undemocratic were anticipated by the Committee's argument that councillors released from involvement in formal committee proceedings would have more time to devote to the affairs of their constituents. In fact the Committee recommended that committees should cease to be directing or controlling bodies, preoccupied as they often were with matters of routine administration. The needs of efficient administration would be more effectively met, in the Committee's opinion, if councillors serving on committees were restricted to a more general, deliberative, representative role, with greater delegation of authority to officers. The Committee specified that the ideal role for committees should encompass the following functions.

1 Making recommendations to the management board on the major objectives of the authority and studying and recommending the means to attain these objectives.
2 Reviewing progress on plans and programmes and on the operation of individual services as the management board does for the whole range of services.
3 Considering the interests, reactions and criticisms of the public and conveying them to officers and if necessary, to the management board.
4 Considering any matters raised by their own members or referred to them by the management board. (ibid., Vol. 1, para. 166)

It was made clear that committees would only take executive decisions in exceptional circumstances and that such circumstances would be clearly defined by the management board.

The Maud Committee was quite direct in its arguments for a radical review of the respective functions and responsibilities of members and officers.

in English local government . . . the word democracy has come to have for many people a special meaning; it is thought to imply that, unless the members determine how the smallest things are to be done, they are failing in their duties. To allow any but the most trivial discretion to an officer is thought to be undemocratic. Hence the cumbrous machinery, the multiplication of committees, the clogged agendas, the long meetings, the neglect of matters of importance and the failure to make full use of the available contacts over the administration and to develop others. (ibid., Vol. 1, para. 72)

The Committee saw the need to attempt a clearer definition of the roles of members and officers. At a superficial level the demarcation seems clear enough: members are concerned with policy and officers with the administration of that policy. However, the dividing line between policy and administration is blurred and any such general criterion is impossible to utilise in practice. Nevertheless, the Committee believed that it was possible to make a realistic distinction between the functions of the representative and the official. Thus, while it was recognised that the overall development and control of services should be the responsibility of members, in the Committee's view: 'the day-to-day administration of services, the decisions in case work, the routine inspection and control should normally be the function of the paid officials and not of the members' (Vol. 1, para. 146). The Committee was prepared to rely on the officer's common sense in recognising the need to refer sensitive issues arising during the course of routine administration to an elected member for decision. Also, this call for greater delegation of executive authority to officers in no way removed the constituent's direct channel of communication to his elected representative should he feel aggrieved.

In summary, the Maud Committee laid the foundations for structural integration in three areas.

1 In the area of policy formulation with its recommendation for a powerful central management board to act as a focal point for the unification of policy and the integration of objectives for the authority as a whole.
2 In the area of committee and departmental structures in its recommendations for the grouping of functions.
3 In the area of central administrative direction in its recommendation for a more powerful chief administrative officer with central directing and co-ordinating power over other principal officers (see Figure 4).

Needless to say such radical proposals found many critics even among members of the Committee itself. For example, in a note of dissent Sir Andrew Wheatley expressed concern over the amount of power which the majority recommendations vested in the management board and the small amount of executive power which the scheme would leave in the hands of committees:

In my view these proposals will vest far too much power in the small number of members who will be members of the management board, and will deprive the great majority of the members of the council of the opportunity of participating effectively in

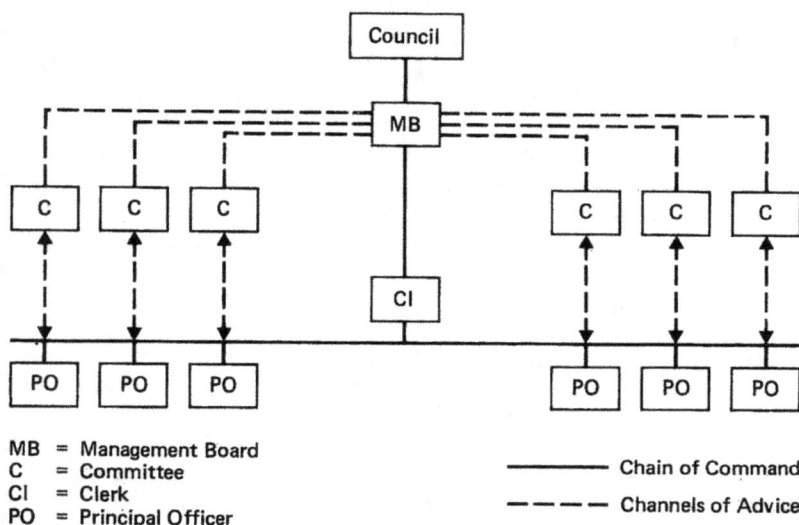

Figure 4   The Maud plan

the formulation of policy and the development of services. (ibid., Vol. 1, p. 154)

In Wheatley's opinion, the minor, deliberative, advisory role envisaged for the majority of members would act as a deterrent to many potential councillors of the quality needed. It was pointed out that such people stand for election in order to take a direct part in the development of services and are hardly likely to find an outlet for their energies in the kind of system which Maud was recommending.

This argument was used to highlight the apparent contradiction between the report's recommendations and the terms of reference which had urged the Committee to find ways of attracting and retaining people of high calibre in local government. In Maud's defence, however, it should be remembered that the calibre of officer is just as important, some would argue more so, as the quality of elected member. The report emphasised that it was the notoriously cumbersome and inefficient administrative machinery which the traditional system had produced that was most likely to deter those with managerial ability and administrative flair from entering the field of local government administration.

It is, of course, a matter of opinion whether the administrative efficiency of local government should take marginal precedence over the needs of local democracy, the exact meaning of which is, as Maud pointed out, a matter of interpretation. The point begs the more fundamental question of what is the primary function of local government? Is it there to provide an additional channel of representative democracy and so overcome the participatory inadequacies of the large modern nation state, or is it there to care for the needs of the handicapped, the unhoused, the elderly, and so on, in the most efficient way possible, given a scarcity of resources? As has been pointed out, Maud saw no such conflict between democracy and efficiency in his recommendations, since increased delegation to officers and the establishment of a compact central managing body in no way affected the traditional channels of communication between councillor and constituent and the terms of any delegation would be controlled by the council as a whole. Moreover, it was argued that under the Maud structure councillors would receive information which was more co-ordinated and integrated and which would give them a much clearer picture of the authority's affairs as a whole, thus increasing their capacity for making rational decisions about broad patterns of resource allocation. If one accepts that the job of the elected representative is to ensure that public resources are used to the best effect and that priorities are ordered in as fair a way as possible then the prerequisites of efficient administration and effective local representation, far from being mutually exclusive, appear supportive and complementary.

Nevertheless, the overall reaction to the report was negative. While the local government establishment largely accepted Maud's broad diagnosis of what was wrong with the system of local government management it disagreed with its detailed proposals, particularly the concept of a central management board with a virtual monopoly of policy-making power, serviced by a similarly powerful officer machinery. The recommendations, it was said, 'leaned far too much towards the needs of administrative efficiency at the expense of local democracy'.

While many local authorities did in fact streamline their committee structures and some even established a form of central policy committee (though none of these were given the same sort of power as the Maud-style management board) nowhere did these innovations resemble an attempt at authority-wide reorientation. They were essentially innovations within the traditional organisational framework. However, the influence of Maud in generating a climate for change must not be underestimated. The Committee had not had to rely on pure theoretical speculation in framing its recommendations. Experiments in new forms of management structure had been undertaken in the field by several authorities, for example, Basildon and Newcastle-upon-Tyne. In such instances the initiative was taken by particularly enlightened and energetic political figures who can quite properly be cast in the role of pioneers. The Maud Report, however, represented an official focal point for the reform movement, a well-documented and well-researched call for the extension of the principles of structural integration to local government in general.

THE REPORT OF THE ROYAL COMMISSION, 1969

The principal contribution of the Royal Commission on Local Government in England to the debate on internal management structures was a general, though not a complete, reiteration of the basic principles put forward in the Maud Report two years before. This is hardly surprising in view of the fact that Sir John Maud chaired both investigations, although by this time he had been elevated to the peerage as Lord Redcliffe-Maud. A commentary on internal management arrangements was very much ancillary to the main business of the Commission, which was principally concerned with the external structure of the local government system. However, the inclusion of such a commentary followed from an anticipation of the managerial problems likely to be encountered in operating the sort of large unitary authorities which lay at the foundation of the Commission's final proposals.

In the area of internal management the Commission was of the opinion that 'far-reaching changes in traditional organisation and methods of work were required' and echoed Maud's belief in the need for a corporate, as opposed to a departmental, approach to the management of an authority's affairs. In addition the Commission believed that any new internal structure 'must remove from members the temptation to cling to their preoccupation with details and with supervision of routine'.

After re-emphasising the interrelated nature of local authority services the Commission stated its firm belief in the need for a central committee, whatever this might be called, to act as a focal centre where a general view could be developed. This central committee was seen as having responsibility for advising the council on general development and the allocation of resources throughout the authority. Also, as 'watchdog of the corporate point of view', the committee would be responsible for effecting co-ordination and, where necessary, unifying procedures.

The Commission, like the Maud Committee, advised a reduction in the number of service committees. However, committees were envisaged as remaining highly influential and the main initiators of policy for the individual services within their special sphere.

The Commission did not believe that there could be any universal method of applying the principle of a central committee, nor could there be any general rules about the relationship which should exist between a central committee and the working service committees. Many factors were seen as determining the exact style of structure and relationships within it. Such factors included the size of the particular authority, the social and economic circumstances of the area and local political traditions. The Commission expressed the hope that there would be 'a wide variety of experiment'. Thus, by being less dogmatic and by emphasising the desirability of flexibility, especially in the sensitive area of the role of service committees, the Royal Commission neatly side-stepped the criticism of power concentration which had been levelled at the Maud scheme.

The Commission was, however, much more in step with the Maud Committee in its advocacy of the appointment of a clerk or chief executive who would be official head of an authority's paid staff. Such an official was again seen as coming from a variety of professional backgrounds including that of general administration. He was seen as the leader of a team of chief officers who would be jointly responsible for 'considering the council's general problems and for co-ordinating action to solve them'. These chief officers would be in charge of groups of services and this would, in the opinion of the Commission, 'reflect the close relationship between the various services and . . . correspond to the reduction in the number of committees'.

In conclusion the Commission observed somewhat prophetically that the success of such an interdepartmental, interdisciplinary approach to internal structure would depend on 'harnessing the enthusiasm of the specialist to the needs of central management'.

Any reaction to the Royal Commission's proposals for internal management was eclipsed by the political response to its major proposals for a general reorganisation of the whole local government system. The Commission had undertaken an impressive amount of research exposing the illogical multiplicity and fragmentation which characterised the existing multi-tier system in which authorities lacked the size, populations and resources necessary to provide the increasingly complex and specialised services demanded in a modern society. The Royal Commission recommended in its majority report that the country be divided up into fifty-eight unitary areas, each of which would be served by a single all-purpose unitary authority, with the exception of specified conurbation areas where a two-tier system was recommended.

Although it was accepted, with minor alterations, by the incumbent Labour government the scheme was rejected by the new Conservative administration which took office in 1970. The Conservatives decided in favour of a two-tier system for the whole country. In rejecting the unitary principle the Conservative government was in tune with both the general body of Conservative party opinion and the opinion of many working in local government. Majority opinion was hostile to reform on such a drastic scale and of such a radical nature. Among the local authority associations, the Association of Municipal Corporations stood alone in support of the unitary scheme. The Conservatives accused the Commission of a preoccupation with the prerequisites of administrative expediency and of failing to protect the democratic and representative character of local government in this country, emphasising the size and potential remoteness of the proposed giant all-purpose authorities. However, it can be argued that the Conservative plan outlined in the White Paper of February 1971 was based not on an objective analysis of the needs of local government but on political expediency. The elected members of the shire counties in rural areas, which were predominantly Conservative, were known to be unhappy at the prospect of being absorbed by new unitary authorities which would, in all probability, be dominated by the urban areas within them which were, in turn, predominantly Labour-controlled.

The Local Government Act 1972, which represented the statutory outcome of the Conservative White Paper of 1971, established four types of local authority – county councils and district councils in the more rural areas of the country, and metropolitan counties and districts in the six highly urbanised conurbation areas. It was intended that the county and metropolitan county councils should have responsibility for strategic planning and for those services such as police and fire which needed to be unified in larger geographical areas than were covered by the traditional local authorities. A major difference between metropolitan and non-metropolitan counties was the fact that the latter were to be responsible for the administration of personal social services and education whereas in the metropolitan areas these were to be the responsibility of the second-tier metropolitan district councils. This crucial difference in the allocation of functions effectively distinguishes the metropolitan and non-metropolitan patterns of local government. It has as its basis the derivation of optimum population levels agreed as being necessary for the effective provision of social and education services (an approach emanating from the research undertaken by the Royal Commission between 1966 and 1969). These optimum levels were set at a maximum of one million and a minimum of one quarter of a million people. Such levels were easily reached by the second-tier district authorities in metropolitan areas which were invariably populous and yet geographically compact. However, outside the metropolitan areas only the top-tier county authorities with their wider geographical spread could attain population levels within the range stipulated. In short, in the metropolitan areas the second-tier districts were to be the major service providers whereas in the country as a whole the top-tier country authorities would occupy this position.

Thus in April 1974, the date when the provisions of the Local Government Act 1972 came into effect, a degree of structural integration was achieved at the interauthority level. The amalgamation of the host of small traditional council units into two major categories – the districts and metropolitan districts – increased, in theory at any rate, the ability of authorities to administer and plan for larger and more realistic geographical, social and economic entities. However, even before the Local Government Act reached the statute book, yet another attempt was made to focus attention on the need to bring about corresponding reforms in the internal management structures of the new local authorities.

THE BAINS REPORT, 1972

In May 1971 a study group was set up by the Secretary of State for the Environment and the four local authority associations. This study group was chaired by Malcolm Bains, Clerk of the Kent County Council, and contained three other clerks, a county treasurer and Mr A. G. Woods, the Company Secretary of ICI. The nature of the group's membership was indicative of its task, which was to offer practical advice and guidance to those who were to have responsibility for the management of the new local authorities. A time of general reorganisation was seen as providing an ideal opportunity for authorities to start from scratch in the design of their management structures and to overcome the inertia of tradition.

In the Bains Report (1972) the need for structural integration and a corporate approach to management was presented as being beyond dispute if local government was to be efficient and effective. However, while Bains was insistent upon a corporate approach to management it did not prescribe a common structural model for all authorities. The report did, nevertheless, recommend certain basic structural features which should be commonly adopted. There were, first, a policy and resources committee supported by four subcommittees and, secondly, a chief executive supported by a chief officers' management team.

The Bains-style policy and resources committee was seen as having responsibility for providing the council with comprehensive and co-ordinated advice upon how the needs of the community could be planned for and met within the resource limits which existed. The committee was to aid the council in the setting of objectives and priorities and subsequently in co-ordinating and controlling policy implementation. In addition, the committee was to have ultimate responsibility for the allocation and control of the major resources of the authority, categorised as finance, manpower and land (including buildings). Unlike the Maud-style management board the policy and resources committee would not have a monopoly of policy formulation. The functional spending committees would be responsible for preparing and submitting policies to the council in their particular areas of responsibility. However, the corporate approach would be protected by the requirement that all important matters of policy or expenditure would also go to the policy and resources committee which would have the opportunity of reporting concurrently to the council. The policy and resources committee was seen as being supported by three subcommittees, each with responsibility for dealing with the more detailed and routine matters within a particular resource area, that is, either finance, manpower or land.

In dealing with the question of the membership of the policy and resources committee and its resource subcommittees Bains skilfully avoided the charge of power concentration and the sort of cabalistic scheme associated with Maud. The solution was found in a complex pattern of interlocking committee memberships designed to maximise the participatory opportunities for elected members at the level of policy formulation and resource control. The group felt that membership of the policy and resources committee should not be limited to the chairmen of major committees; moreover, the report favoured having minority party representation on that committee in those authorities organised along traditional party lines. The report also recommended that membership of the three resource subcommittees should not be drawn solely from those who were members of the parent committee. In a large authority, the report suggested, there might be ten or twelve members of each of the subcommittees, of whom possibly only two would be members of the main committee, with others coming from the operational committees.

Bains agreed with Maud on the need to reduce the number of operational committees in local authorities. Bains favoured the idea of a committee structure based on broad programme areas, that is, wide areas of activity within the authority, aimed at the achievement of a general overall objective. The resulting committee structures would of course vary from authority to authority, whose objectives and therefore programme areas would reflect local conditions and environmental needs. In continuing to allow executive decision-making powers to these programme committees Bains parted company with Maud and thus again neatly escaped being cast in the role of saboteur of the principle of elective control. Indeed, the basis of Bains's criticism of the traditional role of committees is that they do little more than take final decisions. Their involvement in the decision process comes at a time when choices are clear-cut and alternatives reduced to a manageable number. In Bains's view, committees in local government should be more involved in non-decision-making debate at a much earlier stage in the decision process; an involvement which would, in the group's opinion, 'improve the understanding of the issues at stake and therefore the basis of the final decision'.

The concept of the programme committee is central to the Bains strategy of building a structural framework which would support, and indeed make necessary, a corporate approach to the management of a local authority's affairs. Programme committees by their very nature would need to be serviced by several different departments and disciplines or professions and this requirement would, it was hoped, reduce the intercommittee and interdepartmental friction which were so often evident in the traditional separatist structures.

It has already been shown how Bains opened up the opportunities for member participation at the level of policy formulation and overall resource control. However, there remained the problem of reduced opportunities for participation at operational level. Although the Bains programme committees retained decision-making powers their introduction would still mean an overall reduction in the number of committees and therefore a reduction in the opportunities for members to serve in a traditional committee role. The Bains group were well aware of the criticisms which had been levelled at Maud with regard to the competing claims of efficiency and democracy. They were also well aware that their objective should be 'to make democracy as efficient as possible, not to make efficiency as democratic as possible'. The answer to the problem of somehow reconciling the competing claims of committee structure rationalisation and member participation was seen to lie in the concept, already adopted in some authorities, of the informal working group of members. These working groups, which might concentrate on particular aspects of individual services, were presented as providing the backbench councillor with the opportunity to specialise in an area of the authority's work in which he had a special interest. Such groups would also provide a point of reference for the officer wishing to test member opinion on a proposed administrative action. Bains believed that such groups, relieved of the constraints of formal committee procedure, would increase both organisational flexibility and member satisfaction.

It is appropriate, before going on to examine the Bains recommendations for restructuring at officer level, to highlight another area in which Maud and Bains shared a common concern, namely, the area of officer–member relations. Both reports saw a need to clarify respective roles; Bains, however, approached this sensitive subject in a much less absolute and critical way than Maud, emphasising the need for a spirit of compromise:

> Officers must accept that members have a legitimate interest in the day-to-day administration of cases involving their consti-tuents . . . Members must equally realise that the skilled profes-sional officer is not just a servant who is paid to do as he is told. We do not dispute that the major policy decisions must be taken by the elected members, but the officers have a role to play in the stimulation and formulation of policy and in seeing that the members have available the necessary advice and evaluation to make the best decisions. (Report of the Bains Committee, ch. 3, p. 8)

Bains agreed broadly with Maud that there was too much elected member involvement in administrative trivia but emphasised the importance of the constituency role for many councillors who could not all be cast in the role of general policy-makers. For Bains, the answer to this dilemma lay in improving the quality and quantity of the information given to councillors, since lack of information was a prime cause of their frequent excursions into the crevices of the administrative machine:

> The flow of information between elected members and electorate should be a two-way process and the member must be sufficiently well informed to be able to explain the council's actions and policies to his constituents and feed back reaction to appropriate points within the authority organisation. (ibid., ch. 3, p. 11)

Bains believed that a free flow of communication 'oils the wheels of democracy' and would remove the need for members to be constantly 'snapping at the heels' of officers in order to carry out their representative democratic role. A specific recommendation in this context was that council members should be allowed to attend and speak at meetings of committees other than their own and that all committee agendas should be made available to all members.

Bains followed Maud's lead on the need for greater delegation to officers. It was noted that committees often took decisions which could easily have been left to officials. In such a situation the officers' expertise and training was not being fully utilised.

Bains also agreed with Maud that extensive delegation to officers was not undemocratic, since members have the right to amend or withdraw any powers so delegated. Bains points out that in any event the officer exercising delegated authority would have to keep in close contact with appropriate committees (under a programme committee structure he might be responsible to several), and, again echoing the Maud view, that the officer would have to be relied upon to recognise the sort of sensitive issue which might arise during the course of day-to-day administration and which would need to be referred to an elected member for adjudication.

Bains saw the process of management in local government as a scale or continuum (see Figure 5). At the two extreme ends of the scale the respective roles of members and officers are clear enough. However, nowhere along the scale does the balance of control and advice change absolutely. The relationship changes very gradually until a new dominant source of control or advice emerges. Thus at no point on the scale can it be said that everything beyond or before that point is exclusively the province of either element.

With regard to structure at officer level, Bains subscribed to the view put forward by the Maud Committee that there should be one person as head of the authority's paid service and that he should have authority over other chief officers 'in so far as this is necessary for the efficient management of the authority's functions'. Here we find repeated Maud's call for this new position to have a directing as well as a co-ordinating role and to be more than merely *primus inter pares* with other chief officers. Since this implies a very different role from that performed by the traditional town clerk a change in title seemed appropriate. Bains favoured the title of chief executive and saw him as the council's principal adviser, via the policy and resources committee, on matters of general policy. It was considered preferable that the chief executive should not have departmental responsibilities, although it was recognised that he would need a number of personal assistants reporting directly to him. It was also felt that no appropriate disciplinary or professional background could be prescribed for the role and that candidates should be chosen for their proven general managerial ability. It would be the chief executive's responsibility to secure co-ordination of advice on the planning of objectives and services; to ensure the efficient and effective implementation of the council's programmes and policies and the effective deployment of resources; and to keep the organisation and administration of the authority under review in the interests of effective management.

The chief executive's major functional role was seen as the leader of a small team of chief officers, steering them towards common objectives. This management team, consisting of about six principal

Setting of broad policy
objectives. Allocation
of major resources

Implementation of
policy and execution
of plans

| Member | Officer | Member | Officer |
| Control | Advice | Advice | Control |

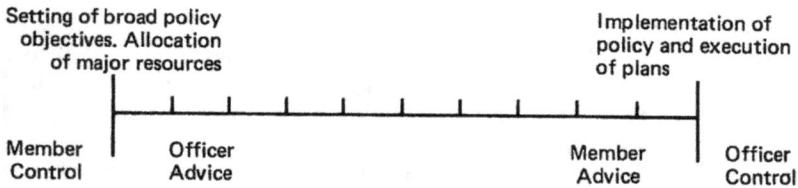

Figure 5   The management process in local government

chief officers, was seen as the focal point of corporate identity within the authority at officer level, the officers' counterpart of the elected members' policy and resources committee. Bains realised that meetings between chief officers already took place with varying degrees of formality in existing authorities. However, Bains saw participation in the principal chief officer's management team as representing a novel and much more demanding experience. Members were to attend not as departmental representatives but as members of a body 'created to aid the management of the authority as a whole'. Bains did not agree with the claim that chief officers from specific departmental or professional backgrounds would be unable to make a contribution to discussions of matters and problems affecting other chief officers, or that they might have insufficient direct interest at any one time to make the team a centre for lively and constructive debate. The Bains justification of the management team as a useful and indeed essential integrative device is summed up in the following quotation from the report.

> We suggest that it is of the essence of the corporate approach to management that Chief Officers recognise that there are few if any major decisions which can be made in isolation without some impact upon others' areas of responsibility. Corporate management requires that the implications for the authority as a whole should be considered and discussed before decisions are taken. It may on occasions be necessary for a Chief Officer to subordinate his own particular interest to that of the authority as a whole. On another level each professional officer has a fund of knowledge and experience which is not only relevant to problems within his own field, but to the solving of problems of other fields as well and it is in the exchange of views and opinions within the management team that a true corporate spirit is likely to develop. (Report of the Bains Committee, Ch. 3, p. 49)

Here, as with the enhanced position of the chief executive, Bains entered the complex area of attitudes and human relations. The extent to which Bains's view was optimistic can perhaps best be judged by reference to the workings of the management team and the office of chief executive in action as described in the case study presented in Part Four of this book. However, at a prescriptive level the Bains group saw the management team as playing a positive role in the central corporate management processes of the authority, receiving instructions from the policy and resources committee and submitting corporate reports to that committee through the chief executive. Bains did not wish to be too specific about the management team's terms of reference. Instead, the group suggested two broad functions: first, the long-term strategic function of considering and advising on what policies the council should be adopting to cope with changing needs and circumstances and, secondly, an overall management, co-ordinative and progress-chasing role. In order to carry out these functions it was expected that the management team would set up a series of interdepartmental working groups which might include a corporate planning group, a research and intelligence group and a manpower and management services group.

Bains put great emphasis on the need to appraise the performance of chief officers in a systematic way at regular intervals. The general function of performance review throughout the authority was taken as warranting the establishment of a separate policy and resources subcommittee with a wide area of responsibility and authority to make detailed investigation into any project, department or area of activity. This subcommittee would be chaired by a member of the policy and resources committee but would generally have a flexible membership reflecting the particular knowledge, skills, or experience prescribed by the nature of the area to be examined. Reports of the subcommittee would be sent to the policy and resources committee and departments and appropriate committees would be given the opportunity to comment upon its findings. Bains went to great lengths to emphasise the constructive effects of performance review for both members and officers. It was envisaged as being essentially a two-way discussion process which would enable the officer to ascertain how he was seen to have performed his duties and to give him the opportunity to make his own comments and suggestions about how he might perform his role more effectively.

With regard to departmental structures, the Bains group noted that having a number of departments grouped together under a director might lead to improved co-ordination and communication between those departments. However, Bains emphasised that the criterion for the grouping of departments must be close service interrelationship and not just a need to even out the workload between directors. Bains did not see the necessity for expanding the programme area principle, recommended as the basis for committee structure, into the sphere of service provision. Any attempt to make the two structures coincide on a programme area basis could, it was thought, reintroduce departmentalism on a grand scale. Bains presented a mixture of grouped and single departments in the same authority as the only logical solution.

However, if committee and departmental structures were not to coincide there would be a need for interdepartmental working groups of officers to service the programme committees whose areas of interest cut across departmental boundaries. Bains saw it as the responsibility of the chief executive and the management team to set up such interdepartmental interdisciplinary groups, each of which would be headed by a senior officer appointed from a discipline appropriate to the specific task or project for which the group was conceived. Using this system, it would be possible 'to bring all the necessary professional skills together into a unified team with a defined objective or task and in so doing strengthen the corporate orientation of the authority'. The significance of introducing this horizontal, transitory element into the management structure can hardly be overstressed since, as we shall see, the concept is basic to a practical assimilation of organic management forms.

Two types of interdepartmental group were envisaged by Bains. These were, first, programme area teams grouped in relation to the overall objectives of the authority and responsible for giving advice on policy formulation and resource allocation and, secondly, project control groups with responsibility for overseeing the implementation of specific items of policy or individual projects. This combination of traditional vertical structure, represented by functional departmental hierarchies, and these horizontal, interdepartmental elements, was to give local authorities the flexibility they required. In organisation and management theory this type of vertical and horizontal design is termed matrix organisation or matrix management and is associated with high levels of organisational flexibility and adaptability. As Bains emphasised:

> The membership of teams (either operating at the level of programme areas or individual projects) can be amended or supplemented, new teams can be set up and existing ones disbanded as circumstances change. Herein lies one of the great advantages of this matrix system of management. By its nature it is flexible and adaptive, unlike rigid bureaucracy which we suggest it should replace. (Report of the Bains Committee, Ch. 3, p. 61)

This structure is illustrated in Figure 6.

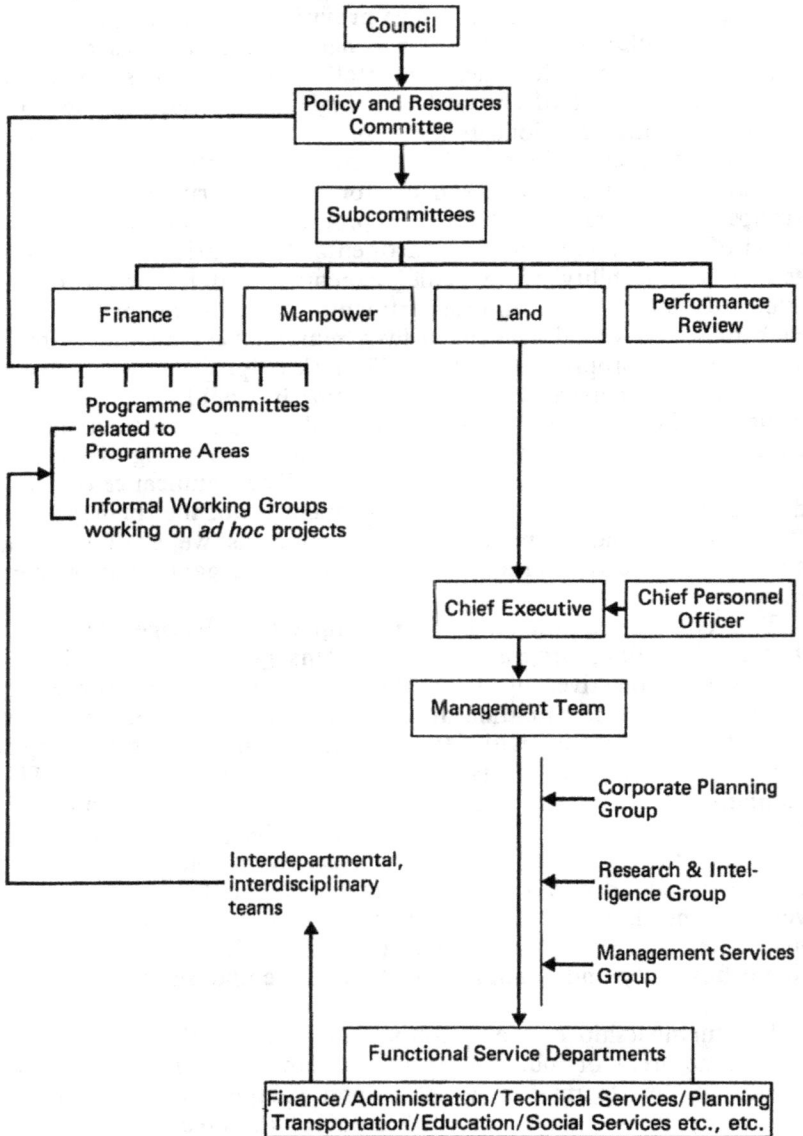

Figure 6   The Bains pattern

THE MATRIX MODEL

Matrix design basically stems from a recognition of the fact that an organisation is, at any one time, both a hierarchical entity designed for functional efficiency and also a complex problem-solving entity which must respond to changing environmental conditions. These two dimensions within an organisation are reflected in what is termed the functional structure and the project structure (Kingdon, 1973). The project structure, represented in the present context by the interdepartmental groups, induces greater flexibility and an increased capacity for problem-solving. This is because expertise is concentrated and authority determined in a way dictated by the nature of the project or subject matter involved. Membership and leadership of such groups is flexible and dependent upon the nature of the immediate project or problem. Those who assume leadership by consensus as to their possession of relevant expertise need sufficient authority to overcome or prevent conflict of interests during projects and problem-solving exercises; exercises which would be characterised by complex patterns of interdependence between different departments. Thus an organisation adopting a matrix form must experience and formally recognise the existence within its managerial structure of a web of authority relationships that violates the traditional command pattern of hierarchical organisation.

The following can be identified as major characteristics of matrix organisation.

1　A set of changing roles for each incumbent rather than a single constant role.
2　A definition of relationships based upon *ad hoc* project needs rather than generalised hierarchical position.
3　Assignments based upon individual expertise rather than fixed task definition.

This description emphasises the project dimension of matrix design which highlights the importance of lateral relationships and group working. The introduction of such horizontal project elements within the organisation assumes a special significance when the introduction of corporate management structures is viewed as an attempt to import organic characteristics into a hitherto mechanistic organisational setting. Burns and Stalker, in describing the essential features of the organic stereotype (1961, pp. 121–2), emphasised the importance of lateral structuring and communication; the adjustment and continual redefinition of individual tasks; and flexibility in the location of authority, which should vary with the location of expertise in relation to the subject matter of a particular problem. The project orientation is also emphasised by Thompson when describing the features of the innovative organisation which, he says, should contain units which represent 'an integrative grouping of various professionals . . . engaged upon an integrative task requiring a high degree of technical interdependence and group problem-solving' (Thompson, 1965, p. 15). Similarly, Greenwood and Stewart, when examining the appropriateness of matrix organisation as a structural vehicle for corporate planning in local government, point to the benefits to be derived from the use of heterogeneous project groups: 'Use of heterogeneous groups secures the diversity of inputs that are required for the diagnosis of complex problems, and places the individual in challenging situations where expertise rather than formal position is of greater importance' (Greenwood and Stewart, 1972, p. 34).

The matrix form advocated by Bains can be seen as representing a possible structural response to the need for local authorities to adopt more organic structures and to increase their adaptive and problem-solving capacity in relation to unstable and complex environmental conditions.

THE RESPONSE TO BAINS

It has been said that it is the task of revolutionary zealots to blaze a trail which more moderate successors can subsequently apply with acceptable modifications. This seems to be an accurate assessment of the relative positions of Maud and Bains. The Maud proposals for structural integration were too much at variance with the traditions of local government in this country. Bains, on the other hand, managed to strike a more acceptable balance between the needs of structural integration, as an essential prerequisite for the achievement of a corporate approach to management in local government, and the more traditional needs of local representative democracy with its attendant demands for maximum councillor participation and control. It is not really surprising therefore that the Bains Report was seen to have more practical impact than the Maud Report. However, it is important to get the response to Bains into perspective. For example, very few local authorities followed Bains to the letter and some of the most crucial concepts in the Bains scheme in fact received a fairly negative response.

In a survey carried out by the Institute of Local Government Studies between 1973 and 1975 the influence of the Bains recommendations during the period of reorganisation was examined (Greenwood *et al.*, 1975). It was shown that generally the new local authorities were not organising their committee structures on the basis of programme areas although the concept had been partly adopted in some authorities. Nevertheless, the survey did show that the call for an overall reduction in the number of committees made by both Maud and Bains had been complied with; whereas the average number of committees for county and county boroughs before reorganisation was seventeen and fifteen respectively, the new county councils averaged only nine, the new districts, six, and the new metropolitan counties and districts both averaged ten.

The idea of informal working groups of councillors as an aid to increased member participation and in-depth inquiry outside the constraints of formal committee procedure was adopted by a relatively small number of authorities – four metropolitan districts and sixteen shire districts. It appeared that local authorities generally preferred the formal committee as the main vehicle for member participation.

The concept of a central policy committee had been widely accepted as had the need for a chief executive with overall directing power over officials. In 1975 practically all local authorities had a chief executive, a management team and a central policy committee, all with Bains-style terms of reference. This was presented in the INLOGOV survey as symptomatic of 'a new orthodoxy amongst local authorities which recognises the need for formal co-ordinating machinery' (Greenwood et al., 1975, p. 55).

The idea of resource subcommittees was widely accepted, although in some authorities the function was granted full committee status. However, fewer than half the new authorities set up a performance review subcommittee. There are two possible explanations for this: first, the fact that most authorities believed that performance review was a matter best left to the appropriate programme or service committee and, secondly, the possibility that local authorities have a better understanding of resource co-ordination which was consequently given more emphasis (through the setting up of committees for finance, land and manpower) than the function of policy appraisal and review. This general reluctance to recognise performance review as a full-blown authority-wide function did not portend well for the subsequent adoption of corporate planning procedures which, as we shall see, centre around a cyclical process of prescription, review and modification.

With regard to departmental structure, the local authorities appeared to share Bains's distrust of directorates, and most of them had retained the traditional form of departmental structure based on professions. As we have seen, Bains believed that the retention of traditional departmental structures was perfectly reconcilable with a corporate approach so long as the structure was supplemented by interdepartmental groups. However, in 1975 it appeared that a surprisingly small number of authorities had set up horizontal project or programme area groups, as Table 3.1 demonstrates.

Table 3.1

	Counties	Metropolitan Counties	County Districts	Metropolitan Districts
	%	%	%	%
Use of project control groups	19·1	50	20·3	45·5
Use of area teams	42·9	33·3	1·9	30·3

Source: Greenwood *et al.* (1975), p. 51.

Such a pattern gives cause for concern since without these horizontal integrating devices the departmental structure will remain unco-ordinated except for the activities of the management team and the efforts of specialist corporate planning staff. It is doubtful whether influence from these two quarters alone would be sufficient to counter the strong centrifugal forces of traditional departmentalism. The fact that many local authorities had not regarded the creation of programme area teams as an important initial step emphasised a danger inherent in any attempt to introduce matrix structure in local authorities, namely, the danger that the horizontal elements of organisational structure may receive inadequate attention and too little organisational emphasis.

Structural imbalance between the vertical and horizontal elements is not the only problem which can accompany the introduction of a matrix design. Clearly the imposition of a horizontal project dimension within an organisation which has previously been structured along purely functional lines will necessitate a considerable change in the behavioural orientation of incumbent managers and participants. In the local authority adopting a matrix structure many officers will, during the course of the new system's operation, be removed from the familiar departmental environment where they are constantly reminded of sectional interests and subject to goal displacement. Instead, they will be placed in an unfamiliar, less permanent, managerial setting, involving equally unfamiliar interpersonal relationships in which the operational concern is less with service provision and more with interdepartmental, interdisciplinary analysis and problem-solving. A matrix structure tends to impose new and unfamiliar expectations with regard to perceptions of group identity and new levels of responsibility upon those charged with its operation. Lawrence and Lorsch's extension of the concept of differentiation into the behavioural sphere discussed earlier involved recognising the presence of bureaucratic organisational value systems or the behavioural traits associated with managers in highly differentiated organisations. An important feature of such behavioural traits was identified as the differences in cognitive and emotional orientation on the part of members of different functional departments, which had been brought about by excessive segmentation and specialisation. The extent to which this behavioural feature can represent a threat to the achievement of structural integration through matrix design is explored more fully in the case study presented in Part Four.

This chapter has been mainly concerned with analysing the movement towards structural integration in local authorities as part of the wider movement towards the adoption of corporate management. This has been set against a general background of theoretical prescriptions for organisational design in relation to organisational task and environmental setting. We now turn to a consideration of the processes of corporate management and planning which such integrated structures are designed to support, concentrating, as before, on analysis within the general intellectual framework of organisation theory.

PART TWO

THEORY AND APPLICATION:
THE PROCEDURAL ASPECT

Chapter IV

RATIONAL DECISION-MAKING AS A THEORETICAL BASIS OF CORPORATE PLANNING PROCESSES

RELATING STRUCTURE AND PROCESS

It is difficult to overemphasise the importance of recognising the interdependence which must exist between the structural and procedural aspects of organisational design and functioning, particularly in view of the supportive or destructive influence that organisational structure can exert upon management process and vice versa. It is essential that structure and process complement each other in a mutually supportive alliance. For example, a managerial process which displays essentially flexible and adaptive characteristics would clearly be stifled if placed within a structural framework which was by nature bureaucratic and mechanistic. Conversely, structural innovation in the direction of more organic forms will be pointless if it is not accompanied by managerial processes and operational norms which have a similarly organic, environmental orientation.

It is often argued that traditionally in local government there has been a marked tendency to concentrate on structural panaceas in isolation, an observation apparently confirmed by the emphasis given to committee and departmental structures and the establishment of specific posts in reports such as Maud and Bains. However, it should be noted that such narrowness of outlook has occurred in interpretation and application rather than in the initial prescription. The Maud Report contained important passages which emphasised that its structural recommendations should be viewed as merely providing a framework for effective management processes. It was specifically recommended in the report that local authorities should adopt a systematic and cyclical approach to the management process which would not leave direction and control to chance and which would ensure that the interests of the whole would be considered at all times. The approach should involve the setting and reconciliation of long-term objectives and a regular review of progress in all fields of activity so that corrective action can be taken in good time when necessary (Report of the Maud

Committee, 1967, Vol. 1, pp. 48–9). However, despite the presence of such passages, the focus of attention following the publication of the report and the debate surrounding its ultimate rejection centred exclusively on its structural features. More recent events suggest that this interpretive bias towards structural solutions continues today. Even though the Bains Report took the process of management as its starting point and deliberately set out to design a related and supportive structural framework, reaction to the report has been characterised by a greater emphasis on setting up committees and posts with Bains-style titles and terms of reference than on getting to grips with a truly systematic and cyclical managerial process.

The main outlets for prescriptions about managerial processes in local government were the various academic pronouncements which appeared in the late 1960s and early 1970s, especially those emanating from the Institute of Local Government Studies (INLOGOV) in Birmingham, and the efforts of bodies such as the Institute of Municipal Treasurers and Accountants (IMTA, now the Chartered Institute of Public Finance and Accounting) and the Local Authorities Management Services Advisory Committee (LAMSAC). These bodies, by studying the problems and providing the opportunities for widespread discussion, helped to generate an atmosphere in which the need for radical changes in approaches to management was accepted. Such pronouncements and discussions usually amounted to the advocacy of a planned process approach to management and, more specifically, the introduction of planning, programming, budgeting systems (PPBS) as the procedural means of meeting the requirements of the newly defined management task of the local authority, with its emphasis on relating the activities of the authority as a whole to the changing needs and problems generated by a turbulent and systemic environment. Thus the move towards more organic structures previously described would be matched by the introduction of a management process with a similarly organic orientation.

The intention in this chapter is to examine the theoretical basis of PPBS as a system of management in local government as a preliminary to a more detailed description of its practical application. This will involve an exploration of another branch of organisation theory, that which is primarily concerned with the processes by which decisions are, or should be, made. For decision theorists like H. A. Simon the structure of an organisation is viewed merely as a device which aids or hinders the decision-making process which lies at the heart of all management activity.

H. A. SIMON AND RATIONAL DECISION-MAKING

At every level of management activity the manager or administrator is concerned with making choices between alternatives, whether this involves seeking solutions to immediate day-to-day problems or the development of broad overall policy. Thus, for Simon, the terms management and decision-making are synonymous. This may seem odd at first sight since it could be argued that the making of a decision, that is, the initial agreement as to which line of action to pursue, is merely one in the overall management process, the next stage being the implementation or execution of the agreed policy. Simon argues, however, that it is impossible to separate the managerial action of decision-making and any subsequent executive stages of the process, since these executive stages themselves involve complex decision functions: 'The task of "deciding" pervades the entire administrative organisation quite as much as does the task of "doing" – indeed, it is integrally tied up with the latter' (Simon, 1957, p. 1).

Simon identifies three basic stages or activities in the decision process:

1 The intelligence activity (using the term intelligence in its military sense)
2 The design activity
3 The choice activity

The first stage in the process represents that part of the administrator's activity which is concerned with becoming aware of situations which require a decision. There is, after all, little point in being skilled in the art of decision if those situations requiring the application of such a talent slip by unnoticed until it is too late for decisive action to be effective. Here we find reflected the environmental orientation associated earlier with the organic approach to management since, in Simon's words, this first stage of the decision process involves 'searching the environment for conditions calling for decisions', which implies an awareness of the need to initiate change in response to environmental instability. The second stage represents the need to discover, analyse and develop the numerous courses of action which it may be possible to pursue in order to achieve a solution. The third stage represents the administrator's action in choosing one particular solution or strategy.

In actual practice each stage in this decision process may contain a microcosm of the whole process. For example, during the design stage the decision-maker may well have to pursue a secondary intelligence activity in order to become fully aware of all alternatives open to him as solutions to the problem identified during the primary intelligence stage. He then has to choose which alternative courses of action to allow within his terms of reference, thus introducing a secondary choice activity prior to the final choice of solutions to be adopted. Thus, although the three stages in the decision process can be clearly identified, the sequence of their implementation may be more complex than the initial analysis might suggest. However, it is clear that the whole spectrum of management activity is inherent in the single process of decision-making.

Simon believed that by analysing the decision sequence and producing a model which increases the rationality and effectiveness of solutions to problems, decision theory can, at the same time, lay the procedural foundations for the most rational and effective process of management.

Simon's work has three basic elements: first, the introduction of the model of pure objective rationality in decision-making; secondly, the production of a more realistic behavioural model comparing the actual behaviour of decision-makers with the ideal model; and thirdly, observations as to how real decision-making behaviour can be brought as close as possible to ideal behaviour.

Simon's description of objective rationality in decision-making follows the well-worn formula of economic theory in that the primary objective is to maximise the amount of satisfaction obtained from scarce resources which can be used in many different ways. The classical economic problem centres on the concepts of scarcity and choice. Resources are scarce compared to wants or needs, thus they not only have a monetary cost but also an opportunity cost, that is to say, the cost represented by the loss of all the alternative uses which are effectively sacrificed when a given resource is committed to a particular use. Thus the rational economic man must ensure that the benefit or satisfaction of need derived from a particular commitment of resources more than offsets the cost of those resources. In a slightly more familiar situation, our decisions as to how to spend our disposable incomes following payday are guided by a continual process of comparing the satisfaction of need which derives from spending a given amount of money on one item with the satisfaction to be derived from spending the same amount on something else. In short, the rational economic decision-maker is continually involved in the identification and evaluation of alternatives. For Simon, good administration is rational administration and the principles to be applied for its attainment must be the same as those used to ensure the optimum use of scarce resources in economic theory:

A fundamental principle of administration, which follows almost immediately from the rational character of good administration, is that among several alternatives involving the same expenditure the one should always be selected which leads to the greatest accomplishment of administrative objectives; and among several alternatives that lead to the same accomplishment the one should be selected which involves the least expenditure. Since this 'principle of efficiency' is characteristic of any activity that attempts rationally to maximise the attainment of certain ends with the use of scarce means, it is as characteristic of economic theory as it is of administrative theory. The 'administrative man' takes his place alongside the classical 'economic man'. (Simon, 1957, pp. 38–9)

Thus, according to Simon, rational decision-making in administration consists in 'the selection of preferred behaviour alternatives in terms of some system of values whereby the consequences of behaviour can be evaluated' (Simon, 1957, p. 75).

Simon's normative model sets out the desirable sequence of stages which should follow on the identification of a problem. Those stages are:

1 List all the alternative courses or strategies one might pursue.
2 Determine all the consequences that follow upon each of the strategies.
3 Evaluate these sets of consequences, choosing the alternative which facilitates the maximum attainment of one's goals at the lowest cost.

However, just as economic models are often criticised for being convenient and manageable abstractions from the real world with their heavy reliance on all other things being equal and their tendency to ignore the unpredictable nature of many variables which are conveniently viewed as constants, so the model of objective rationality assumes too much of the decision-maker in the real world. Simon appreciated the utopian character of the model and specified three broad areas in which actual behaviour must fall short of objective rationality.

1 Rationality requires a complete knowledge and anticipation of the consequences that will follow on each choice. In fact, knowledge of consequences is always fragmentary.
2 Since these consequences lie in the future, imagination must supply the lack of experienced feeling in attaching value to them. But values can be only imperfectly anticipated.

3   Rationality requires a choice among all possible alternative behaviours. In actual behaviour only a very few of all these possible alternatives ever come to mind. (Simon, 1957, p. 81)

Thus in reality administrative man cannot be objectively rational:

> The capacity of the human mind for formulating and solving complex problems is very small compared with the size of the problems whose solution is required for objectively rational behaviour in the real world – or even for a reasonable approximation of such objective rationality. (Simon, 1957, p. 188)

THE CONCEPT OF BOUNDED RATIONALITY

Simon introduces the concept of bounded rationality to describe how decision-makers behave in reality. The concept emphasises that the rationality of the decision-maker will remain subjective within a more closely delimited and less open-ended frame of reference than that assumed in the model of objective rationality. Moreover, in his decision process the administrator satisfices rather than maximises. By this Simon means that the administrator is concerned more with finding satisfactory solutions to problems than with finding solutions which might be considered optimal. The difference between the two approaches is 'the difference between searching a haystack to find the sharpest needle in it and searching the haystack to find a needle sharp enough to sew with' (Simon and March, 1958, pp. 140–41).

Thus, while rational economic man strives to select the best alternative from all those available to him, administrative man is concerned with making a decision which appears satisfactory. Once the latter has discovered such a satisfactory solution then his search is terminated. He will not continue to examine alternatives in the hope of discovering an ideal solution.

A whole range of factors will determine the point at which a decision satisfices. A consideration of these factors led Simon to consider the 'psychological environment of choice'. Simon observes that:

> It is impossible for the behaviour of a single, isolated individual to reach any high degree of rationality . . . individual choice takes place in an environment of 'givens' – premises that are accepted by the subject as bases for his choice; and behaviour is adaptive only within the limits set by these 'givens'. (Simon, 1957, p. 79)

For rationality to be achieved the decision-maker must experience a period of hesitation preceding choice, during which behaviour alternatives, knowledge of environmental conditions, consequences and anticipated values must be the focus of attention. However, this hesitation-choice pattern indicates a relatively sophisticated level of behaviour. If consciously pursued the hesitation-choice pattern may well lead to inaction since the individual, conscious of his inability to consider all relevant factors and despairing of rationality, might hover between possible choices until the time for effective action was passed.

The stimulus-response pattern takes us nearer to what really happens:

> In fact, choice and action usually take place long before attention has been given even to those elements in the situation that are within grasp. A stimulus, external or internal, directs attention to selected aspects of the situation to the exclusion of competing aspects that might turn choice in another direction. (Simon, 1957, pp. 89–90)

Such stimuli will determine the particular focus or bias which the decision-maker, with his limited span of attention, will bring to his perception of problems. In an organisational/administrative setting the stimuli creating a particular focus or bias are numerous.

1 Factors of a personal/individual nature – individuals' beliefs, values, education, intellectual capacities, etc.
2 The influence of informal groups, their conventions and behavioural norms.
3 Influences of an organisational kind such as formal divisions of work, standard practices and procedures, channels of communication for information and transmitting the decisions of others within the organisation, organisational training, etc.
4 External pressures exerted upon the organisation, and its whole environment.

Simon points out that such stimuli need not necessarily be random and arbitrary but can be planned and controlled so as to serve broader ends.

STRUCTURING THE DECISION-MAKING ENVIRONMENT

The suggestion that the stimuli affecting the perceptions of decision-makers can be manipulated has significant implications, for it implies that an organisation can, to some extent, structure the decision-making of its members. In other words, members can be placed in a psychological environment which will adapt their decisions to the organisation's objectives and will make sure that they are provided with the information needed in order to make decisions correctly. Thus, in an organisational setting, the administrator can be organisationally rational, in that his decisions will approach, as closely as possible, rationality judged in terms of the organisation's objectives and values. The organisation can simplify the rational decision process by structuring the choices open to individuals, providing information, and infusing its values into the administrator. Thus the administrator can be provided with both a constraint upon the range of alternatives to be considered and a standard for the evaluation of expected outcomes. It follows from this that one should always:

> judge a procedure, an arrangement of functions, a recruitment policy or a training scheme by its contribution to good decision-making. If these are well devised they will make it more likely that the 'relevant' considerations will be taken into account by the right people at the right time. (Brown, 1971, pp. 153–4)

The notion of organisational rationality, therefore, involves placing the organisation members in an administrative environment that will structure or manipulate their decision processes so that they will achieve rationality in terms of the organisation's objectives and requirements for future survival and growth.

For all its remoteness from empirical reality, Simon's model of pure rationality still has prescriptive value. The model emerges as a regulative ideal against which actual decision processes and organisational decision-making environments can be measured and if necessary improved. There is plenty of scope for enhancing the level of rationality in decision-making and one can move towards an ideal even though one may not be fully able to attain it. After all, a decision becomes more rational to the extent that a decision-maker extends his examination of the alternative courses of action open to him and the consequences of those alternatives, and attempts to clarify his goals and objectives. A danger that concerned Simon was the lack of a corrective to the narrow perspective of many organisations. The need consciously to extend the search for alternative solutions and strategies and to anticipate and evaluate as thoroughly as possible the consequences of specific policies is particularly critical in the public sector. Whereas an organisation in the private sector has to think primarily in terms of the values and objectives necessary for its own welfare and survival, an organisation in the public sector ought to operate in accordance with a comprehensive system of community values and thus promote a symmetry between organisationally correct values and socially correct ones. In order to make sure that some relevant factors are not excluded from consideration Simon would stress the importance of centralised controls and central review to encourage a comprehensive view and to minimise some of the dangers inherent in narrow departmentalism. In an organisational setting the decision-making process involves interaction between different groups and organisational units. This raises problems of co-operation and co-ordination to ensure that all the organisation members are acting to secure the same set of preferred consequences or objectives. The more complex the organisation the more difficult this becomes. Here we see a direct correlation between the requirements of organisational rationality in procedural terms and the need for structural integration and a corporate approach discussed in the previous section.

Dunsire has pointed to the affinity between Simon's rational model and some of the techniques now employed as aids in the making of decisions in the public sector. Using the three elements or stages of Simon's decision model as reference points, Dunsire refers to categories of decision aids which:

1 Help to widen the range of options considered.
2 Assist in the prediction and presentation of logical empirical consequences.
3 Assist in the ranking and marshalling of outcomes for evaluation. (Dunsire, 1973, p. 118)

In the first category are included the group of techniques that fall under the general heading of operational research, which has been successful in encouraging fresh and clear-eyed approaches to problems and has often generated surprising options, quite outside the range that would normally have been considered by the organisational decision-maker. In the second category are the increasingly sophisticated projection techniques based on systems analysis or network analysis, which attempt to enable the decision-maker to see into the future with much more reliability than would be the case if all he had to rely on was intuition and educated guesses. Networking or planning techniques and the estimating side of budgeting, with the aid of machines and computers, enormously increase the human capacity to look ahead. Cost-benefit analysis is identified as a technique to facilitate an objective consideration of alternative ways of allocating resources and an evaluation of their consequences, expressed where possible in monetary or quantitative terms, thus making it possible to choose that alternative which has the greatest net benefit. As Dunsire points out, in actual fact, all these techniques would be used together in an overall corporate planning system such as programme budgeting.

Programme budgeting is one of a family of general management systems all of which are based on the general management philosophy of long-range planning. Although such systems tend to vary in emphasis the procedures or stages involved in their operation follow a common pattern.

1 The organisation identifies needs and problems in its environment.
2 Objectives are formulated in relation to those needs.
3 Alternative ways of achieving the objectives are identified.
4 These alternatives are subjected to a process of evaluation to gauge the probable effect on resource usage and environmental impact.
5 Decisions are made on the basis of this information and action initiated.
6 Results are monitored and, if necessary, adjustments and revisions undertaken in relation both to strategy and overall objectives. Thus the whole cycle begins again.

This then is the kind of systematic and cyclical approach to the process of management advocated in both the Maud Report and the Bains Report. The need in local government was for policy planning, the process whereby an authority can plan and adjust its activities so as to meet the needs and problems of its environment. Policy planning, like rational decision-making, is an ideal, but an ideal which the application of systems such as programme budgeting can help to achieve, emphasising as they do the importance of knowledge of the organisation's environment and the need to set and reset objectives.

The sequence of stages followed in these planning systems relates to Simon's model of rational decision-making in so far as it gives formal recognition to the need to consider alternative courses of action, to evaluate the consequences of those alternatives and to choose that course of action which brings the greatest net benefit. However, the procedures for long-range planning modify the model in an important way. By implanting the need for review and information feedback, the procedures allow for the decision-maker's less than perfect knowledge.

It should be clear by now that rationality in decision-making is largely dependent upon the gathering and assimilation of information: information about the organisation's environment, about possible alternatives, about the consequences of alternatives, about the evaluation of output as well as input. Management systems such as programme budgeting provide a basis on which the information available can be structured and from which the search for new information must start. 'Why is this activity being undertaken? What is the objective that is being met in this activity? Are there other activities that could be undertaken that would be directed at the same objective? How effective is this activity in meeting the objective and at what cost?' By asking such questions, the planned process of management can expose ignorance and partial knowledge. As was pointed out earlier, certain techniques such as cost-benefit analysis can provide some of the answers and form an integral component of planning systems like programme budgeting. What these planning systems do is to apply such analytical, evaluative and forecasting techniques systematically. They help place the decision-maker in a structured and programmed administrative environment which reflects the needs of rationality, or at least the more subjective variant of organisational rationality, while at the same time recognising the limitations to its achievement. They provide an administrative environment which produces the kind of organisational stimuli or influences, referred to earlier, which will create a bias towards greater organisational rationality in the decision-making process and therefore in the management process as a whole.

Before leaving this discussion of rational decision-making as a theoretical basis of programme budgeting and related systems of management, it should be noted that merely placing the decision-maker in an appropriate administrative environment does not guarantee success. Although an organisation can help the decision-maker by providing an environment of givens, a framework of reference points and values which can produce an optimal decision in terms of the particular organisation's needs, rationality is still limited by the capacities and whims of its human members. The behavioural element, the orientation and perceptions of the organisation's members, is of paramount importance. This is all the more so since planning systems like programme budgeting with their inherent demand for self-criticism and the need for a creative dissatisfaction with the status quo are as much attitudes of mind as formal systems of management.

Chapter V

FROM THEORY TO PRACTICE – PROGRAMME BUDGETING IN LOCAL GOVERNMENT

ADVANTAGES OF FORMAL PLANNING SYSTEMS

The management philosophy of long-range corporate planning emphatically rejects the idea that an organisation can only react to external changes in its environmental or market situation as these occur. Rather, it is based on the premise that by taking suitable actions today an organisation can significantly and favourably influence the position in which it will be at a given point in the future. Planning is decision-making. It is the determination of goals and the specification of means to achieve those goals. A plan is, by definition, some predetermined cause of action over a specified period of time. The planning function is essential given that an organisation's adaptive process cannot be instantaneous. Nevertheless, planning remains one of the most vulnerable of management activities. This is because planning, and especially long-range planning, is an activity permeated with uncertainty and difficulty. It requires a conscious effort to penetrate the future, to forecast what is unknown, to predict and prescribe action for coping with novel problems and conditions which may or may not materialise. Such activity is far less comfortable and inviting than those aspects of the management process which offer the refuge of routine and certainty. At best, managers procrastinate about planning; at worst, they do no planning at all. Simon himself refers to 'Gresham's law of planning' (a variation of Gresham's Law in economic theory) which states that the easier, less demanding routine work drives out the more difficult planning work. This is because the planning situation is relatively unstructured and the manager, robbed of any recourse to set procedure and precedent, must fall back on such intangible qualities as judgement and intuition. In Simon's words:

A completely unstructured situation, to which one can apply only the most general problem-solving skills, without specific rules or direction, is, if prolonged, painful for most people.

Routine is a welcome refuge from the trackless forests of unfamiliar problem spaces. (Simon, 1960, p. 39)

The main advantages of introducing a formal planning system such as programme budgeting into an organisation are twofold. First, by introducing a set pattern and sequence of stages to be followed an otherwise unstructured and uncomfortable management activity is imbued with a certain amount of programming and routinisation. It is Simon's contention in his later work that more and more elements of such managerial qualities as judgement, intuition and creativity, traditionally the organisation's only assets in tackling strategic planning decisions, are now capable of being programmed and of being incorporated into structured planning systems. This has been made possible through advances in mathematical analysis and forecasting techniques, computer simulation, and so on. Thus a great deal of the uncertainty and difficulty can be removed from the planning process. The second major advantage associated with the establishment of a formal planning system lies in its use as a means of achieving organisational rationality in the decision process. A comprehensive statement of the advantages of formal planning, which highlights this particular overall quality is given by Steiner.

Effective planning prevents ad hoc random decisions. Effective planning gives an organisation a structural framework of objectives and strategies, a basis for all decision-making. Lower level managers know what top management wants and can make decisions accordingly. An effective planning organisation provides a powerful channel of communications for the people in an organisation to deal with problems of importance to themselves as well as to their organisation. (Steiner, 1966, p. 5)

Effective planning is thus seen as producing organisationally rational decisions. It is equated with the presence of a formal system of management which consciously produces a structural framework of objectives and strategies, widens the basis of choice and improves communications between different levels of management and between the organisation and its environment.

WEAKNESSES OF TRADITIONAL PLANNING IN LOCAL GOVERNMENT

Planning has always existed in local government. It would have been difficult indeed to control and administer resources and activities on the scale applicable to most local authorities without some conscious regard to what had been achieved in the past and what needed to be achieved in the future. The main criticism of traditional approaches to planning in local government has centred on the fact that they usually took the form of a series of isolated, departmental exercises which lacked any common framework of reference apart from the central control of financial input. Lack of co-ordination meant that plans prepared by different departments were often subject to a wide degree of variation in such significant areas as time-spans and basic projection assumptions and could quite feasibly be pulling resources in opposite and irreconcilable directions. A common result of this fragmented approach was for plans to be prepared within the confines of a particular department's primary interests, with little or no regard for implications for the forward planning of other departments. For example, the siting of a housing development without regard to educational, leisure and transportation problems, or the determination of living environments without proper awareness of social welfare considerations (as was the case with high-rise flat developments). In short, the plans produced did not represent the results of strategic exercises designed to ensure the effective operation of the authority as a whole facing the common problem of coping with a complex and turbulent environment. Often the initial stimulus for undertaking planning exercises came not from a recognition of the needs of the authority but from the dictates or requests of central government departments, a factor which reinforced departmentalism and encouraged a fragmented approach to problems.

Further weaknesses of traditional planning in local government lay in the lack of adequate data and research and the fact that planning exercises were normally based on an assumed continuation of the status quo with regard to current activities and objectives and were thus restricted to the planning of marginal adjustments to existing policy. Rarely were the activities and objectives of the authority subjected to comprehensive critical review.

The lack of adequate data and research is well illustrated by the following passage from the Seebohm Report on Personal and Allied Social Services:

In the past there has been little real planning in the personal social services and this has had unfortunate effects. Some of the problems we saw and heard about (for example, those connected with immigration) appeared to have been aggravated because they had not been foreseen, though they surely could have been, and because in consequence arrangements to deal with them had been made too hurriedly and too late. The planning of the personal social services cannot be undertaken successfully without research which identifies emerging trends, assesses long-term repercussions, and estimates the character and dimension of future needs. (Report of the Seebohm Committee, 1968, p. 142)

The piecemeal nature of traditional planning was the subject of a commentary by the management consultants McKinsey & Co. when they were engaged in the design of a new management system for Liverpool Corporation in 1969.

> The Council's two formal planning vehicles tell only how much is to be spent. Nowhere is there a comprehensive statement of the expected effects of the Corporation's total expenditure in terms of standards and coverage of services. Moreover, because most of the budget figures are derived from previous years' results, continuation of the present pattern of activity is assumed as the starting point for the budgetary process. A comprehensive review of existing services and approaches is seldom, if ever, undertaken. (McKinsey & Co., 1969)

CORPORATE PLANNING AND STRATEGIC DECISION-MAKING

Corporate planning was seen as a method of introducing and sustaining a central integrated planning function which would take the needs of the local authority in its particular environmental setting as its starting point and would include environmental research and the marshalling of relevant data as an integral element in the overall planning process. Skitt has defined the process in the following terms.

> Corporate planning means planning as an authority rather than by departments in the major areas of the authority's work . . . it implies that planning is carried out in the knowledge of defined and agreed objectives, that the plans once formulated are plans for action, and are flexible and responsive to changing needs. (Skitt, 1975, p. 5)

Corporate planning implies some degree of subservience on the part of departments and service committees in the area of strategic decision-making or policy planning. The management consultants Urwick, Orr & Partners have outlined the distinction between strategic policy planning, which is the responsibility of the corporate management machinery, and tactical policy planning, which remains a more departmental and service committee responsibility. In their opinion, strategic policy planning includes decisions upon:

the relative emphasis to be given to each main type of activity; the general nature of the projects to be pursued; and the degree of priority which they should be given. This involves the type and level of decision which has a major impact on your rate of spending. It should be limited to broad judgements, guiding and where necessary initiating action in the light of the relative needs of all the services within the scope of the corporation, and setting the pace and general direction in which each should develop. (Urwick, Orr & Partners, 1971, p. 27)

Tactical policy planning on the other hand, consists of the preparation of detailed plans and policies.

The fact that corporate planning or strategic policy planning takes place at an authority-wide, interdepartmental level serves to highlight the importance of the sort of integrative structural devices (central policy committees, management teams, etc.) discussed in the previous section. It reinforces the point that structural and procedural arrangements need to be mutually supportive. Structural reforms of the type discussed earlier generally answered the traditional criticism that local government was structurally fragmented and unco-ordinated. What concerned the advocates of procedural reform was the need to encourage a more imaginative and creative approach to strategic decision-making once the necessary structural prerequisites had been met.

PROGRAMME BUDGETING – THE CYCLE

Both management consultants and academics were united in their advocacy of planning programming budgeting systems as the appropriate procedural vehicle for the introduction of corporate planning and more effective strategic decision-making in local government.

Definitions of PPBS abound. A comprehensive one was published by LAMSAC:

A planning, programming, budgeting system (PPBS) is a management system, designed to assist members and officers in taking decisions about the use of resources by the monitoring of results and the feedback of this information to assist in the updating and revising of plans. It is not a technique but a comprehensive system of corporate planning and controls which harness analytical techniques to the needs and processes of management. The emphasis is on providing timely and relevant information rather than a specific management structure. (LAMSAC, 1972)

The definition issued by the IMTA puts slightly more emphasis on the specific elements of PPBS.

Programme budgeting is primarily a system associated with corporate management which identifies alternative policies, presents the implications of their adoption and provides for the efficient control of those policies chosen. It embraces several established concepts and analytical techniques within the framework of a systematic approach to decision-making, planning, management and control. The principal features of programme budgeting are that it relates to objectives, it relates to output, it deals comprehensively with all relevant data, it emphasises the future and it emphasises choice. (IMTA, 1973)

A diagrammatic representation of its sequential stages illustrates the systematic and cyclical characteristics of programme budgeting (see Figure 7). Stage one, the identification of strategic problems, relates to the initial intelligence activity of the decision process discussed earlier. Just as the decision-maker must make himself aware of problems that require solution, so the local authority must have an information system which provides knowledge of new or changing problems in its environment. Without such environmental intelligence the authority cannot be sure that past objectives are still valid and that the services it is providing are really the most effective in relation to public needs.

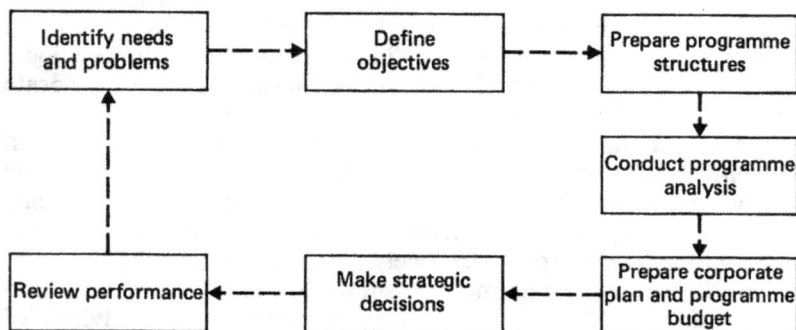

Figure 7 Sequential stages of PPBS

A clear understanding of the nature of the problems which must be faced is a prerequisite for the establishment of objectives or goals. For example, if the strategic problem identified is one of housing shortage, then the objective set might be 'to provide five hundred new council houses during a specified period of time'. In practice, objectives at the primary formative stage of the programme budgeting cycle are much more general, for example, 'to provide for the physical welfare of the inhabitants of the local authority's area', in which case the provision of housing would appear as a second level objective. This distinction between highly general and more specific objectives forms the basis of the programme structure of the authority.

The programme structure has as its main purpose the clarification of the relationships which exist between overall organisational objectives and activities which contribute towards their achievement. In other words, it is an attempt to display graphically the relationship between ends and means. Programme structures are therefore normally hierarchical designs moving down from the most general, broad objectives through layers of more specific sub-objectives right down to specific management tasks. The concept of management by programme is perhaps made clearer by reference to an actual example of a typical programme structure. The structure shown in Figure 8 is based on the leisure programme area of the London Borough of Islington. The other programme areas adopted by Islington were social services; transport; health, safety and protection; planning and development; housing; and general services.

As an initial step in encouraging a more imaginative and creative approach to strategic decision-making, management by programme is useful since it affords the decision-maker an overall view of the authority's activities. As we shall see later, when this is combined with a similarly programme-based budgetary presentation it is an aid to a clearer perception of existing and possible resource allocation patterns. The approach aids the achievement of a corporate orientation on the part of decision-makers by illustrating the inter-relatedness of the work of specific departments and committees in the context of overall objectives. For example, it may be made obvious from the programme structure that several departments are contributing to a particular sub-programme but are not co-ordinating their efforts effectively. An obvious instance in relation to the leisure programme area shown in Figure 8 may be a need to improve the degree of co-ordination between the activities of the education department and the social services department in the provision of swimming therapy courses for handicapped children.

Stage four of the PPBS cycle, that of programme analysis, equates with the decision activity of design, that is, the activity of examining and evaluating alternatives. As we have seen, rationality in decision-making is primarily concerned with the search for information about alternatives and outcomes; programme analysis represents the stage in the PPBS cycle which is concerned with the compilation of such information.

To promote the availability of, and enlargement of opportunities for, the varied enjoyment of leisure time by the inhabitants of the Borough

SUB OBJECTIVES

1. Physical Recreation

1. Outdoor relaxation

Provision of parks

Gardens

Playgrounds (adventure and conventional)

2. Sports and games

Sports centres

Playing fields.

3. Swimming baths

Provision of pools

Swimming instruction

Turkish baths & saunas

4. Special facilities

Holiday projects

Award schemes

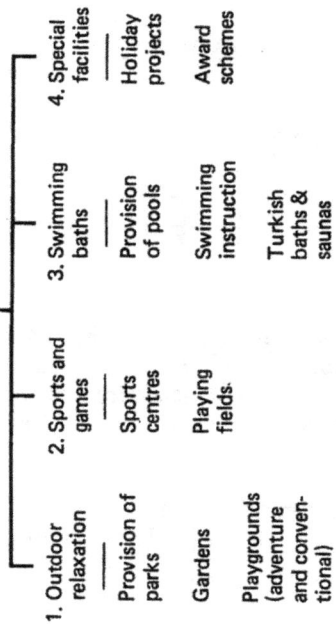

2. Social and Cultural Recreation

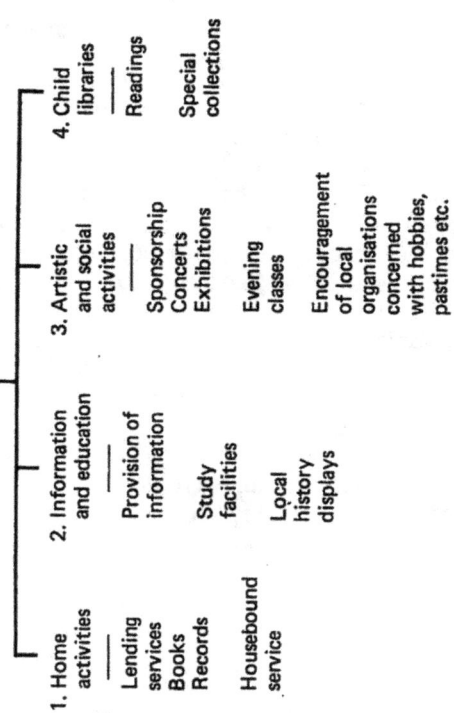

1. Home activities

Lending services
Books
Records

Housebound service

2. Information and education

Provision of information

Study facilities

Local history displays

3. Artistic and social activities

Sponsorship
Concerts
Exhibitions

Evening classes

Encouragement of local organisations concerned with hobbies, pastimes etc.

4. Child libraries

Readings

Special collections

Figure 8   Programme structure: leisure programme area of the London Borough of Islington

Programme analysis is the comprehensive investigation of a problem or situation, to provide the information necessary in making an informed decision. It is particularly concerned with seeking out and assessing (in quantitative terms where possible) the implications of various courses of action, so as to identify the action or actions which are likely to contribute most to the objectives of the programme under consideration, relative to the resources to be used. (LAMSAC, 1972)

Programme analysis is seen as an ongoing activity rather than a strategy to be adopted when a specific problem arises within a programme area. Ideally, all programmes should be subjected to regular in-depth analysis so that:

1   Crises can be anticipated and avoided.
2   Changing needs can be identified and catered for, thus ensuring that current operational objectives are in fact still the most appropriate.
3   Scarce resources can be seen to be employed in the most effective way in relation to needs and overall organisational objectives.

However, the demands made on managerial and technical expertise by these comprehensive analytical exercises are such that their application on a regular across-the-board basis would be impractical. Thus programme analysis is normally entered into only after specific problems have arisen.

An initial step in the process of programme analysis involves the presentation of an issue paper. This comprises a general survey of the problem area to be tackled together with a preliminary plan of action for further analysis. The LAMSAC report on PPBS sets out the key factors which should be considered at the issue paper stage:

1   *The problem*
    What is the real problem in terms of public need? What are the causes of the problem? Who are the groups affected (classified by age group, social group, or geographical location)? What is the size of the problem at present and is it likely to get greater or smaller in the future?
2   *Objectives*
    Clarification of the authority's objectives in the programme area concerned. If more than one objective is involved what are their relative priorities?

3 *Quantification*
How can progress towards achieving the objectives be measured? It is important here that relatively intangible criteria should be described as well as criteria which are more easily quantifiable.

4 *Current action*
Who is currently doing what? Specifically:
(a) What specific activities are already being undertaken (or are under consideration) by the council which are relevant to this problem? What are their costs? What effects are they having on the problem? How do these activities relate to what others are doing?
(b) What other governmental agencies (central and/or local), or other sectors of the community, are involved in attempting to meet the need? What are they doing? How much effect are they having?

5 *Other factors*
What other factors or constraints exist which might affect the problem? (Such factors may be of a political, chronological or economic nature.)

6 *Possible alternatives*
What alternatives might be used to achieve the objectives? What programmes or services might be able to meet some or all of the need? What are their major characteristics? (LAMSAC, 1972, p. 15)

This last element is particularly important since the generation of as comprehensive a range of alternatives as possible is central to the whole rational approach to decision-making and the incompleteness of knowledge of alternatives in a practical decision-making situation was a principal determinant of the limits to objective rationality. It is at this stage of programme analysis that the chickens of bounded rationality come home to roost. The danger of overlooking a valid alternative is always present. Utilisation of the following techniques is presented as reducing to some extent the possibility of expensive oversights.

1 Brain-storming sessions.
2 Exhaustive searches of relevant literature including newspapers and professional journals.
3 Contacting and canvassing the view of members of the public, professional bodies, pressure groups and those on the shop floor or out in the field who are currently involved in the work being done.
4 Interauthority comparisons; what have others achieved when faced with a similar problem?

There is, of course, no foolproof method which guarantees the generation of alternatives. In the final analysis the thoroughness of the operation will depend on the flexibility and imagination of the executive management concerned.

The issue paper provides the framework for more detailed analysis of the costs and benefits of alternatives. Here, programme analysis must utilise appropriate analytical techniques. Such techniques are the aids to decision-making which Simon identified as incorporating into programmed analysis elements of judgement and intuition. An obvious example is the technique of cost-benefit analysis, which compares and projects the costs and benefits, monetary, social and economic, of different policies or projects in accordance with standard methods of quantification. As will be shown later, a major criticism of PPBS as an approach to strategic planning in local government is that, because of its inevitable reliance on such complex and highly technical management aids, the system places the decision process almost exclusively in the hands of the planning experts, the technocrats of policy formulation. Of course one need not be an expert in cost-benefit analysis or any of the other analytical techniques in order to benefit from the information produced by their application. It is true however, that a working knowledge of the theoretical basis of such methods does facilitate a more accurate assessment of the relevance of a particular technique to a specific problem and a more penetrating interpretation of results. Even the most sophisticated analytical and forecasting techniques cannot prevent the intrusion of value judgements. Indeed, the need to admit both professional and political value judgements into the process of formal programme analysis is reflected in the recommendation that interim reports on analysis exercises be issued and decision-makers invited to supply 'explicit weights for value judgements used in the analysis, in place of the analyst's assumptions' (IMTA, 1971).

The results of the programme analysis should provide decision-makers with sufficient information for them to make choices which are organisationally rational; that is, choices based on as wide as possible a survey of alternatives and their evaluation structured within the requirements of stated objectives and organisational value judgements. Specifically, the presentation of the results of programme analysis should contain the following:

1 The final statement of objectives.
2 Any important assumptions made, together with information on the data generation sources and methods. Coupled with this should be information on how variations in assumptions might affect the results.

3 A summary of the findings, including summarised direct financial costs, indirect financial costs, and the social costs and benefits for each alternative considered.
4 Where possible, a recommendation.

The setting of objectives and the establishment of programme structures and programme analysis provide the raw material for the compilation of the ultimate source of information for the taking of strategic decisions, namely, the corporate plan and programme budget. The corporate plan represents a statement of an authority's present and future policy, including information on expenditure and resource commitment and expected outputs for a current or base year and a number of years ahead. As a source of comprehensive information for those with responsibility for taking policy decisions the corporate plan should contain the following specific elements.

1 A statement of the main problems facing the authority and a description of the policies adopted for tackling them presented in the format of agreed programme structures.
2 A presentation of expenditure information for the current year and future years in terms of objectives and programmes rather than in terms of specific items and departments, thus enabling decision-makers to see more clearly the patterns of resource commitment in relation to specific policy options.
3 Provision of information on the commitment of other resource elements, such as land and manpower, so that the total resource requirements and implications for every programme can be ascertained.
4 Provision of guidelines and indicators as to the present and expected outputs of programmes so that decision-makers can see what is being gained or might be gained from a given pattern of resource allocation.

Thus the corporate plan provides decision-makers with a comprehensive data base from which to judge the future implications of particular decisions, the scope for the expansion of services, or perhaps the need to curtail certain services and activities where the ratio between resource input and output is disappointing or unacceptable.

It is the provision of the data needed to complete this input/output equation which is most significant for the purposes of strategic decision-making and effective resource allocation. On the input side the most important element will be financial expenditure. Traditional financial budgetary presentations in local government have centred on showing the allocation of funds between departments and on detailing the breakdown of expenditure within departmental totals. This itemising approach is suitable if all one wants to do is to monitor and control the rate at which resources are being expended by particular departments and to make sure that money is only being spent on authorised activities and for purposes agreed by the council. The approach does not, however, meet the requirements of corporate planning, which needs instead to relate resource allocation patterns to the programmes and policies which have been adopted as a means of achieving stated objectives. This is the essential difference between a programme budget and a traditional budget. The programme budget presents expenditure on the basis of objectives and programmes rather than on specific items of expenditure within departmental boundaries. Of course, budgetary presentation must be related to the varying requirements of management control and strategic decision-making. There is still a need for assessing unit cost on a departmental basis, an exercise which is complicated by the interdepartmental nature of programme areas. Thus, basic information on costs and performance needs to be presented in different ways for different purposes. Most authorities have recognised this problem and have solved it by running different budgetary presentations simultaneously. One budget is departmental and itemised and is used for internal control purposes while the other is based upon objectives, follows the format of programme structures and is largely for use as an aid to medium-term plan-making. Both presentations therefore concentrate on those areas of information which are potentially most relevant and helpful to particular levels of control.

The output side of the effectiveness equation is rather more problematic in local government and indeed in the public sector generally. This is because the outputs or products of service functions such as education and the personal social services are notoriously difficult to identify and measure. It is easy to confuse indicators of workload or activity rate, for example, number of children taught by each teacher or number of cases handled by each social worker, with true indicators of programme output, which are more closely related to the environmental effectiveness of a programme in terms of its objectives. Some possible indicators of programme output are given below:

Programme – Transportation
Objective – To provide adequate transportation facilities, having regard to the needs of safety, efficiency and the social, environmental and amenity effects of schemes.

Elements	*Output indicators*
1 Improvement of highways	Journey time
	Vehicle-operating costs
	Comfort and accidents
2 Snow clearance	Journey time/Journeys lost
	Accidents due to skidding
3 Protection of pedestrians	Accidents to or involving
	pedestrians
4 Road safety education in	Accidents to schoolchildren due
schools	to their non-observance of the
	highway code.

Inputs for the above programme would include money spent on road-surfacing equipment; the wages of road gangs, etc.; money spent on building pedestrian subways and on the introduction and maintenance of new types of pedestrian crossing; and money spent on arranging school visits and perhaps on the employment of a full-time schools road safety liaison officer.

Ideally both the input and output sides of the effectiveness equation need to be expressed in the same terms. Here the techniques developed in the area of cost-benefit analysis can in theory, provide some assistance. Ingenious ways have been devised for reducing the costs of such things as traffic jams and road accidents to monetary terms by computing the monetary value of lost working hours, wear and tear on vehicles, increased fuel consumption, and so on. In this way, it is suggested, the cost of building a ring road around a notorious traffic bottleneck can be compared with the probable savings to the motorist and the local economy in general. Thus the input and output sides of the equation can be expressed in the same monetary terms. However, as will be shown later, the worth of such exercises in the monetary quantification of social costs and benefits is, to say the least, open to debate.

The monitoring of inputs and outputs as a check on levels of effectiveness and efficiency forms the basis of the sixth and perhaps most important stage of the programme budgeting cycle, that of review of performance. The results of this activity provide the feedback of information which, if effectively absorbed and acted upon, starts the whole planning cycle once again. Changes in the environment such as new legislation, social changes, changes in economic conditions, and so on, may necessitate a reassessment or modification of overall objectives or the adjustment of specific elements within programme areas if, for example, expected outputs are not forthcoming.

All this, of course, requires a fairly sophisticated organisational information system, a system which collects, collates and disseminates information in such a way that valid and relevant control and assessment data are injected at appropriate points into the programme budgeting cycle and thus the decision-making process. Much useful information about effectiveness can be gathered despite the lack of suitable means of precise output measurement. For example, much can be learned from the analysis of complaints brought by the public, of questionnaires and of public opinion surveys. Ideally, the organisational information system should be a centralised affair involving a central data bank into which all contribute what they can and from which all may draw what they need. Thus, expensive duplication of research can be avoided. much useful cross-referencing can be undertaken and there will be an overall improvement in the communication of information within the total organisation.

In the review of performance the first and the final stages of the programme budgeting cycle merge as one, since the same exercises which produce information and clarify performance levels may also identify new or changing needs and strategic problems. Thus the cycle is completed and can begin again on the basis of the most up-to-date knowledge and information.

Programme budgeting can be seen as meeting the procedural requirements of the three related prescriptive areas identified earlier, namely, the need for an environmental orientation, the need for a corporate approach (made necessary by environmental conditions and characteristics), and the need to achieve organisational rationality in the decision-making process. The emphasis placed on the specification and regular adjustment of objectives on the basis of environmental intelligence means that the authority adopting programme budgeting would be explicitly giving recognition to the turbulent nature of its environmental setting and also taking steps to focus its problem-solving capacity upon those areas of activity and environmental interaction crucial to its survival and development. The grouping of activities into programme areas related to overall objectives would serve to highlight the interrelationships which exist between the activities of different departments, thus encouraging a corporate approach to the design and development of strategic plans. The programme structure would also assist the decision-maker in his perception of the relationship between ends and means, that is to say, what specific activities are contributing or could contribute to what particular objectives. Programme analysis and the greater emphasis placed on the identification and measurement of output would make explicit the need to recognise the importance of assessing or estimating the environmental impact of activities, again subscribing to a central theme of environmental orientation. The identification and evaluation of alternative programmes and activities would assist the decision-maker to select the most effective programme in relation to corporate objectives, thus helping to ensure that resources are used in the most effective way. The compilation of the corporate plan and programme budget would show the decision-maker the full cost-benefit implications of past and current policies, thus providing the raw material for a much wider and deeper consideration of priorities and alternative courses of action. Finally, the formal recognition of the need for monitoring and review would help to ensure a constant flow of information between the authority and its environment and the kind of cyclical dynamism which is essential if the authority is to keep abreast of the changing problems and needs generated in the community it serves.

THE PRACTICAL IMPACT OF PPBS – AN ASSESSMENT

This, then, was the procedural model, the method by which planning and policy-making in local government could be changed from a piecemeal, ill-defined activity into an explicit programmed exercise based on the major premises of rational decision-making. The type of organisational structure recommended by Bains was designed to provide the structural framework within which such procedural qualities could be reinforced and supported. The structural elements of a central policy and resources committee, a chief executive, management team, interdepartmental groups, and so on, would assist overall planning and control, encourage long-term co-ordinated action and a corporate view of needs and resource allocation. However, in assessing the extent to which PPBS has been adopted as a system for corporate planning in the post-reorganisation period, we find evidence of the structural interpretive bias mentioned at the outset. Research carried out by the Institute of Local Government Studies has shown that in some authorities the mere establishment of certain structural features, such as a central policy committee and a management team, has been deemed equivalent to an adoption of corporate management and planning. Insufficient regard to procedural requirements has sometimes led to situations where, because magic solutions fail to appear, corporate management is deemed to be a failure (Greenwood *et al.*, 1977).

In fact the whole picture with regard to the extent to which PPBS has been adopted in local government is somewhat confused. The same INLOGOV research identifies three categories of authority in this context, each distinguished by the observed degree of commitment to the adoption of a full corporate planning process.

The first category includes authorities which continue to adhere to the traditional departmental approach while at the same time outwardly displaying the structural features of a chief executive, a management team and a policy and resources committee. Within such authorities, particularly prevalent amongst counties and shire districts, the office of chief executive is often indistinguishable from that of the traditional town clerk, the incumbent remaining essentially *primus inter pares* in his relationship to other chief officers. The management team meets infrequently and is concerned only with matters of administrative co-ordination. Members of the team are, first and foremost, departmental delegates and there is little emphasis on developing among them a collective responsibility for the management and planning of the current and future activities of the authority as a corporate whole. The policy and resources committee co-ordinates at a low level and is in no way the fountainhead of corporate policy. A chief executive of one authority within this traditionalist category is quoted as saying: 'Corporate management is all a matter of attitude. We have no corporate planners, no central units, no fancy gimmicks and we have absolutely no intention of having them' (Greenwood *et al.*, 1977, p. 25). Faith is vested in the native wit and intelligence of the service professional as a means of ensuring that the authority administers its resources in the most effective way and provides services of a quantity and quality needed by the community.

Authorities falling within the second category have achieved a kind of half-way house, having adopted a very gradual approach to the introduction of corporate planning. Examples of authorities in this position were found across the whole spectrum of local government units. Here the policy-making initiative is divided between traditional service departments and organisational units operating at a corporate level. Matters of so-called ongoing policy are left with the appropriate department, but matters involving new policy or a substantial variation in policy are seen as rightfully residing in the territory of the corporate machinery. Thus the corporate Bains-style elements of the organisation have an explicit and creative role to play and are not just parodies of prescriptive models or the results of meaningless relabelling exercises. In such authorities the chief executive is more interventionist and positive in his scrutiny of what is and what is not passed on to the management team by departments. Further structural indications of this type of authority's long-term intention of eventually adopting a complete corporate approach to management and planning are provided by the existence of more specialised corporate devices such as corporate planning and research and intelligence units.

The third category of authority includes those which have already adopted a comprehensive system of corporate planning. They tend to be found mainly in metropolitan or urban areas. In such authorities the corporate system is 'the centrepiece of the policy-making and advising process'. The departmental structure is seen only as an outlet for policy implementation and the overriding plan is to produce

> an overall corporate plan for the authority which is as all-embracing as possible. The aim is an explicit policy-making system with a systematic process of policy review, an increased concern for environmental analysis, the explicit identification of the authority's objectives, the exposure of the contribution of different departments to the same objectives, and a concern with performance and output management. (Greenwood *et al.*, 1977, p. 31)

Interdepartmental groups are prominent in the analysis of alternative courses of action and the management team displays a corporate orientation acting as a repository for specialist advice in the task of co-ordinating and developing corporate strategy. The chief executive, while often still involved in the central administration of service functions, is cast primarily in the role of policy adviser and director. The policy and resources committee is interventionist and directive in character, fulfilling the role of custodian of the corporate plan. The documentation produced by such authorities is indicative of their commitment to a corporate planning process based on the programme budgeting model. It invariably includes comprehensive statements of current and future need, research reports, issue analyses, different budgetary forms and presentations, statements of service output and new methods of costing.

From this analysis it is clear that one cannot generalise about the acceptance of PPBS as a procedural route to corporate planning in local government. It is even more perilous to accept the advocacy of PPBS without giving a great deal of thought to the system's drawbacks and weaknesses, both in terms of its practical operation in local government and, indeed, its intellectual foundation in a model of rational decision-making. It is to a consideration of such problems that we now turn.

Chapter VI

PROBLEMS AND ALTERNATIVES

THE RISK OF DEPOLITICISATION

It is the political function of local government which is often put forward as the major justification for its continued existence. After all, central government field agencies would be quite capable of administering services at a local level, but would they be sufficiently flexible and responsive to the variety of conditions and needs which exist in particular areas? Such agencies probably would not have the time or the inclination to constantly accommodate and attempt to reconcile conflicting local opinions about what needs are most pressing in an area and what priorities ought to be established. Central government could never be as sensitive and adaptable as local councils following the decrees of elected representatives who have placed their manifestos before a local electorate and who rely for their security of tenure upon the continued support of those who live within their areas. One of the main benefits of having a separately elected level of local government is that it can act as a reconciler of community opinion through the machinery of local politics. This facet of local government is the more important in view of the fact that public agencies usually have a monopoly of the service they are providing and operate outside the normal economic market place where the discipline of the price mechanism identifies demand and need. In local government, it is argued, the rule of consumer sovereignty manifests itself instead through the discipline of the ballot box.

All this is very well in theory and, of course, the objection can be raised that when people bother to vote at a local election (on average only about 40 per cent of a local authority's eligible voters) then more often than not they are using the local election as an opportunity to pass an interim verdict upon the actions and policies of the national government and are not making a comment on local issues at all. Clearly it is true that where local authorities are dominated by strong national parties, as is the case in most urban areas, then national issues can colour the outcome of a local election; but this does not invalidate or weaken the present argument. It can still be asserted that local elections produce elected bodies which are sensitive to local conditions and the demands and interests of the local population. Newton's research into local politics in Birmingham confirms both the points raised above. First, city councillors showed that they believed national issues and the popularity of their party nationally to be by far the greatest influences on local election results. However, councillors also believed that, since local factors are the only ones which they can control, their record on local issues can make that small but perhaps critical difference in a close-run election race.

Success often rests on a small handful of votes because turnout is low, and because swings are often quite large. This uncertainty puts the councillor on his guard and concentrates his attention wonderfully on those things he can influence . . . He cannot bring down prices or increase wages . . . but he can do his best to improve conditions in his ward. (Newton, 1976, p. 19)

If politicians believe that their response to local issues and demands can have some effect on the next election result then they will be more likely to attempt to accommodate and reconcile conflicting local opinions. Thus the political basis of local government decision-making remains important and it is the need to protect and retain this functional quality which distinguishes a major category of criticism of the implantation of systems such as PPBS into local government.

Critics of PPBS argue that its introduction threatens to depoliticise the entire decision-making process in local government. It is argued, for example, that in most corporate management systems the objectives used are often the expression of politically non-contentious goals formulated at the top of the organisation, 'to assist in achieving and maintaining the optimum standard of community health and well-being for people in the city' or 'to enrich the lives of the people by the optimum personal development of each individual'. Such objectives, often formulated by officers and submitted to councillors for ratification, have not been generated from within the political system. They emerge from a consensus view of society, an assumption that needs, once identified, are uniform throughout the community. Real conflicts of interest and diversity of need, which would be apparent in objectives emanating from within the political system, are aggregated out and lost within broad categorisation exercises used to identify targets of achievement required for management control purposes. Objectives arrived at in this way are more likely to reflect professional and administrative values than community values.

It is not just the generality of the objectives used or the particular values which they reflect which provide grounds for criticism. The very attempt to specify objectives at all is deemed to be counterproductive. Undue emphasis on overall objectives is adjudged to polarise issues and hinder the process of reconciliation and compromise which is an integral part of practical politics. It is much easier to reach agreement about specific policies than to agree about what such policies are designed ultimately to achieve. For example, a proposal to provide additional youth clubs for a community as part of a broader leisure and recreational facilities programme may have an appeal to most shades of political opinion. However, if one attempts to specify the broad objective of such a proposal one may generate heated argument as to whether youth clubs are designed to keep young people off the streets (which has definite law and order connotations) or whether they are designed to assist in the personal, social and cultural development of their members (an interpretation far more acceptable to those of a more liberal persuasion). As we shall see later, many critics argue that the best policy is that which one can secure general agreement upon and not that which emanates from a previously conceived notion of what is to be achieved and how different achievements can be valued and compared.

Thus it seems that, on objectives, systems like PPBS cannot win. On the one hand politically neutral, overgeneralised objectives are seen as preventing the recognition of real conflicts and diversity of opinion in the community, conflicts which are exposed more effectively through the workings of the political system. On the other hand too much emphasis on specifying objectives to the point at which they can be subject to political interpretation is seen as generating avoidable conflict and acting as a political barrier to compromise and pragmatism.

The intrusion of professional and administrative values into a traditionally democratic and political decision process forms the basis of another platform of criticism, that which challenges the value-free pretensions of corporate planning techniques. Critics argue that the introduction of long-range planning and the use of sophisticated projection and evaluation techniques has increased the influence of the professional and the technician in the political process. It is true that advocates of corporate planning and PPBS have gone to great lengths to emphasise that the purpose behind the introduction of such systems is to strengthen and improve the quality of analysis and information upon which the politician can base his decisions and not to usurp in any way his prerogative of final choice. The aim is to improve the politician's ability to make rational choice, not to pre-empt this action. The criticism is not so easily answered however. For example, evaluation of alternatives is clearly a political activity, but the range of alternatives presented for evaluation will have been filtered already through professional value judgements. Elected members must be placed in the hands of the professional planners who are more familiar with the complex techniques used. For instance, it was noted earlier that a councillor need not be an expert in cost-benefit analysis in order to benefit from the information which the technique may provide; however, a corollary of expert knowledge of a technique is knowledge of its limitations and without this knowledge a penetrating lay assessment of results is virtually impossible. The way in which results are presented is bound to influence final decisions and this lends weight to the claim that 'corporate planning and policy planning are supporting the emergence of a new supremo profession which can operate with great entrepreneurial freedom largely outside the political and public debate' (IMTA, 1973, p. 17). Councillors, it is argued, may find themselves relegated to the fringes of decision-making or, if they attempt to retain their dominance, becoming so bogged down in technicalities that their decision-making capacity and their ability to govern will be seriously impaired.

Another issue which critics associate with depoliticisation is that of output measurement and the expression of social costs and benefits in monetary terms. It was pointed out earlier that ideally the two sides of the effectiveness equation, input and output, should be expressed in comparable terms, monetary if possible. It was also noted that techniques such as cost-benefit analysis provide a theoretical framework within which such comparisons as between the cost of a new bypass, in terms of capital expenditure and loss of environmental amenities, and the benefits, in terms of time saved waiting in traffic jams and so on, can be made. Eminent critics such as Peter Self (1970) have described such activities as marking a 'tendency to convert genuine political and social issues into bogus technical ones'. In Self's opinion the 'statistical and theoretical gymnastics' used to place monetary values on such things as increased noise levels, reduced journey times, the destruction of churches and even the special benefit to future generations of preserved historic houses is indeed 'nonsense on stilts'. Self dismisses the use of the monetary standard as a 'confidence trick – to exploit the ordinary man's respect for the yardstick of money in what are actually non-monetary situations'. He goes on to argue that such valuations must remain highly arbitrary, since a very wide range of values can be offered for each and every one depending upon innumerable opinions and assumptions. The sort of valuation required would involve a series of social or political judgements of which there are as many variations as there are people in Britain. For Self, the kind of information provided by techniques such as cost-benefit analysis must remain of dubious value and can never be regarded as conclusive: it must be seen for what it is – the result of a 'dubious and esoteric art, whose main use is to provide ammunition for some policy viewpoint' (Self, 1972, p. 268). Self concludes that greater rationality in the final decision is not helped but hindered by the use of notional monetary figures which either conceal relevant policy judgements or else simply involve unrealistic and even artificial degrees of precision.

For Self, the great danger lies in the attempt to translate genuine political problems into technical terms more susceptible to analysis by the techniques familiar to the professional planner and analyst. Such developments may allow the political process to be dominated by the persuasive powers of the technocrat. In Self's opinion, the introduction of systems such as PPBS, with their heavy reliance on complex quantitative models, represents 'a shift of social power and prestige towards managerial and professional experts and away from local politicians' (Self, 1971).

In conclusion, one can identify the following as important weaknesses of PPBS:

1 Incapacity to deal with conflicting non-commensurate values (other than through neutralising the issue when possible by seeking out value-insensitive alternatives).
2 Neglect of the problem of political feasibility.
3 Strong attachment to quantitative models and theories.

Critics argue that in view of these failings PPBS is of doubtful value as a system for dealing with political decisions and public policy-making since the latter is essentially concerned with the expression and reconciliation of subjective values and, quite often, the accommodation of the irrational · but politically expedient solution.

CHARLES LINDBLOM AND THE SCIENCE OF MUDDLING THROUGH

The risk of depoliticisation has been presented as a problem existing at an essentially practical level. We now turn to an examination of those critical statements which attack PPBS on a more fundamental conceptual plane. Basically these are statements which challenge the utility of the rational decision model upon which systems like PPBS are based and propose more realistic and less demanding alternatives which are seen as being more appropriate and potentially more effective in the area of public policy- and decision-making.

Perhaps the most definitive critique of Simon's model of rational decision-making is contained in Charles Lindblom's exposition of

'The science of muddling through' (1959). Lindblom's paper, as its title suggests, challenges the rationalist assumption that any approach to management and decision-making which is not under the strict control of some central overall co-ordinating body or confined within a rigid framework of cyclical procedures and comprehensive soul-searching, must be chaotic, wasteful of resources, and doomed to a painful progression from crisis to crisis.

It seemed strange to Lindblom that the literature on decision-making persistently emphasised an approach which was impossible to practice. More than this, it seemed that the procedural realities of decision-making were dismissed rather too abruptly as mere reflex actions with no logical foundation or pattern. For Lindblom the answer was simple. If one could subject this procedural reality to academic formulation and show that there was in fact a scientific basis and logical pattern underlying the apparently muddled, haphazard actions of decision-makers, then one could produce a legitimate and infinitely more practical theoretical model. In the event, 'muddling through' was the rather unsophisticated term used to describe what was, in Lindblom's opinion, the highly scientific approach of 'successive limited comparisons'.

Lindblom used the term root and branch analysis when comparing the rational comprehensive approach with that of successive limited comparisons. The difference between the two approaches was likened to the difference between pulling the whole tree up by the roots in order to check on its progression towards maturity and assessing progress by merely examining the growth of the branches. The rational model is founded on the need for regular comprehensive analysis, each time returning to re-examine fundamental assumptions and objectives from the ground up, as it were, whereas the branch method, which Lindblom saw as lying closer to what actually happened in organisations, builds out continually from the current situation, step by step, by small degrees.

An important feature of the branch method is the fusion of the objective setting and policy choice stages which remain separate and sequential in the rational comprehensive model; that is, one decides first on objectives to be attained and then decides upon a policy which maximises such attainment. Lindblom's argument is that the process of deciding objectives and marshalling values cannot be separated from the actual choice of alternative policies, for the following reasons:

1 There will always be a lack of real agreement with regard to what specific objectives and values should be sought and applied. [As we have seen, this is a particular problem in the public sector.]

2   It is virtually impossible to rank and express a preference for conflicting values other than in terms of marginal gain or sacrifice, that is to say, how much of one value is worth sacrificing in order to achieve a little extra of another value.

As Lindblom puts it:

> I know of no way to describe, or even to understand, what my relative evaluations are for say, freedom and security, speed and accuracy in governmental decisions, or low taxes and better schools, other than to describe my preferences among specific policy choices that might be made between the alternatives in each of the pairs.

Thus, in reality, the decision-maker makes specific or incremental comparisons; the choice is between a policy which, if implemented, produces more or less of a particular value than is being produced by existing policies. By operating at the level of marginal preference in terms of specific policies the decision-maker need not attempt the sort of comprehensive analysis of objectives and values required in the rational, root method. He need concentrate only upon the extent to which alternative policies reflect differences in values at the margin. In consequence, Lindblom observes: 'His need for information on values or objectives is drastically reduced as compared with the root method, and his capacity for grasping, comprehending and relating values to one another is not strained beyond the breaking point.'

For Lindblom, the futility of attempting a completely comprehensive investigation of policy alternatives and consequences forms a major platform of criticism of the rational, comprehensive, root approach to decision-making. In the branch approach the consideration of alternative policies is restricted to those which differ only marginally from the policy already in operation, thus reducing drastically the number of alternatives to be considered and simplifying the depth of investigation which needs to be undertaken into each alternative and its probable consequences. It is necessary only to study those respects in which the proposed alternative and its consequences differ from the status quo. Lindblom notes that the latter approach is in line with the observed reality of policy development, which rarely moves in leaps and bounds but displays instead a pattern of gradual development through incremental change. But should such a descriptive theory be attributed prescriptive value?

Supporters of Simon can point to the dangers inherent in this narrow, deliberately exclusive approach to decision-making and graphically conjure up pictures of overlooked consequences and ill-used affected parties. Lindblom is quick to counter such charges claiming that 'even if the exclusions are random, policies may nevertheless be more intelligently formulated than through futile attempts to achieve a comprehensiveness beyond human capacity.' Great faith is placed in the process of partisan mutual adjustment as the most effective way of ensuring that important consequences of particular policies are identified and evaluated. Through this process, policy is moulded by the arguments and accommodations of interested or affected parties whose selfish interest makes the exposure of sensitive consequences almost automatic. Thus the more participants in a decision the better. A multiplicity of participants means that there is more chance of picking up and remedying the adverse consequences of any previous decision, on the grounds that every interest has its watchdog, whether it be a pressure group or an administrative agency. What is overlooked or neglected by one participant will be the major concern of another. Through the mechanism of mutual adjustment, co-ordination of policy can be achieved without the guiding hand of some centralised policy body inspired by some notion of a dominant common purpose. For Lindblom, reliance on mutual adjustment amounts to a practical recognition of the reality of the power structure in a pluralist society. Innovation is hard because it is difficult to get political support for a policy that is too radical for established interests. Incrementalism as a strategy is more likely to command agreement and meet the requirement of political feasibility.

Although reliance on the mutual accommodations and adjustments of partisan protagonists is by no means a failsafe method of identifying a correct policy (for example, it assumes that all interests are equally organised and articulate, which they clearly are not) for Lindblom it still represents a preferable and more effective alternative to a centralised attempt at 'super-human comprehensiveness'. It will often accomplish an adaptation of policies to a wider range of interests than could be done by one group centrally. For these reasons Lindblom holds that policy-making through incremental adjustment, in spite of its apparent defects, is more realistic, less pretentious and certainly as rational as the root method of comprehensive analysis.

> In the root method, the inevitable exclusion of factors is accidental, unsystematic, and not defensible by any argument so far developed, while in the branch method (incrementalism) the exclusions are deliberate, systematic and defensible. Ideally, of course, the root method does not exclude; in practice it must.

By proceeding through a series of incremental adjustments the possibilities of serious error which haunt the rational model are considerably reduced. The decision-maker is constantly building on past experience and his knowledge of the status quo rather than taking large leaps into the dark in pursuit of new or modified objectives. The 'suck it and see' approach of marginal incrementalism through successive limited comparisons, because it is founded essentially upon empirical observation, releases the decision-maker from an over-reliance upon theoretical devices and models as a means of anticipating and evaluating consequences.

For Lindblom, muddling through is indeed a science, a systematic and legitimate approach to decision-making and policy formulation. It is, and ought always to be, 'for complex problems the principal reliance of administrators'.

As Lindblom's model is prescriptive as well as descriptive there is a clear conflict with regard to the question of whether an approximation to comprehensive central control and review or to bargaining between multiple decision influence centres is most conducive to the maximisation of benefits. Structurally the implications of Lindblom's model are the exact opposite of those contained within the model presented by Simon. Placed within the context of the preceding discussion of decision-making in local government, the conflict is between decision-making and policy planning through central policy committees and management teams attempting to operate from an authority-wide viewpoint, and something more akin to the traditional departmental approach. In the latter situation, departments and service committees bargain for resources and have to put forward their own convincing arguments for incremental adjustments in spending and service provision. The microcosmic reflection of the council's political composition on service committees firmly linked in a self-supporting alliance with spending departments meant that the benefits of administrative competition and political mutual adjustment could be experienced in the authority's decision and policy formulation process. Also, as was demonstrated earlier, the introduction of programme budgeting as a practical manifestation of the rational, root approach called for radical changes in traditional budgetary procedures. The change was away from the conventional 'last year's allocation plus x per cent' formulation towards a more fundamental cyclical examination of the continued relevance, validity and effectiveness of existing resource allocation patterns. In fact the incrementalist approach lies at the heart of the traditional budgetary process. The conventional 'last year plus x per cent' formulation for budgetary allocations means that new commitments can be entered into without endangering existing commitments, all of which will have beneficiaries keen to defend them. Changes in the direction of commitment emerge through a series of incremental budgetary adjustments, each of which will trigger off a supportive or obstructive reaction from affected parties, thus bringing the mechanism of partisan mutual adjustment into operation to shape and mould the emergent policy.

Many criticisms can be levelled at incrementalism both as a descriptive and a prescriptive concept. As description, it is difficult to reconcile its assertions with the radical and sudden change which does sometimes occur in the field of public policy. Moreover, the extent to which a policy variation is incremental or radical is a question of subjective judgement. For example, a member of an extreme left wing group active in local politics may regard changes introduced by a Labour-controlled council merely as incremental tinkerings with the system; on the other hand, the same changes may be viewed by a more conservative element as radical and dangerous departures from a more or less acceptable status quo. Also, the theory cannot account for policies which are clearly not the result of mutual adjustment in any sense at all. Such policies may have been bulldozed through by the controlling political group with as little debate as possible, or debated behind closed committee room doors with interested parties claiming insufficient involvement and lack of opportunity for positive participation (a claim heard more and more in the field of local government policy-making). As a prescriptive concept it is criticised because of the dangers inherent in having a formal theoretical support for conservatism and even inertia in periods of severe social, economic and political change and turbulence. Dramatic change may sometimes call for equally dramatic adaptive policy responses which are unlikely to be the product of an incremental approach of limited successive comparisons. The validity of incrementalism is inextricably linked to the existence of a consensus with regard to the satisfactoriness of the status quo, and this, once again, is mainly a question of subjective assessment.

DROR AND THE OPTIMAL COMPROMISE

There are many theorists who point to the oversimplifications contained in both the rational and incremental models. Both models are really extremes, the first being too utopian and unattainable, the second guilty of encouraging inertia and conservatism dangerous within the context of an epoch of unprecedented social and economic change. Both models are one-dimensional in that each places the emphasis either on rational or on more sensory, less tangible criteria. A logical compromise between the two extremes, which is held to be more suitable in both prescriptive and descriptive terms, is based on a multidimensional approach. By this is meant an approach which accepts the potential contribution, value and legitimacy of both rational and extrarational components in the decision process and consequently gives each area formal recognition in its prescriptive exercises.

The most famous multidimensional model is that developed by Yehezkel Dror (1968). Dror's optimal model attempts to integrate and supplement the strengths of the models previously discussed while avoiding their weaknesses.

The model contains two interesting features. First, it is based on an economically rational approach. The cost, in terms of resource commitment, of approximating as closely as possible to pure rationality must be more than offset by the potential benefits. Thus, the extent to which it is possible to approximate to the rational model or to which one has to settle for something closer to the incremental model and successive limited comparisons depends on the availability of resources and inputs and on the law of diminishing returns – the economic law which states that, after a point, the benefits gained from the further commitment of resources to a particular purpose become less than the benefits which could be gained by commiting those additional resources to some other purpose. The ruling criterion, therefore, is one of economic feasibility. Secondly, it contains extrarational as well as rational components. The extrarational components of decision-making are viewed as an important supplement to the rational components. In his model, Dror allows for the potentially important contribution of such things as intuition, hunches, and so on. Such qualities are necessary because of the need for creativity and innovation and because, in some instances, extrarational processes may actually be more conducive to the achievement of optimality than rational processes.

The actual process for optimal decision-making is divided into a number of phases, many of which appear at first glance to equate with Simon's stages of pure rationality. For example,

1   Establishing operational goals with some order of priority.
2   Establishing a set of other significant values with some order of priority.
3   Preparing a set of major alternative policies.
4   Preparing reliable predictions of the significant benefits and costs of the various alternatives.
5   Comparing the predicted benefits and costs of the various alternatives and identifying the best ones.

However, in all these phases there are important divergencies from the rational model. For instance, in relation to the establishment and ranking of operational goals, the goals aimed at in the optimal model would not be as concrete and quantified as they would have to be within the framework of the rational comprehensive approach. As Dror puts it:

> Insofar as different operational goals are based on different, unrelated final values and so cannot be reduced to commensurable (quantitative and qualitative) terms, extrarational value judgements and intuitive evaluations will provide the main methods for developing this phase. (Dror, 1968, pp. 176–7)

Similarly, in considering other significant values, that is to say, significant values which are not directly part of the problem or policy under consideration, extrarational processes are formally recognised as probably the most effective way of establishing a cut-off horizon for values to be considered thus preventing a situation where so many values need to be included that effective policy-making becomes impossible. The values considered must, for practical reasons, be limited to those which will probably be affected in some major way. Extrarational processes become very important when policy-makers have had no experience on which to base their predictions.

A further important way in which the optimal model differs from that of pure rationality is that fewer alternatives are considered at the stage at which alternative policies, solutions or strategies are set out for evaluation. However, as Dror emphasises, the term 'optimal' implies more than 'satisfactory', that is, more than a limited search for alternatives which ends with the discovery of one the net benefits of which are considered to be 'satisfactory' in the circumstances (satisficing behaviour). Dror suggests that one answer to the problem of somehow delimiting the search for alternatives could lie in the principle of economic feasibility mentioned earlier. Specifically, one should only continue the search for as long as one is reasonably sure that by so doing an alternative will be discovered, the benefits of which will more than offset the opportunity cost involved in the continued effort. Such predictions about the probable outcomes of extended search are, however, impossible to make with any certainty. Dror looks elsewhere for a rationale to bound the search for alternatives and concludes that in the optimal model the search should be continued until an alternative is discovered which provides a net output that is not only satisfactory but 'good'.

We should continue searching until we either find such an alternative or conclude that we can find no such alternative within the means at our disposal, in which case we must mobilize additional resources for the search or change our standard of 'good'. (Dror, 1968, p. 178)

In preparing reliable predictions of the significant benefits and costs of various alternatives the potential contribution of extra-rational factors is again emphasised. In the optimal model the object is to construct as reliable a set of predictions as possible 'within the limits set by economical allocation of resources'. This set of predictions must contain the following elements for each alternative:

1   The foreseeable benefits and costs, with an explicit estimation of how probable their occurrence is.
2   An indication of how valid those predictions are, including a critical examination of the assumptions on which they are based.
3   An indication of how probable it is that unpredictable conse-quences will occur, with some informed guesses about the main direction they might take, as well as an estimate of how valid the indication is and an explicit examination of its assumptions.
4   A clear demarcation of the cut-off horizon (in terms of time, territory and spheres of social activity) on which each of the above predictions and estimates is based; some indication of what the long-range spillover and chain-reaction consequences might be; and an evaluation of how reliable this indication is and the assumptions on which it is based.

Clearly, both rational and extrarational components are utilised in the construction of these elements. Dror emphasises that in the optimal model, as in the rational model, all available rational tech-niques and knowledge should be used to help reduce uncertainty in the prediction of the costs and benefits of alternative policies. However, in the optimal model, the limitations of such rational techniques and the inevitable continued existence of areas of uncertainty are explicitly recognised in the formal inclusion of judgements and hunches as separate and legitimate sources of information. As Dror points out:

the more complex and novel the alternatives are, the less will rational methods be able to predict their effects, and the more must (and should) judgements, hunches, and similar extrarational processes be relied upon, after they have been nourished by the findings of the rational methods. (Dror, 1968, p. 183)

The choice of that policy or decision which brings the greatest net benefit represents the final stage of the pure rationality model. It may or may not represent the final stage in optimal policy-making, since the search for alternatives has been more limited. Should none of the identified alternatives prove acceptable then the search can be extended. However, the degree of acceptability is determined by the process of comparison and evaluation and, since the criteria used in the optimal approach are much less refined than those used in the rational model, it is more likely that a group of policies having broadly similar costs and benefits may appear equally acceptable. It is accepted in the optimal model that the criteria for comparison and evaluation can be little more than 'rough orders of priority' since there is no completely rational and objective way of comparing different types of benefits and costs which differ from one another 'not only in substance, but also in their chronological distribution and in the reliability of the predictions of their likely occurrence'. It follows that comparative evaluation of costs and benefits must rely more on extrarational than on rational processes. If, as has already been suggested, this produces several alternatives which appear equally 'good' then the optimal policy maker must seek to reduce the number of such alternatives by either 'synthesising a better composite alternative', choosing one alternative in a random way, or by letting choice be guided by intuitive guess.

Some areas of Dror's model may seem unclear and confusing. For example the introduction of the ill-defined concept of 'goodness' as an ultimate determinant of acceptability and an indicator of search frontiers in the quest for alternatives. Dror's problem, however, is one of attempting to give formal academic expression to qualities and criteria which, although recognised intuitively by a real decision-maker in a real situation, nevertheless remain difficult to define in a prescriptive exercise. But, for Dror, as long as they mean something to decision-makers in the field then their importance must be formally recognised and appreciated.

CONCLUSIONS

In a sense, all three models discussed in this section have been concerned with the concept of bounded rationality as described by Simon, that is, the extent to which pure rationality in decision situations can, or should, be sought. For Simon, rationality is bounded by human capacity but can be approached within a given organisational setting (organisational rationality). For Lindblom, any attempt to achieve rationality is doomed to failure by the sheer complexity of problems and the fact that marginal incrementalism as a practical reality is clearly superior. Dror has tempered both extremes with a recognition both of the dangers inherent in an incrementalist strategy during a period of rapid change, and the futility of attempting to rely completely upon rational formulae and quasi-economic calculation in a process which must continue to rely to a large extent upon such intangibles as intuition and hunch.

In the context of local government decision processes the present reality probably approaches Dror's model more than any other. As we have seen, the prescriptive writings of the rational school as reflected in the design of planning systems like PPBS have made a dent in, but have not completely penetrated, a traditional approach characterised by a lack of analysis and marginal incrementalism. It is now generally recognised that rational techniques should be employed in an effort to reduce the amount of uncertainty surrounding policy decisions. More analysis probably takes place now than ever before. However, there is still a heavy reliance upon professional judgement and feel for ensuring effectiveness. Much faith is still placed in the native wit and intelligence of officers and the political judgement of elected members. Thus it can be argued that Dror's rational and extrarational components exist side by side in local government decision-making. The question remains as to the balance between components and, as the INLOGOV research referred to earlier has shown, this varies considerably from authority to authority.

In these first two sections the concern has been to analyse, within the conceptual framework of organisation theory, recent organisational innovation in local government. This analysis has so far centred upon the development of more organic structures and procedures as an attempt to increase local government's capacity for effectiveness in changing conditions. The interdependence which must exist between the structural and procedural aspects has been emphasised already but the ultimate effectiveness of such reforms lies in yet another area where organisation theory provides both prescription and analysis. This is the cultural area which encompasses the values, beliefs, goals and expectations held by the human members of the organisation. It is all too easy to treat human relations studies as an isolated side-show, something to be considered when the more important structural and procedural aspects of organisational design and functioning have been worked out. However, as will become apparent from the case study presented later, the success or failure of structural and procedural innovations in any organisation will be determined to a large extent by the degree of commitment experienced by the human participants.

The following section will be devoted to an examination of some of the basic concepts underlying this important branch of organisation theory and the implications of such concepts for two important aspects of modern local government management, namely, the introduction of change within an organisation and the effective development of the manpower resource.

PART THREE

THEORY AND APPLICATION:
THE CULTURAL ASPECT

Chapter VII

ORGANISATIONAL CULTURE AND VALUE SYSTEMS

ORGANISATIONS AS SOCIAL SYSTEMS

The sociological approach to the theory of organisations sees them essentially as miniature societies, that is to say, as identifiable social entities formed when a group of independent individuals 'combine and interact, in an ordered fashion, for the purpose of achieving certain goals' (Parsons, 1964). This viewpoint therefore contends that many of the characteristics which are attributed to human societies at large are also identifiable within the social organisations which form important sub-units of those societies. Thus, just as different societies have different cultural beliefs or dominant ideologies about important aspects of social interaction and activity, so organisations, having particular origins and specific purposes, develop dominant ideologies governing such things as what are desirable goals and outlooks for their members, what behavioural patterns are helpful and acceptable and which are not, and so on.

The idea of organisational culture rests firmly on the conception of organisations as social systems. But what is a social system? How is it defined? What are the principal characteristics which distinguish it from an *ad hoc* collection of individuals all intent on pursuing their own best interest? It is necessary to seek an answer to these basic questions before we can proceed to a discussion of the practical effects and implications of the concepts of organisational culture and value systems and their interrelationship with the structural and procedural aspects of local authority organisation.

Olsen defines a social system as:

a model of a social organisation that possesses a distinctive total unity beyond its component parts, that is distinguishable from its environment by a clearly defined boundary, and whose sub-units are inter-related within relatively stable patterns of social order. (Olsen, 1970, pp. 228–9)

The most important element in this definition is the requirement of 'stable patterns of social order' since this implies the need for recurrent and ordered social interactions between organisational sub-units. Since the smallest and most basic of these organisational sub-units will be represented by the individual human member then an important distinguishing characteristic of a social system or a social organisation emerges as the existence of an ordered and patterned system of human interrelationships. These patterns of social ordering are established and maintained by the individual's observance of the behavioural rules and norms which apply to his particular organisational role, that is, his position and functional capacity within the organisation. Such compliance with role expectations, by which is meant role enactment in accordance with the expectations both of the organisation and other role incumbents, is the result of the process of organisational socialisation.

In the widest sense, socialisation refers to the process whereby an individual, with a potential for a very wide range of behavioural patterns, is led to develop actual behaviour patterns which are within the range of what is customary and acceptable according to the general standards of his family, school, church, work group and country. Thus we are born human beings but we have to be taught to be social beings, to be accepted as members of our society. This process of social learning takes place through the constant reinforcement of social rules of behaviour as the individual encounters various types of social situation. When the individual first enters a new social situation, for example, joining a new company or any other form of work organisation, his actions will be rather random. He may imitate the actions of others working within the organisation, assuming that the rules which govern their behaviour should also govern his. However, the newcomer's actions must remain uncertain until others begin to react to them. By evaluating these responses the individual has some means of assessing the relative appropriateness of his own actions and behavioural patterns. The individual soon learns through his interaction with others in the organisation what patterns of behaviour are acceptable, praiseworthy and likely to bring the rewards of approval, recognition and security, and those which are unacceptable and are likely to generate disapproval. In the extreme case, organisational rules and norms may be internalised by the individual, that is to say, accepted by him as his own personal standards of action: they become part of his personality. The process of organisational socialisation is extremely important since, as Schein points out, 'The speed and effectiveness of socialisation determine employee loyalty, commitment and productivity. The basic stability and effectiveness of organisations therefore depends upon their ability to socialise new members' (Schein, 1968, p. 2).

An organisation's behavioural rules and norms are the product of its central value system or culture. Generally, this will have developed as a response to the organisation's needs for survival and functional efficiency: 'the survival and operational requirements of an organisation are more likely to be satisfied through the enactment of socially responsible roles [in organisational terms] than through the random actions of autonomous and self-orientated individuals' (Olsen, 1970, pp. 113–14). Thus an organisation experiencing, during the course of its development, an overriding need for the rational division of functions and the efficient processing of a multitude of similar operational tasks will probably have developed a dominant ideology or culture with all-encompassing, precise and rigid expectations for all organisational roles. On the other hand, an organisation with a much less formal orientation will have developed cultural expectations limited to broad outlines and general guidelines with regard to behavioural norms and organisational role enactment. It follows from this that a direct correlation and supportive alliance will invariably exist between the dominant structural and procedural characteristics of an organisation and its cultural make-up. An understanding of an organisation's cultural blueprint is therefore crucial to any subsequent analysis or successful manipulation of its structural and procedural characteristics.

The complexity of the concept of organisational culture prevents the construction of any succinct working definition. It is possible however, following Harrison (1972), to describe some of the functions which an organisation's culture performs.

1 It specifies the goals and values toward which the organisation should be directed and by which its success and worth should be measured.
2 It prescribes the appropriate relationships between individuals and the organisation, that is, it makes specific what the organisation should be able to expect from its people, and vice versa.
3 It indicates how behaviour should be controlled in the organisation and what kinds of control are legitimate and illegitimate.
4 It depicts which qualities and behavioural characteristics should be valued or vilified, as well as how these should be rewarded or punished.
5 It shows members how they should treat one another – competitively or collaboratively, honestly or dishonestly, closely or distantly.
6 It establishes appropriate methods of dealing with the external environment.

TYPES OF CULTURE

Harrison, in an effort to establish a conceptual framework for the discovery and understanding of ideological conflicts within organisations, presents a fourfold classification of dominant cultural types. These types may be termed the power culture, the role culture, the task culture, and the person culture.

The organisation having a dominant *power culture* is characteristically driven by a need to dominate its environment and conquer all opposition. Those in authority within such organisations require absolute control over subordinates. A good example is provided by the autocratic family firm employing a form of paternalistic enlightened despotism which amounts to the power orientation within a velvet glove and which rapidly transforms into the iron fist if challenged or threatened in any way. The organisation has little need for precise, standardised rules and procedures since the smooth execution of its operations is facilitated through obedient and rapid responses to the central dictates and commands of key individuals. These key commanders will invariably have won their positions through their success at playing the organisational power game. As individuals, they will normally be power-oriented, politically minded, willing to take risks, and they will not hold security very high on their list of priorities for job satisfaction. They are judged on results and results alone and must be psychologically equipped to take the strain and survive in a highly competitive atmosphere. Organisations with power cultures have important advantages. They are very successful at co-ordinating the individual efforts of many for the achievement of organisational goals determined exclusively at the top of the organisation. They are, on the face of it, good at adjusting rapidly to new technologies or environmental changes. Size, however, is their greatest enemy. The organisation can become too large and complex to remain under the sole command of an all-powerful elite. Subordinates, influenced by the sole criteria of power acquisition and retention, may keep and utilise crucial information for reasons of self-aggrandisement. In short, the organisation may itself fall victim to its own ruthless value system. The organisation might be very effective in the short term but will lack long-term stability. Too much depends on the strength of individual personalities and a charismatic system of authority.

Harrison sees the difference between the *power culture* and the *role culture* as being similar to the difference between a dictatorship and a constitutional monarchy. The byword in the power culture is blind unquestioning obedience; the norm in the role culture is obedience to legitimate authority operating in accordance with rational rules and procedures. Consistent adherence to agreements, rules and procedures replaces the ruthless competition and conflict of the power culture as the best means of attaining organisational goals. Although both the power and role cultures are characterised by an authoritarian atmosphere, both placing great emphasis on formal hierarchy and status, in the latter this emphasis is tempered by an equally strong commitment to the need for legitimacy and legality. In the role culture nothing depends on the whim of the power hungry individual. Conformity to rules, respect for precedent and accompanying predictability are valued just as highly as competence. Results are important but the means by which results are obtained remain equally important, in some cases more so. As Harrison puts it, 'the correct response tends to be more highly valued than the effective one'. Clearly, this cultural setting corresponds directly to the bureaucratic system of organisation described earlier, with its emphasis on legitimate authority emanating from a particular office or position rather than from an individual incumbent, and displaying a preoccupation with means rather than ends. The role culture offers security and predictability to the individual. However, it also tends to reward the satisficer, since performance beyond the precise limits prescribed for a particular organisational role is unnecessary and even actively discouraged in view of its possible disruptive effects. The role culture is well suited to a situation where the need to cope with large-scale operations is more pressing than the need to remain flexible. It is effective where the development of technical expertise within a rational division of labour is more important than product innovation and the constant redeployment of skills to meet new problems as and when these arise.

In organisations where a *task culture* predominates, the goals of power acquisition and precise role enactment are replaced by the goal of task accomplishment, an overriding need to carry out specific organisational assignments and achieve prescribed superordinate goals. Nothing is allowed to prevent this. Power and command structures, though remaining necessary, are not held to be inviolable. The ideological commitment to authority, order and precedent is replaced by a commitment to solving the problem or getting the job done. In consequence, all rules, procedural norms and formal structures are constantly evaluated in terms of their actual or potential contribution to the achievement of these aims. If existing authority structures or procedures are seen as more of a hindrance than a help in a given task situation then they are simply replaced by more appropriate arrangements. The byword in this cultural setting is flexibility governed by the varying demands and requirements of changing problems.

Clearly, the task culture corresponds to the organic model of organisational design and is particularly supportive of the matrix project group approach. However, matrix design really combines the role and task cultures within the same organisational framework. It is based on a recognition of the equally important requirements of logical ordering and centralised command systems on the one hand, and organisational flexibility for the purposes of task accomplishment on the other. An organisation based exclusively upon a task culture would be able to achieve very little central control over day-to-day operations, working methods, use of resources, and so on. Such a situation with minimal central co-ordination may be acceptable in the rare eventuality of there being a plentiful supply of resources. However, in the more realistic situation of resource scarcity the lack of central control and co-ordination would lead to the disintegration of the task culture. The various task groups would be forced to compete for available resources and a power culture would begin to emerge, eventually manifesting itself in open conflict between individual team leaders.

In the fourth cultural type, that which is *person oriented*, the goals of power acquisition, adherence to established procedures and task accomplishment are all subservient to the goal of meeting the psychological and social needs of the individual members of the organisation. Here the organisation–participant relationship is turned completely around. Instead of the organisation using the collective efforts of its members to achieve organisational goals, the organisation is itself used by its members to fulfil personal needs which they would not be able to fulfil while acting outside the organisation. A group of eminent scientists joining together for the purpose of some collective research effort provides an example, as does any group practice of professionals, doctors, lawyers, and so on. Such organisations can be very unstable, since membership and compliance with organisational rules is strictly voluntary. Formal recognition of authority is discouraged, instead: 'individuals are expected to influence each other through example, helpfulness and caring.' The organisation may be disbanded at any time when it ceases to provide a system within which members can 'do their own thing'.

Clearly the dominant culture of an organisation, because it influences and shapes the attitudes, beliefs and values of participants, will have a profound influence on the effectiveness of that organisation both in terms of its internal operation and its interaction with the wider environment in which it exists. It has already been suggested that an organisation's culture will have developed largely as a response to the organisation's needs for survival, growth and the achievement and maintenance of functional efficiency. Thus in local government the successful processing of large-scale operations, involving the establishment of routine procedures and requiring uniformity and consistency rather than adaptability, was facilitated not only by the development of hierarchical, mechanistic, structural and procedural patterns but also by an infusion into the organisations of supportive behavioural norms associated with a role culture. These supportive behavioural norms will have been strengthened over time through the continuous reinforcement processes of organisational socialisation. However, as we have seen, the role-oriented culture with its mechanistic structural counterpart is insufficiently flexible to adapt rapidly to external changes. Stability is achieved at the expense of adaptability. The task culture, which corresponds more closely to the organic model of organisational design and functioning, is much better suited to dealing with complex changing environments.

It follows that cultures as well as structures and procedures need to be related to environmental context if an organisation is to be fully effective. However the creation of an ideal, organisation-wide cultural setting is impossible. Different cultural atmospheres meet different needs which exist concurrently in most organisations. Harrison illustrates the point by outlining the qualities required of the 'ideal' ideology or culture.

The 'ideal' ideology would possess some power orientation to deal smartly with the competition, a bit of role orientation for stability and internal integration, a charge of task orientation for good problem-solving and rapid adaptation to change, and enough person orientation to meet the questions of the new recruit who wants to know why he should be involved at all unless his needs are met.

While such a cultural setting remains utopian, Harrison believes that some form of cultural composite still provides the answer for organisations which need to maintain internal stability but at the same time need to be able to respond rapidly and effectively to changing environmental conditions. Such organisations may have to be composed of units which are ideologically homogeneous within themselves yet still quite different from each other. The introduction of a matrix design can be seen as such a compromise solution to this problem. Structural stability is provided by the presence of a role-oriented framework (the functional dimension) and operational flexibility by the establishment of task-oriented project groups (the project dimension).

The big problem which accompanies such cultural composites is the conflict and ideological struggle which is bound to occur when the two cultural and operational settings come into contact with each other. For example, matrix systems often suffer from attempts by the role-oriented functions to over-control the task-oriented functions. The role culture will invariably be successful principally because organisations attempt to operate matrix structures without having taken steps to ensure that participants are committed to the underlying culture. In short, role-oriented people cannot simply be plunged into a task-oriented system and expected to operate it successfully. If the matrix system is to work then appropriate structural and procedural reforms must be accompanied by equivalent cultural retraining and adjustment. There is an urgent need to avoid or overcome the problems of cultural maladjustment which can occur when changed conditions or new interpretations of an organisation's primary task demand not only radical structural and procedural innovations but also a fundamentally different overall orientation from that which had evolved since the organisation's inception.

In old-established organisations such as local authorities the cultural evolutionary process will be well advanced and, like most things which have evolved over time rather than been created at one stroke, the most fundamental cultural aspects will be potentially very difficult to dislodge or modify. Thus there is a very real danger of radical reforms being introduced in the areas of internal structuring and procedures with little or no revisionary effect being felt in the area of organisational culture. In consequence, cultural maladjustment will cause attitudes and behavioural patterns to have a destructive rather than a supportive effect upon the whole reforming effort.

The practical consequences of cultural maladjustment will be explored in more detail later. At this point we halt at the position that, following structural and procedural reform, organisational cultures must be somehow manipulated and adjusted so that the three aspects of organisational design and functioning, the structural, the procedural and the cultural, are in balance and are mutually supportive. Here we are talking about influencing the way in which organisational participants behave and relate to one another in the work situation, bringing about a change in their values, the way they see the organisation and their role within it. In fact, we are prescribing fundamental alterations in every area in which organisational culture has an effect. Such conscious, deliberate manipulation of values, prejudices and behavioural patterns requires expert knowledge about human motivations and interrelationships, about the behaviour of individuals and groups. Such knowledge is found in the field of human relations studies and behavioural science and it is necessary to understand some of the major tenets of this branch of theory in order to appreciate the particular form of the practical managerial strategies designed to achieve cultural adjustment.

THE BEHAVIOURAL APPROACH

Behavioural science is a multi-disciplinary approach to the study of human behaviour in social settings. It is essentially an extension and development of the human relations movement which had its origins in the United States in the late 1920s.

In 1927 Elton Mayo, Professor of Industrial Research at Harvard University, was responsible for the initiation and direction of the famous five-year research programme conducted at the Hawthorne plant of the Western Electric Company in Chicago. Although the initial purpose of the Hawthorne experiment was to examine the relationship between varying physical work conditions and levels of productivity, by 1932 the research had produced results which not only surprised the researchers but which carried a message of great significance for organisation and management theory generally.

As a preliminary to the Hawthorne programme the productivity of selected groups of female workers under varying conditions of lighting was tested. The researchers were puzzled when productivity rose for all groups under test regardless of whether lighting had been improved or caused to deteriorate. Mayo and his team, in an effort to explain the mystery, concentrated their attentions on a smaller, single group of workers and attempted to prove the existence of a correlation between the outputs of individuals and such physical factors as diet and hours of rest. During the experiment the output of the group went up but no correlation was observed to exist between output variations and such physical circumstances. Undeterred, Mayo introduced, over a period, improved working conditions for the group, shorter hours, longer rest periods, and so on. The workers responded and output increased. Then, after eighteen months of steadily improved conditions, the test group was suddenly subjected to a return to the conditions which had applied at the beginning. The expected drop in output did not, however, take place. Instead, the workers achieved an all-time productivity record.

After much argument and analysis Mayo and his colleagues concluded that the expected relationship between physical working conditions and productivity had been overridden by a third factor, the attitude of the workforce, the way the workers under observation felt about the work they were doing. Their very involvement in the experiment, the research team's obvious reliance on their help and co-operation, had given them a new sense of purpose and value. They felt part of a team out to solve an important problem, rather than seeing themselves as so many anonymous cogs operating within a soulless impersonal machine.

Intrigued by these results, the researchers, in an effort to learn more about group processes, studied a team of male workers operating under a group piecework incentive plan. It was observed that the importance of the economic incentive in such a situation, which called for the maintenance of maximum productivity levels by every team member, was less than the need of each individual to win social acceptance and security within the group. In order to gain such acceptance and security all group members had to conform to a collective productivity norm established by the group. The sense of social isolation experienced by nonconformists was heightened by the use of such terms as 'rate busters' for those who worked too hard and exceeded the productivity norm, and 'chisellers' for those who did not pull their weight and fell below the targets. Moreover, the presence of a self-policing, closely knit group identity was reflected in the hostility reserved for a 'squealer', someone who informed a supervisor of some breach of the general discipline code by a fellow worker.

Initially, the Hawthorne experiments set out to prove, in line with classical assumptions, that workers will respond predictably to certain physical working conditions and types of incentive. If the results of the experiments had been more in line with conventional managerial wisdom then the neat and comfortable conclusion could have been reached that in order to increase productivity all one needs to do is manipulate, in an appropriate way, the structural or procedural framework of operations. However, the results that were obtained indicated the existence of a much more complex situation with regard to worker motivation. Specifically, it had been shown that response to change in the work situation can only be fully understood, and therefore predicted, if it is seen in terms of the attitudes, goals and social interactions which exist within the work groups which the changes are likely to affect (Mayo, 1933; Roethlisberger and Dickson, 1939).

The conclusions drawn from the results of the Hawthorne research programme had a great influence on management and organisation theory. They certainly had the effect of making the study of organisations more complicated. The term 'human relations school' is itself really a collective label for three sub-schools, all of which have a behavioural orientation but which differ in terms of analytical emphasis. For example, the Chicago sub-school places more emphasis on the possible effect of the wider social environment upon organisational behaviour. Its principal advocates, such as W. L. Warner (1947) of the University of Chicago, adopt a broader conceptual focus than that adopted by Mayo and the orthodox school, emphasising the importance of such factors as social class, race, religion and family upbringing in the study of organisational behaviour. However, the orthodox and Chicago schools remain broadly similar in their continued emphasis on the need to study the determinants, whether these are found inside or outside the organisation's boundaries, of sentiments, of how people feel and think; sentiments are seen as the principal factors governing behaviour in organisations. The interactionist sub-school, however, strives to turn the emphasis away from sentiments and towards the study of observed behaviour, the study of what people actually do and how they interact with each other. For interactionists such as Arensberge (1957) and Whyte (1951), the most appropriate focus for study was on the observation and measurement of the manner in which participants contact each other. At one extreme, interactionist theory sees sentiments and feelings as being always a by-product of interaction patterns. At another extreme, interactions, activities and sentiments are seen as being at least on an equal footing.

Despite all these variations in emphasis the human relations school, taken generally, had the effect of dismissing the classical concept of the workforce as a collection of hands or brains which, if properly ordered and controlled, would produce predetermined results. Instead, managers were confronted with the prospect of harnessing the efforts of participants whose behaviour was greatly influenced by complex social and psychological forces and as such was often unpredictable. The secret of organisational success, it appeared, lay in gaining an understanding of group behaviour and individual motivation and in concentrating on improving morale and the achievement of commitment rather than on the imposition of discipline and the rigid application of mechanical operational procedures.

The barrier presented by classical management assumptions about human motivation to the achievement of such behavioural objectives as high morale and strong commitment was highlighted by McGregor in his analysis, *The Human Side of Enterprise* (1960). In McGregor's opinion the validity of management as a profession depends upon its ability to base its practices on the expertise and empirical research findings of the behavioural sciences. In other words, management should make maximum use of the body of theoretical knowledge about people at work which has continued to grow and develop since the days of Hawthorne.

For McGregor, the starting point must be an examination of the way the manager sees himself in relation to his job of managing and organising human as well as material resources. The manager is bound to hold a set of fundamental beliefs or assumptions about human nature. In accordance with these assumptions, he will judge the kind of responses one might reasonably expect to follow the application of particular managerial strategies. In order to illustrate the way in which such assumptions affect approaches to management and, in turn, the effectiveness of organisations, McGregor developed two theoretical models of human nature in relation to the work situation. These models he called theory X and theory Y (McGregor, 1960, pp. 33–57).

Theory X is seen as representing the view of human nature underlying the classical approach to management and organisation and a view still frequently held by managers. It is based on the following assumptions.

1   The average human being has an inherent dislike of work and will avoid it if he can.
2   Because of this inherent dislike of work most people must be coerced, controlled, directed and threatened with punishment to get them to put forth adequate effort toward the achievement of organisational objectives.
3   The average human being prefers to be directed, wishes to avoid responsibility, has relatively little ambition, wants security above all.

It is certainly true that many observed behavioural patterns in organisations apparently lend credibility to such assumptions about human nature. For example, constant pressure for longer holidays and higher wages, unwillingness to co-operate with management and resistance to strategies designed to increase productivity and organisational effectiveness. However, McGregor holds that such behavioural characteristics are in fact the manifestations of frustration caused by an approach to management which is based on an incorrect, or at least grossly oversimplified, concept of human motivation.

The subject of human motivation is extremely complex. However, even a basic outline of current ideas about what motivates people in the work situation is sufficient to demonstrate the inadequacies of the theory X assumptions.

To begin with, human motivation is inextricably linked to human need. We are motivated to effort by the desire to satisfy needs. These needs, in their most fundamental form, are of a basic physiological nature, for example, the need for food, shelter and physical security. As these basic needs are satisfied other needs, of a more complex social and egoistic nature, become important. Social needs include the need for a sense of belonging, the need for acceptance by one's colleagues, the need to give and receive friendship. Egoistic needs relate to the way in which we see ourselves: for example, our self-esteem, need for reputation, recognition and the deserved respect of our fellows.

It was the strength of such social and egoistic needs as determinants of behaviour which was encountered during the Hawthorne experiments. Then it was seen that a small cohesive group with a sense of purpose can be extremely effective and productive. This was because this kind of work situation was meeting the social and, to some extent, the egoistic needs of the workers involved. If these needs are not met then the individual worker often becomes resistant, antagonistic and unco-operative. Such a situation tends to develop if, for example, the individual is isolated on an assembly line with little or no group affiliation and no contact with an end product to which he can relate. Similar behavioural characteristics emerge in situations where the individual is subjected to rigorous codes of practice and discipline which leave little room for personal development and creativity.

The negative behavioural traits associated with a state of social and egoistic deprivation can work against the organisation. Participants will be resistant to change; they will be unwilling to accept responsibility. The major outlet for their frustrated energies will be found in making unreasonable demands for economic benefits. The traditional response to such attitudes and apparent hostility towards the organisation has been a reliance on direction and control, on promises and incentives, on threats and other coercive devices. However, such strategies mistake effects for causes and only serve to exacerbate the situation, since they reinforce the very approach to management and organisation which has produced these behavioural consequences.

The assumptions underlying McGregor's theory Y imply a far more complex task for managers than those associated with theory X. Theory X calls for a firm hand and a judicious application of the carrot and the big stick. In contrast, management in accordance with theory Y involves a recognition of the complexities of human motivation and behavioural response and also an appreciation of the need to integrate and bring into balance the goals of individuals and the goals of the organisation.

The assumptions of theory Y are as follows:

1   The expenditure of physical and mental effort in work is as natural as play or rest. This contradicts the traditionally held view that people inherently dislike work and suggests that in the right conditions work may be a source of great personal satisfaction.

2 External control and the threat of punishment are not the only means for bringing about effort towards organisational objectives. Man will exercise self-direction and self-control in the service of objectives to which he is committed.

3 Commitment to objectives is a function of the rewards associated with their achievement, for instance the rewards of self-fulfilment and self-esteem as well as the more obvious economic rewards represented by wages.

4 The average human being learns, under proper conditions, not only to accept but to seek responsibility.

5 The capacity to exercise a relatively high degree of imagination, ingenuity and creativity in the solution of organisational problems is widely, not narrowly, distributed in the population.

6 Under the conditions of modern industrial life the intellectual potentialities of the average human being are only partially utilised.

An important conclusion reached from this alternative résumé of human nature is that 'the limits on human collaboration in the organisational setting are not limits of human nature but of management's ingenuity in discovering how to realise the potential represented by its human resources' (McGregor, 1960, p. 48). Management must seek to achieve integration of the needs of the individual and those of the organisation. Management must create conditions in which 'the members of the organisation can achieve their own goals best by directing their efforts towards the success of the enterprise' (McGregor, 1960, p. 49).

McGregor's theme is taken up by Argyris (1962 and 1964) who begins by re-emphasising that the classical organisation is founded on impersonality and the thesis that 'effectiveness decreases as emotionality increases'. In other words, the classical approach is based on the belief that the more emphasis that is placed on human relations and social considerations the less rational and therefore the less efficient will the organisation be in the pursuit of its goals.

For Argyris such organisations represent social systems which lack 'interpersonal competence'. In other words, because of their deliberate blindness to social and emotional factors and influences, the organisations lack the capacity, or competence, to deal frankly and openly with interpersonal behavioural problems. This means in turn that they lack the ability to adjust successfully to the social and egoistic needs of participants:

If individuals are in social systems where they are unable to predict accurately their interpersonal impact upon others, and others' impact upon themselves, they may begin to feel confused.

'Why are people behaving that way toward me?' 'Why do they interpret me incorrectly?' Since such questions are not sanctioned in a rationally dominated system, much less answered, the confusion will tend to turn to frustration and feelings of failure. (Argyris, 1962, pp. 43–4)

Far from representing a barrier to the achievement of organisational effectiveness, recognition of the emotional interpersonal side of organisation can, in Argyris's opinion, avoid a great deal of frustration and antagonism. Such feelings among organisational participants, it is pointed out, serve to misdirect and waste a considerable amount of emotional energy which could otherwise be directed at the achievement of organisational goals. For example, the presence of interpersonal uncertainty and mistrust causes participants to devote a great deal of time and energy to activities designed to defend their own position. Their behaviour is characterised by conformity reinforced by a desire not to expose themselves to unnecessary risk by rocking the boat or by adopting adventurous and novel approaches to work problems. Such a defensive outlook causes participants to become preoccupied with protecting the interests of their own group or department. As participants become more department- or group-centred intergroup and interdepartmental rivalries develop, rivalries which become magnified by the general atmosphere of mistrust, conflict and uncertainty. The same defensive strategy encourages participants to postpone or withdraw from complex problems which involve dealing with uncertainty and to play it safe by concentrating on easier problems.

Thus conflict among individuals and groups, excessive conformity, and avoidance of risk and uncertainty are important products of low interpersonal competence. Such characteristics will clearly reduce the organisation's capacity for flexibility and adaptation and will also decrease the possibility of achieving meaningful and constructive co-operation between departments. Argyris concludes that reform strategies introduced to increase organisational effectiveness must be designed to influence values and the form of interpersonal relationships within an organisation as well as to change structural and procedural characteristics. One can introduce changes in departmental design and introduce procedures which require a strong element of interdepartmental co-operation, and so on, but 'none of these changes will have any lasting effects unless the inputs [values] are appropriately influenced' (Argyris, 1962, p. 53). For Argyris, the most appropriate influence is in the direction of increasing interpersonal competence. In practical terms this means the active encouragement of an atmosphere of open communication and mutual understanding of functions and roles that permits internal flexibility and freedom. It also means the development of a pervasive attitude that welcomes change as a means of growth and advancement within the demands of the external environment.

Argyris concludes that any successful approach to the introduction of change in an organisation must represent a comprehensive package involving the modification of structure, process and culture. However, in view of the fundamental and potentially obstructive nature of dominant attitudes and values, the ideal approach should focus initially upon the cultural aspect.

The research findings and conclusions of such writers as McGregor and Argyris indicate the direction in which cultures and value systems need to be manipulated if organisational effectiveness is to be increased and cultural maladjustment avoided. The problem remains, however, of how to translate such theoretical prescriptions into practical management terms.

It has been shown that in terms of practical management application behavioural science has two important aspects. First it prescribes a means of improving organisational productivity and effectiveness by generally being aware of human relations problems and catering for the social and egoistic needs of the individual. Secondly, it prescribes ways of successfully introducing and assimilating change within an organisation. Both aspects can be seen as having a particular relevance for local government, which is labour-intensive and which has undergone a period of rapid change and adjustment. However, as will become clear from the discussion which follows, the transition from broad theoretical prescription to practical management application in local government has been less obvious in this behavioural sphere than in the areas of local government structure and process.

Chapter VIII

FROM THEORY TO PRACTICE –
MANAGING THE HUMAN RESOURCE

PERSONNEL MANAGEMENT AND APPLIED BEHAVIOURAL SCIENCE

The most obvious platform for the practical application of behavioural science theories and the area of local government in which their potential contribution has been most advocated is that of personnel management. In the discussion which follows, the relationship between personnel management and applied behavioural science is examined and particular attention is given to highlighting the behavioural science foundations of four major areas of personnel work which have featured prominently in prescriptions for the development of the function in local government.

Personnel management in its embryonic form appeared in the guise of welfare work aimed at mitigating to some extent the poor working conditions which formed part of the legacy of the Industrial Revolution. Initially, its development was hindered by a general vagueness on the part of both management and welfare practitioners with regard to the exact role of the welfare worker. Attempts by welfare workers to involve themselves in the formulation of management policy or to force major improvements in conditions of employment often led to clashes and a summary dismissal of their suggestions as 'unrealistic and visionary rather than practical and of immediate consequence' (Crichton, 1968, p. 20). However, shortly before the First World War momentum was gathering within the welfare movement for a consolidation and clarification of its identity and in 1913 a Welfare Workers Association was established as a permanent focus for the dissemination of welfare expertise.

The intensification of production during the First World War led to the first formal investigation of the effects of working conditions on the individual worker and in 1916 the Home Secretary was empowered to make orders requiring some welfare provision in factories or workshops. Unfortunately, the resultant growth in demand for trained welfare workers was not matched by a corresponding growth in theoretical knowledge. Literature on the subject was scarce and newly appointed welfare workers often found them-selves with little or no knowledge of their work, under employers who knew even less and regarded them as an expensive and unneces-sary luxury. When peace came and restrictions were lifted, many employers disbanded their welfare departments with relief.

Nevertheless, attempts to professionalise and define the welfare function continued. In 1917 the Central Association of Welfare Workers had been formed and soon displayed its dedication to furthering the recognition of welfare work as part of the overall function of management and to developing the identity of the welfare worker as part of the management team with a legitimate expertise.

After 1925, conditions in industry changed dramatically and the role of the welfare supervisor underwent a metamorphosis from a narrow welfare function to a broader, labour management role. The atmosphere of depression and high unemployment stimulated the need for rationalisation and efficiency. At the same time, the theory of management was becoming more complex and scientific in approach. The classical approach reigned supreme and pro-claimed the need for clearly defined organisational structures in which jobs and roles would be delineated with equal precision and clarity. The need for a scientific approach to recruitment, selection and training, coupled with a need for satisfactory industrial rela-tions, gave impetus to the need for an extension of the role of those already concerned with the human factor in enterprise. It was logical for the welfare function to develop into the wider function of labour management and the Institute of Industrial Welfare Workers adopted the title of the Institute of Labour Management in 1931.

The value of a specialised labour management function became even more obvious during the Second World War. War conditions produced a complex web of new labour legislation and a multitude of human problems. Labour managers helped to ensure that all statutory requirements were being complied with and also tackled such tasks as recruitment, wage negotiation and training. By 1943 the number of welfare and personnel officers, as they were increas-ingly being called, stood at almost five and a half thousand, three times the estimated figure for 1939.

The war years witnessed a movement towards self-identification in the field of labour or personnel management. The work of a planning and development committee of the Institute of Labour Management resulted in the publication in 1945 of a definition of the work and objectives of the Institute. Personnel management was defined as being that part of management which is primarily concerned with the human relationships within an organisation and which, by catering for the well-being of the individual, enhances the effective working of the organisation. Such definitional exercises were, however, more expressions of aspiration than descriptions of reality in achievement.

The postwar period was one of rapid development in the field of personnel management and, once again, a pioneering era was accompanied by a change of name. The Institute of Labour Management became the Institute of Personnel Management in 1946.

During this period the call in management generally was for advice from specialists. The specialists in the field of personnel management responded to the call with a growing awareness that little was known about the factors which influence men at work, both as individuals and as members of groups.

However, the raw material for such an understanding was emerging through the studies being carried out by human relations and behavioural theorists in the 1950s and early 1960s into the psychological and sociological aspects of industrial problems. These developments were making a growing contribution to the understanding of people at work, the interrelationships between individuals and groups and, indeed, the very nature of the work organisation. The social and behavioural sciences appeared to be providing the intellectual basis for an expertise in human relations which would, if harnessed, enable the personnel manager to make a positive contribution to the development of managerial policy.

A growing awareness of this latent creative role for personnel management provided the setting for a protracted and involved debate within the ranks of personnel officers concerning the question of exactly what was the correct or desirable level for personnel management involvement in the overall process of management. From the debate there emerged a consensus on the need for personnel management to be more involved and to be less of an advisory function located at the periphery of the management process.

In 1963 the Institute of Personnel Management, in a statement on the 'Definition and aims of personnel management', described the function as seeking 'to bring together and develop into an effective organisation the men and women who make up an enterprise, enabling each to make his own best contribution to its success both as an individual and as a member of a working group' (*Personnel Management*, March 1963). The Institute also stressed that the function was concerned with the human and social implications of change, both internal, in terms of organisational structure or working methods, and external, in the wider sense of economic and social change in the community. In an editorial comment accompanying the Institute's statement Joan Woodward called for the greater involvement of personnel specialists in policy discussions. She emphasised that every management decision has repercussions for the relationship between an organisation and its employees. Thus it follows that at the point where management decisions are being made then the human and social implications should be recognised.

In 1964 Tom Lupton was to argue at length that the personnel function had the intellectual raw material to underpin its demands but that radical changes would have to take place before the benefits could be harnessed.

In a pamphlet entitled *Industrial Behaviour and Personnel Management*, Lupton asserted that personnel management should increasingly become the application of behavioural science to problems of the structure and functioning of organisations. For Lupton, effective personnel managers must possess the skill to analyse the social and psychological problems which occur in organisations, particularly those which accompany technological and economic change. Lupton wished to see the emergence of the personnel manager as a social analyst, exercising a preventative rather than a remedial function, forecasting the social problems which might emanate from specific technical policy decisions and advising on how these problems can be handled. In Lupton's view:

> The recognition of the policy-making role of the personnel manager depends upon the extent to which he can demonstrate that he possesses a degree of expertise in the systematic analysis of the social consequences of economic and technical decisions which other members of top management do not possess . . . only if he has a good working knowledge of the theories of the behavioural sciences, and an ability to apply this knowledge to the analysis of the problems of the organisation, will he generate confidence in his ability as a professional. (Lupton, 1964, p. 48)

Development of the creative, analytical role prescribed by Lupton has characterised the continued evolution of personnel management from the mid-1960s to the present time. The personnel specialist is viewed more and more as enacting a key role in the organisation, translating and adapting behavioural science knowledge into effective managerial practice. It is to a more detailed examination of some of these areas of managerial practice that we now turn.

ASPECTS OF PERSONNEL PRACTICE

A whole range of activities and techniques have been developed to assist in the effective utilisation and development of human resources. The techniques used in such specialised areas as recruitment and selection, education and training, staff assessment and appraisal and the pursuance of good industrial relations and good employer–employee communications can all be seen as making an important contribution towards improving the effectiveness of the organisation through the application of behavioural science expertise.

Well-thought-out recruitment policies and sophisticated selection techniques can help to avoid the placing of square pegs in round holes, and this is good for the individual and the organisation. Attention to this area can also ensure that the organisation does not find itself devoid of personnel with the particular skills required for its future growth and development. A systematic, planned approach to recruitment may involve visits to educational institutions, such as schools, colleges and universities; the skilful use of advertising and the projection of the sort of image most likely to attract people of the quality required; and accurate job specification. The process of selection can be greatly assisted by the skilful design of application forms, since their completion can highlight immediately the best and worst qualities of an applicant and so reduce abortive interviewing to a minimum and help in the speedy compilation of manageable short lists. T. P. Lyons has noted that

> We have as yet a great deal to learn in the interpretation of private and employment life patterns as indicators of personal qualities and behavioural characteristics, but it is possible to envisage the time when these skills have been so developed that, with the necessary facts elicited by the right questions being asked, purely personal interaction will be the sole purpose of an interview. (T. P. Lyons, 1971, p. 52)

Handling the interview situation itself requires a certain amount of behavioural knowledge and skill. An interview is, after all, a largely artificial confrontation and, if run badly, will hardly provide a true picture of a candidate's likely attitudes and behaviour in a normal work situation. Interviewing techniques have been developed to penetrate and, if possible, altogether dispense with the conventional interview atmosphere. Interviewers must be aware of their own shortcomings: for example, a belief that they can sum a man up in a moment or a tendency to be blinded by superficial characteristics such as appearance. A hypercritical or over-hostile approach to questioning, for example, commenting upon aspects of a candidate's application details with apparent incredulity, will invariably bring about a reciprocal hostility on the candidate's part. Such a situation will not be conducive to meaningful communication.

The group selection approach calls for even greater behavioural science skills. The approach is based on conclusions drawn from the observation of candidates in a group situation which gives them the opportunity to demonstrate their capacity for successful personal interaction and co-operation.

The connection between well-planned training and the achievement of organisational effectiveness through the development of the human resource is self-evident. However, the connection will only be achieved if the organisation has a system for the identification of the training needs of employees and the ability to satisfy them once they have been identified.

French describes the training process as a 'complex combination of many sub-processes concerned with increasing the capabilities of individuals and groups in contributing to the attainment of organisational goals' (French, 1970, p. 477). Training is thus a particularly well-defined area in which the personnel function can influence the way in which the individual responds to the demands and challenges of his job. The process is usually concerned with either providing participants with the basic skills and knowledge required in carrying out the various specialised activities which together contribute to the overall task of the organisation, or with the broader development of general managerial and supervisory skills. Both aspects of the training process are now highly developed and some would argue that the training function should be seen as a separate specialised entity running parallel with the general function of personnel management. In terms of the actual organisation and control of training resources and internal training provision, such functional differentiation and the establishment of separate training departments can be justified. However, if one looks at training as an ongoing programme with the overall objective of improving the total of the employee's contribution and self-fulfilment, then it is clear that, at least at the level of identifying training needs and the formulation of long-term training policy, the function remains integral to personnel management.

Cuming lists the following among the main objectives of a planned training programme.

1　Keeping participants informed about the current technical demands of their jobs.
2　Providing information about the organisation's policies and activities so that the individual has a knowledge of overall objectives and can appreciate the nature of his own contribution.
3　Taking steps to ensure that individuals have a good knowledge of the techniques and methods of management appropriate to their organisational role and how these might best be applied under existing conditions.

4 Instructing participants in the principles of personal leadership and developing their ability to exercise them effectively.
5 Teaching participants to cope successfully with changing conditions. (Cuming, 1968, p. 161)

In order to achieve these objectives the personnel manager must be able to assess the training needs and potential of employees. He must have the skill to relate these to the requirements of the organisation and to the training facilities available, whether these exist within the organisation or outside, in professional training and educational establishments. It is also an important part of the training skill to be able to assess the probable effectiveness of different techniques and approaches to training in specific situations and when dealing with particular individuals.

The identification of training needs and the assessment of the potential of individuals are perhaps the most difficult facets of training policy. Both tasks are made much easier if the organisation has a well-developed system for staff assessment and appraisal. Such a system provides an opportunity for the frank and open discussion of an individual's role, level of satisfaction and performance. Appraisal is, however, a very sensitive area of management and must be handled with considerable skill if it is to avoid being regarded as a one-sided punitive exercise by those who see themselves as being on the receiving end. Effective assessment and appraisal must be based on a two-way partnership approach on the part of superior and subordinate, with both being prepared to admit faults and identify areas where improvement is required. Regular appraisal sessions facilitate a reintroduction of personal contact in situations where normal operational relationships may of necessity remain distant and depersonalised.

As a formal process of management, assessment and appraisal has the following objectives:

1 The identification of any misunderstanding or conflict between the individual and his superior with regard to job definition and areas of responsibility.
2 The detection of any shortfall in the individual's performance as compared with previously agreed performance objectives and standards.
3 The frank and open discussion of the reasons for such shortfalls and the achievement of agreement on appropriate corrective action such as additional training in specific areas, skills or techniques.
4 The agreement of future performance objectives and standards.
5 The discussion of the individual's aspirations and future career development within the organisation.

6 The provision of data for the organisation with regard to managerial resources and manpower planning.

Clearly, exercises designed to achieve these objectives can assist in the achievement of self-fulfilment and job satisfaction on the part of participants. At least such discussions can, if approached in the right spirit, help to remove some of the causes of the frustrations and misunderstandings which, according to the observations and prescriptions of behavioural science, can lead to a reduction in the level of organisational effectiveness.

An extremely important area of modern personnel work, where behavioural science expertise and particularly a knowledge of group behaviour is of immediate value, is that of industrial relations. The successful management of industrial relations can be seen as lying in the recognition and understanding of intergroup relationships and the presence of conflicting interests and the fact that, in reality, the behaviour of individuals is affected by their consciousness of group membership.

Disputes can often be interpreted as an expression of the conflicting interests of the employee group and the management group. An understanding of the work group as a social entity with its own values and behavioural norms, which may or may not be consistent with those set for the group by higher authority, can assist in the mitigation of the worst effects of long-term disagreement and help in the formulation of compromise solutions. The manager without such an insight may adopt a hostile stance which could cause attitudes to harden, reinforcing the group identity in a 'them and us' situation. Lupton points out that:

> The problem of industrial relations is to find ways of so regulating the relationship between contending interests as to give to each full recognition and the satisfaction of freely pursuing its own interests as it sees them, while at the same time, and by the same process, seeking to maximise the general interest. In other words, to have civilised disagreement about the things to be disagreed about and civilised recognition of common interest. [This is] partly a recognition that organised conflict of interest is a means of releasing and canalising emotional energy just as much as a method of affecting compromise between points of view. (Lupton, 1964, p. 38)

In the emotive atmosphere of modern industrial relations the application of such skills in conflict resolution and management becomes increasingly important. It represents an area where the role of the personnel manager as an applied behavioural scientist becomes as pertinent as his role as interpreter of statutory requirement.

Good industrial relations are inextricably linked to good communications within an organisation. The end product of communications in this context is to convey to employees the nature of the task of management and the overall objectives of the organisation and the conveyance to management of the goals and aspirations of employees. The setting-up of joint consultation machinery provides structural recognition of such a two-way communications system, as does the recent movement for greater industrial democracy and worker representation at the higher levels of policy formulation. However, merely ensuring open two-way communication by way of structural devices does not solve all the problems. This will not always promote mutual confidence and co-operation. Sentiments as well as facts are communicated and these can act to distort the messages which are transmitted. Differing points of view and perspectives on particular problems, coupled with the often large differences in relative power positions between participants, can cause a continuation of feelings of suspicion and resentment.

It is the role of the personnel manager to advise on the probable effectiveness of various communications patterns which might be established within his organisation. To give such advice he must have a good knowledge of the types of communication block which can and often do occur.

Development in all these areas has shaped the modern personnel management function. It is now recognised almost everywhere as a professional management specialism which concentrates on the development of the human resources of the organisation through a practical application of behavioural science knowledge.

ORGANISATION DEVELOPMENT AND THE MANAGEMENT OF CHANGE

Clearly, a well-developed personnel management function will, as Lupton stressed, be concerned with adjustment to changing economic, social and technological conditions. However, the practical application of behavioural science prescriptions in the area of change management has given rise to a separate body of techniques and the emergence of distinctive management strategy known as organisation development.

Organisation development or OD, as it is conventionally abbreviated, represents an educational strategy which concentrates on the people variable within organisations. It is a comprehensive approach to the management of organisational innovation and change and has within its purview values, attitudes, interpersonal relations and organisational climate as well as the structural and procedural aspects of change (Bennis, 1969).

Defining OD in a form which is at once precise and comprehensive is difficult. The definitions provided by Bennis and Beckhard are perhaps the most useful: 'OD represents a response to change, a complex educational strategy intended to change beliefs, attitudes, values and structure of organisations so that they can better adapt to new technologies, markets and challenges' (Bennis, 1969, p. 2). 'OD is an effort – planned, organisation-wide, and managed from the top – to increase organisation effectiveness and health through planned interventions in the organisation's "processes" using behavioural science knowledge' (Beckhard, 1969, p. 9). Beckhard's definition, in particular, highlights the salient features of any OD process:

1 It is essentially a planned process.
2 It is managed from the top of the organisation.
3 It has as its aim the improvement of the organisation's effectiveness and state of health.
4 It pursues this objective through the application of behavioural science knowledge.

In the terms of Beckhard's definition a planned approach to the introduction of change rules out any sudden and violent rejection of traditional structures, roles and values. Such sudden upheavals can alienate participants and introduce an almost anomic state, resulting from the sudden disappearance of previously internalised values and cultural reference points. A planned approach also rules out long-term incremental strategies whereby small *ad hoc* changes in structure and procedures are introduced to meet specific contingencies as they arise; this is in the hope that the aggregate effect of such adjustments will be the development of the organisation as a whole in roughly the right direction. Such an approach is often termed 'passive adaptation'. In contrast, the planned OD programme proceeds from a systematic study and diagnosis of the organisation and its problems and focuses on the development of strategic plans for improving its operational effectiveness and attaining the most efficient use of its resources.

Top managers and administrators will often have achieved success in their careers because they have learned to live by the traditional values of the organisation; they will have been in tune with the predominant culture and will have adopted appropriate behavioural norms. It is thus often difficult for them to contemplate modifying or even discarding those values. Often, the top administrator sees the maintenance of the status quo as his prime responsibility, but OD demands that the status quo be challenged and, if necessary, changed. The need for an OD programme to emanate from top management is thus self-evident and crucial, as Beckhard points out: 'Top management must have knowledge of and commitment to the goals of the programme and must actively support the methods used to achieve the goals' (Beckhard, 1969, p. 10).

The ultimate objective of OD is given as that of improving the effectiveness and health of the organisation. The implication is that organisations can display symptoms of ill-health in much the same way as living organisms. The question thus arises as to what constitutes a healthy organisation? Bennis (1969, p. 15) refers to the development of organic systems as representing a primary goal of OD, thus associating organic characteristics with the healthy organisation. This view is also held by Beckhard, whose comprehensive catalogue of the features of the healthy, effective organisation conveys the impression of one which is adaptive and responsive, with a well-developed problem-solving capacity and, using the concept developed by Argyris, displaying a high degree of 'interpersonal competence' so that organisational effectiveness is not impaired by interpersonal difficulties (Beckhard, 1969, pp. 10–11).

Finally, OD achieves its goals through planned interventions using behavioural science knowledge. An intervention in this context refers to a deliberate interference in the organisation at a specific point in order to arrest current ineffective operation:

> A strategy is developed of intervening or moving into the existing organisation and helping it, in effect, 'stop the music', examine its present ways of work, norms, and values and look at alternative ways of working. (Beckhard, 1969, p. 13)

Partin includes the following amongst the principal types or areas of intervention which may be used in varying combinations depending on the specific needs of the particular organisation:

1 Training: procedures involving direct teaching or experience-based learning.
2 Process consultation: watching and aiding ongoing processes and coaching to improve them.
3 Confrontation: bringing together units of the organisation (persons, roles or groups) which have previously been in poor communication.

4 Data feedback: systematic collection of information which is then reported back to the appropriate units as a basis for diagnosis, problem-solving and planning. (Partin, 1973, pp. 7–8)

The most important areas of intervention in terms of social or cultural adjustment and those which, as will be shown later, have the greatest significance when assessing the relevance of OD to the problems of local government are those of training and confrontation. It is from these two general areas that the techniques of team development or team building, and the management of intergroup conflict emanate.

The importance of the work group as a focal point is emphasised by the following assumptions which Beckhard lists as being basic to the initial diagnosis of organisational problems and the subsequent development of an appropriate OD change strategy:

1 The basic building blocks of an organisation are groups [teams]. Therefore the basic units of change are groups.
2 An always relevant change goal is the reduction of inappropriate competition between parts of the organisation and the development of a more collaborative condition.
3 One goal of a healthy organisation is to develop generally open communication, mutual trust, and confidence between and across levels.
4 'People support what they help create.' People affected by a change must be allowed active participation and a sense of ownership in the planning and conduct of change. (Beckhard, 1969, pp. 26–7)

Because of these basic assumptions about organisational functioning and the underlying importance of group processes most OD change programmes take as their starting point the improvement of group or team effectiveness. This is usually inaugurated through the application of a technique which is variously called group dynamics training, sensitivity training or, most commonly, T-group training.

T-group training takes place in an unstructured group setting where participants examine their interpersonal relationships. It has as its goal the transformation of groups from *ad hoc* collections of competing individuals into single problem-solving entities. It sets out to mould effective working groups which will possess the capacity to make swift, well-judged decisions. The primary concern is with building a group norm which facilitates open and free discussion of the differences which exist between members of the group in so far as such differences form the bases of potential conflict between them. When exposed openly these differences are often shown to represent the legacy of old-established, though often groundless, prejudice, misconception, or simple ignorance and misunderstanding about the problems, goals and expectations of other group members.

The T-group approach is presented as being particularly useful as an initial group learning exercise when new teams are being established either as new organisational units or temporary project teams. Beckhard (1969, pp. 28–9) traces the stages through which such new teams invariably pass as their operation becomes established. To begin with there is a fair degree of confusion as to roles and relationships within the team. The participants are usually specialists, having a particular technical competence required for the completion of the project or functioning of the unit, and they concentrate their attention exclusively within that area of competence. Team leaders are usually preoccupied with completing the team task successfully and do not pay much attention to the relationships existing between the team members. All this means that when interpersonal problems and conflicts do finally develop the team will already be deeply involved in its operational activities. At this stage the damage inflicted by interpersonal conflict can be great and the treatment of the malady costly and disruptive. There are thus great advantages to be gained if a new team is obliged at an early stage in its operational life to examine itself in a frank and open way, to assess collaboratively how it is going to work as a unit, to decide what working relationships are to be established and discover what are going to be the primary concerns of individual team members. It is believed that a team which has subjected itself to such self-scrutiny at an early stage will have fewer interpersonal problems, will be more effective in the achievement of its goals, and will be more meaningful to its members.

Work groups as well as individuals can experience conflict. A major problem affecting organisational effectiveness is the amount of time and energy devoted to competition and fighting between groups. The reduction of such inappropriate competition is the main purpose of managing intergroup relationships. Intergroup problemsolving through confrontation meetings proceeds on much the same basis as T-group training. Groups may be asked to state frankly how they see themselves and other groups or other departments with whom they interact and to speculate on how they may appear to other groups. The groups are then brought together to be confronted with and to discuss openly each other's perceptions. Again, the process often results in the removal of misconceptions and resentments that have accumulated over long periods.

OD interventions are conventionally seen as being prescribed and monitored by an external consultant who enters into a relationship with the client organisation for the purpose of helping it to help itself. Usually called a change agent, this consultant is seen as occupying a role similar to that of the psychoanalyst. He begins by identifying the symptoms of the client, expresses these symptoms in such a way that possible underlying causes become apparent, and then takes remedial action. Jones (1969, p. 19) describes the working concept of the change agent when he points out that the term covers 'helping professionals whose role involves the stimulation, guidance, and stabilisation of change in organisations'. More specifically, the change agent is concerned with introducing a planned change process which moves through three phases – the unfreezing phase, the changing phase, and the refreezing phase (Schein, 1969).

Within each of these phases of change management certain skills are employed to achieve the desired ends. In the unfreezing phase the change agent must help his client group to become aware of the need for change. The change agent must seek to encourage the development of an atmosphere in which participants are aware of the potential benefits to be derived from the proposed change and feel a commitment to the change strategy and a responsibility for making it work. It is also important during this phase that the agent and the client collaborate in diagnosing the situation, the behaviour or the performance which is to be modified. In the second phase appropriate action or intervention is planned, introduced and its effectiveness monitored. The final phase of refreezing involves ensuring that the improvements achieved, especially when they have required the introduction of new perceptions and behavioural patterns, will have continuity. This necessitates integrating, as far as possible, new responses and perceptions into the normal value system of the unit or organisation. In a sense this is directly related to the thoroughness with which the unfreezing process was undertaken.

The emphasis on the external consultative nature of the change agent's role, which characterises most of the literature on OD, follows from a belief in the need for complete objectivity and detachment in any diagnosis of organisational problems. It also follows from a recognition of the amount of professional expertise required to perform the role effectively. The need for detachment is easy to understand, especially in the event of a clash occurring between the requirements of organisational effectiveness and the managerial philosophy predominant within the client organisation. The prescribed role of external consultant stems from the need for the temporary involvement of an outside skill, namely, that of the applied behavioural scientist. The question arises, however, as to how rapidly such an outside consultant can become familiar with, and be accepted by, the organisation. The suitability of the external consultancy role must turn on the question of acceptance on the part of the organisation. Not only must the change agent become completely familiar with the nature of the client organisation's goal structure, authority relations, communications patterns, and so on, but he must also gain the confidence of participants. This need for acceptance and credibility is emphasised by the collaborative nature of the agent–client relationship referred to briefly earlier and prescribed as essential if OD is to be successfully introduced. The relationship must involve 'mutual trust', 'joint determination of goals and means', and 'high mutual influence' (Bennis, 1969, p. 13). The ease and speed with which such a relationship between an organisation and an external consultant can be achieved will largely depend on the strength of the organisation's current administrative values and the extent to which these are at variance with the basic values and assumptions underlying the OD approach. Indeed, in situations where this variance is extremely pronounced OD exercises may be considered wholly inappropriate. In other less extreme situations it may still be argued that OD would be potentially more effective if introduced through the mediation of an internal specialist. This could be someone who would already have an identity and a certain amount of acceptance within the organisation but who would, at the same time, have a knowledge of the scientific basis of OD work. In the light of previous discussion of the development of personnel management as a professional discipline, an obvious candidate for the role of internal change agent would be the personnel officer. The integration of the personnel management function and the role of change agent would serve to link OD to other important aspects of human resource management. However, a major problem with the concept of an internal specialist change agent is the inevitable identification of the incumbent with the established hierarchy and power structure. Such identification may assist in the establishment of a constructive relationship between the change agent and top management but it may act as a barrier to open communication and co-operation on the part of the workforce in general. The constructive aspects of OD interventions may be lost sight of as some participants sense that they are being manipulated for the purpose of securing the goals and aspirations of top management.

In a sense, the need for the change agent to establish a relationship of trust with both top management and the workforce enhances the proposition that the role be assumed by the personnel specialist. After all, the requirement does little more than reflect the type of role conflict which has been a constant feature of the development of personnel management. The conflict between the personnel manager's role as guardian of workers' welfare and his role as a tool of management has its roots in the initial clashes between the early welfare workers and less welfare-conscious employers and, later, the need for personnel managers to gain recognition as a legitimate part of the management team. This conflict of roles has never been resolved in general terms and, in the final analysis, its resolution must rest with the individual personnel manager confronted by a particular situation. What can be stated in general terms, however, is that because of this history of conflict personnel managers are used to being the men in the middle, often acting as conciliators and communicators between levels of management and between management and workforce. Because of their training in behavioural science and the human aspects of organisation they will be more familiar than most with the organisation's overall power structure and be able to appreciate the significance of the authority relationships which exist within it. For these reasons they will probably be in the best position to undertake the function of change mediation from the inside.

It has already been implied briefly that OD should not be seen as a panacea immediately applicable to all organisational problems. The types of planned intervention discussed earlier can only be effective where there is a basic sympathy on the part of the organisation with the ultimate objectives of the exercise.

The potential effectiveness of OD will be determined by the state of cultural readiness within the organisation in which it is applied. Bennis presents a framework of reference points within which an assessment of cultural readiness can be made. These reference points are:

1   The legitimacy of interpersonal relationships within the organisation.
2   The nature of the control and authority system presently employed by the organisation.
3   The presence and intensity of conflict within the organisation.
4   The nature of the organisation's internal boundary system and the degree of cultural variation between sub-units.
5   The change agents' probable relationship with the organisation.

It has been shown that T-group techniques and conflict management focus on improving the performance of a group by the inclusion of interpersonal relations as a legitimate element of data. However, as an initial step the organisation must acknowledge that such interpersonal considerations are relevant to the effective performance of the organisation's tasks. Again Bennis points out that

In many client systems interpersonal phenomena are not considered appropriate to discuss, germane to the task, or legitimate
as a focus of enquiry . . . There are still many situations where
interpersonal influence is regarded as invalid, illegitimate, or
an invasion of privacy. (Bennis, 1969, p. 45)

In such situations the application of OD techniques would clearly
be a barren exercise.

Similarly, if the organisation's control and authority system is
too rigid then it may be too much at variance with the values of
OD with its emphasis on informal, flexible authority structures.

To a certain extent OD practitioners differ from conventional
human relations theorists in that they believe in the constructive
as well as the destructive qualities of conflict within organisations.
Whereas pioneer human relations theorists preached harmony,
understanding and the abolition of conflict within organisations,
OD is firmly based on the proposition that the presence of conflict
is inevitable and, indeed, that the expression of conflict is desirable,
in a controlled setting, as a route to good organisational health.
However, most practitioners are in agreement about the inadvis-
ability of introducing OD programmes in situations where conflict
between organisational sub-units is intense. This is because in such
situations the organisation is likely to be under severe stress and OD
could conceivably be introduced as a tool or weapon in the power
game or it could be used later as a convenient scapegoat (Bennis,
1969, p. 46).

A successful OD programme must involve the whole system of
the organisation and not just unusually receptive parts of it. Only
by the acceptance and application of OD strategies by the whole
organisation can situations be avoided where OD values and assumptions are internalised in one part of the organisation only to be
rejected by, and cause disruption in, an adjacent part of the system.
The basic problem is one of variation in the degree of receptiveness
of sub-units and this problem is heightened where the client
organisation is traditionally differentiated and multi-functional.
This is because, as was shown earlier, differentiation can manifest
itself in the form of values and behavioural orientation as well as
in the more obvious form of structural and functional boundaries.

The final point of reference focuses on the relationship between
the change agent and the client organisation. The most important
considerations are, first, the basis upon which guidance from the
change agent is accepted and, secondly, the realism and practic-
ability of the expectations of the client organisation's management.
For example, if guidance is accepted by sections of the organisation
through fear or as the result of intimidation of some kind, or if

participants have unrealistically high result expectations of OD intervention techniques, then the exercise will not be based on a firm enough foundation. As a consequence the achievement of any real improvement may be stifled by premature outbursts of cynicism or, in the case of superficial acceptance on command, will be reduced to a temporary alleviation of problems which will reassert themselves when the coast is clear.

Chapter IX

PERSONNEL MANAGEMENT
IN LOCAL GOVERNMENT

THE ESTABLISHMENTS TRADITION

The ability of local authorities to benefit from a practical application of behavioural science ideas is largely dependent upon the extent to which the concept of a positive and creative personnel management function has been developed in local government.

The Bains Report devoted an entire chapter to the subject of personnel management and identified it as 'an area of management which has not hitherto been given sufficient recognition in local government'. In the field of personnel management local government was seen to have lagged behind industry and even other areas of the public service, a fact which was all the more worrying in view of the labour-intensive nature of local government work (Bains, ch. 6).

Fowler (1975) identifies some reasons for the stunted development of personnel management in local government compared with its development in private industry and commerce. He observes that the principal influences which provided the direction and momentum for the development of modern personnel management have either simply 'passed local government by' or have been felt by local authorities at a much later stage. For example, the pressures for efficient manpower management which was experienced during both world wars was not felt in local government 'the production pressures and consequent personnel problems of large-scale factory work did not apply to the thousands of generally small-scale authorities' (Fowler, p. 88). In the field of industrial relations the private sector has a long history of conflict. The disruptive effect of strikes was magnified as industry became increasingly technological and was characterised by greater economic interdependence. The sheer economic cost of disputes, coupled with the growing realisation that their root causes could be extremely complex and psychological, gave an impetus to the development of industrial relations expertise within individual companies. In local authorities, on the other hand, industrial conflict and militant union activity has been a fairly recent phenomenon. The spate of labour legislation which characterised the 1950s and 1960s provided an impetus for the development of specialist interpretative and advisory skills within personnel management. However, this legislation had a less pronounced impact in local government. Most of it was aimed at formalising the employer–employee relationship and encouraging fair employment practices and improved working conditions. In local government, the traditionally formalistic employment practices meant that most of these legislative requirements on contracts of employment, written schedules of employment conditions, and so on, were already being complied with. In this area at least, local government practice was in advance of general industrial practice. It is significant, however, that these particular aspects of personnel work stem from the need for control and the keeping of accurate records, functions which fitted well within the rather narrow establishments role which has been the closest public sector equivalent to the industrial and commercial personnel management function.

Traditionally, establishments work has displayed a distinctly negative orientation, concentrating on the control of staff numbers and the day-to-day administration of conditions of service and disciplinary codes. The local government establishments function had its origins in the Report of the Hadow Committee (1934). This represented the outcome of an inquiry into the apparent lack of any co-ordinated staffing policy or administrative machinery for dealing with staffing matters in local authorities. Hadow recommended that each local authority should set up a committee which would have exclusive responsibility for recruitment and training, gradings and promotions, conditions of employment and disciplinary procedures. Following this recommendation, all local authorities either set up establishments committees to carry out these functions and appointed establishments officers to service them, or extended the range of work of finance or general purposes committees to include the basic establishments functions.

Hadow was explicit about the location of responsibility for even the most detailed aspects of establishments work. This was to rest with members rather than officers. For example, in the area of appointments it was recommended that members should be concerned with selection procedures even at the most junior levels which had traditionally been left exclusively in the hands of senior officers. The clerk was seen as the most appropriate source of co-ordinated advice for the establishments committee, a view which reflected the feeling that such advice, when requested, should be of a very general, non-specialist character.

The emphasis on member control in establishments matters served to set the pattern for the future development of the establishments function in local government. It has already been suggested that local government remained largely sheltered from the influences which acted to broaden and professionalise the personnel management function in industry. In addition, the emphasis in local government establishments work reflected the principal concerns of councillors rather than the widening interests of a developing specialist function of management. Councillors were concerned with the achievement of economy in the use of manpower, the need to retain a detailed control over staff numbers, appointments and promotions and the administration of codes of discipline. In short, the overall emphasis was on control rather than development.

This basic pattern of establishments work remained virtually unchanged up to the 1970s, despite the appearance of major reports on local government management and staffing arrangements.

The Maud Report of 1967 made only a passing reference to the establishments function and then only to emphasise and reinforce the importance of its role in controlling staff numbers and ensuring the most economic use of manpower. The Mallaby Report, also published in 1967, was more directly concerned with staffing matters in local government and as such might have been expected to advocate at least a broadening of the basis of establishments work in order to bring it more into line with current best practice in the field of personnel management generally. It is surprising, therefore, that, far from attempting to bring about such a change, the Mallaby Report made a positive and direct contribution to the continued retardation of personnel management in local authorities.

For the most part, Mallaby departed little from the original concept of establishments work put forward by Hadow. Mallaby, too, stressed the importance of the controlling aspect of the establishments function, recommending that authorities should ensure that they had 'adequate arrangements for central establishments control to ensure the economic use of staff and to keep a check on the numbers and gradings of staff within departments' (Report of the Mallaby Committee, para. 437). In its subsequent discussion of the executive work of the establishments function, Mallaby restricted itself to the observation that major advantages could be sustained if a central establishments organisation in each local authority provided a number of executive services in the areas of training, recruitment, welfare and record keeping for individual departments and for the authority as a whole. Mallaby's description of the role of the establishments officer appears at first sight to be based on a recognition and acceptance of the specialist and professional nature of establishments/personnel work. For example, the establishments officer is described as 'a man who is to advise principal officers on their staffing needs, and who in the last resort may have to suggest to the Clerk that principal officers' proposals should be challenged'. The importance of the position is apparently reinforced by the requirement that establishments officers should have the status and capacity to undertake the role effectively (Report of the Mallaby Committee, para. 440). However, these exhortations were immediately followed by the denial that any relevant training or qualification for personnel or establishment officers in local government existed and the recommendation that establishments work 'should not become a new specialism in which officers make a career divorced from other duties' but should remain firmly within the province of the lay administrative officer. By lending support to the view that establishments work in local authorities should remain of a non-specialist, non-professional character, Mallaby helped to perpetuate the minor administrative image of personnel management in local government.

It is difficult to reconcile this view of establishments work with Mallaby's later call for substantial improvements in almost every area of personnel management. Mallaby stressed the need for improved recruitment and selection techniques, improved and better planned career structures, especially for the lay administrative officer, a more sophisticated and visionary approach to training and a more effective use of management services. As Fowler puts it: 'No small-scale establishments branch, lacking top management status and staffed by lay administrative officers, could hope to pick up and develop the range of difficult – and necessary – improvements in manpower management proposed in the Mallaby report' (Fowler, 1975, p. 69).

BAINS ON PERSONNEL MANAGEMENT

In contrast, the call in the Bains Report was for the replacement of the conventional establishments man with the more positive and creative concept of the personnel manager, as it had been developed elsewhere. Bains saw the human problems of management in local government as being in no way different from those in industry, and yet the resources devoted to the solution and, more important, the prevention of those problems in local government were seen to be generally inadequate. The establishments officer had been a prisoner of his rather restricted traditional role, unable to widen the range of his involvement; and this restriction had effectively deterred those with experience or training in the wider aspects of personnel management from entering local government establishments sections. It was suggested that, as an initial step, the title 'establishments' be replaced by that of 'personnel management' since this title would more accurately reflect the function which

Bains believed the department should perform and would also be more likely to attract suitably qualified staff (Report of the Bains Committee, para. 6.21).

Bains identified the following specific areas of personnel management where substantial development was needed in local government.

1 Recruitment and selection
2 Education and training
3 Industrial relations
4 The human and social implications of change

On the subject of recruitment and selection Bains believed that there was a real need to critically examine traditional processes and to keep abreast of developing techniques. In particular, substantial benefits were seen to lie in the application of expertise in the areas of man and job specifications, the design of application forms and the development and expansion of interviewing skills.

The need for effective staff appraisal and assessment was recognised as lying at the heart of a systematic approach to education, training and career development within local government. Although the training of professionals in local government is looked after by appropriate professional bodies, the local authorities themselves must look to the training of generalist administrators and manual staff. There must be an effective system for identifying potential and specific training needs for such employees, and local authorities, it was argued, must adopt a more positive approach to the development of the potential of members of staff as individuals. Bains advocated a system of regular secondments and exchanges of staff between different types of authority, between the civil service and local government and even between local government and private industry, as a means of broadening the outlook of individuals and of fostering an awareness of the problems which are faced by others in different organisations and sectors.

In the field of industrial relations the role of the personnel officer as a channel of communication between the council and the trade unions was emphasised. He was seen as having a particular responsibility for developing 'an atmosphere of mutual trust and confidence between the authority and its employees'. The personnel officer was envisaged as performing an advisory role in the conduct of negotiations and in the development of industrial relations policy generally. Bains saw the presence of such a focal point for advice as helping to ensure consistency and continuity in industrial relations and as aiding the higher levels of management to maintain an awareness of the general industrial relations climate throughout the organisation.

The fourth area identified by Bains centred on the 'human and social implications of change'. The identification of this area is particularly significant since, by its introduction, Bains can be seen as prescribing a role of change mediation for local government personnel officers. Earlier, Bains had identified two broad aims of a positive personnel management function. These aims were: '(a) To promote the effectiveness of the human resources within the short and long term, and (b) To create and maintain a climate in which changes which are to the advantage of the [organisation] can be achieved' (Report of the Bains Committee, p. 65, para. 6.8). The emphasis in the second of these aims is on climatic adjustment and, by implication, the conscious and deliberate management of the organisational culture and value system. The report went on to ask the question: 'In how many authorities is there anybody who can advise on the effect of organisational change upon employees and on how managers should be trained to manage change?' (para. 6.9). The report asserted that the answer was likely to be 'very few' but pointed out that: 'At the time of a total re-organisation . . . the need for an understanding of the "human and social implications of change in internal organisation" could hardly be overemphasised' (p. 72, para. 6.29). On the same theme, J. D. Stewart (1974) has argued that the role of change mediator, which is implicit in the modern personnel management function, is equally valid and indeed essential within the context of local government. Stewart emphasises that a local authority's personnel policy must create a situation where: '(1) Personnel will be aware of the need for change, and (2) where there will be an attitude in which change is accepted' (Stewart, 1974, p. 89). The emphasis is on responsiveness to the need for change, not just recognition of that need. To be responsive, personnel must be assisted to attain the skills, the knowledge and the attitudes which enable an effective response to be achieved. The prescription for an effective local government personnel management function in this area corresponds closely to the requirements for effective change management described in the earlier discussion of organisation development, the implication being that local government personnel officers should act as internal specialist change agents.

Bains recommended the setting-up of new personnel departments in local authorities and stressed the urgency of the need to appoint suitably qualified chief personnel officers who should have direct access to the chief executive and who should not be subordinated to any other chief officer. Recognition of the specialist, professional status of personnel work was evidenced in Bains' recommendation that:

Chief officers in other departments will normally be expected to accept and act on the advice of the personnel department on matters within the latter's specialist knowledge in exactly the same way as they would normally accept the Treasurer's advice on financial matters. (p. 73, para. 6.36)

Bains admitted that, in the short term, the influence and actual contribution of the new personnel departments would be dependent on the acquisition of adequate staff resources. It was noted that relatively few existing local government staff were adequately qualified to carry out the kind of sophisticated personnel management function which the report was advocating. Accordingly, Bains recommended the immediate instigation of recruitment drives and training programmes and, again, the secondment of appropriate senior staff to industry or other areas of the public service where the function had reached a higher stage of development.

The Bains Report concludes its discussion of personnel management in local government with the short but highly prophetic statement that 'the new local authorities will need personnel managers of high quality if the human problems of re-organisation are to be overcome'.

POST-BAINS DEVELOPMENTS

In 1973 the Local Government Training Board (LGTB) produced a booklet entitled *Personnel Management in the New Local Authorities*, which contained a comprehensive statement of the new look personnel management function in local government. This document also highlighted human relations activities as a major category of personnel work. The term 'human relations activities' was seen as covering a wide area, from industrial relations work and the maintenance and improvement of communications between employer and employee, to the application of organisation development and the mediation of change and conflict. The LGTB recognised that it was too much to expect the average personnel officer to become familiar with, and practice, the whole range of behavioural science skills. It did point out, however, that the personnel officer's training, if properly organised, should enable him to make intelligent use of some of the conclusions reached in that field. To meet this challenge the LGTB itself produced a comprehensive package on personnel practice designed to assist authorities to implement their own internal training programmes. In addition, it began developing closer links with the Institute of Personnel Management, and tuition for IPM examinations was offered through the NALGO Correspondence Institute.

In 1974 the LGTB reported a disappointing response to these developments on the part of local authorities. In fact, developments in local government personnel management since 1974 have been influenced by a whole range of economic, logistical and attitudinal problems which have combined to produce a less than enthusiastic response despite so many official exhortations. In order to plot these developments in the post-Bains era we turn now to an analysis of the actual impact of such exhortations in a particular local authority and then to an assessment of the extent to which the conclusions reached can be applied to local government in general.

At the time of reorganisation, Birmingham District Council followed the general pattern of many other local authorities and established a central personnel department. Whereas it is true to say that most of the criticisms and observations of the Bains committee with regard to the lack of development in the field of personnel management applied to Birmingham, it would be misleading to suggest that the report's recommendations came as a complete surprise or a startling revelation. The minutes of the former Establishments Committee reveal that work was being carried out and progress made in several of the areas of personnel work which Bains identified as requiring improvement in local authorities. For example, in Birmingham much attention had already been given to the rationalisation of personnel procedures and the establishment of joint consultation machinery in the field of industrial relations. However, there is little doubt that the publication of the Bains Report lent additional impetus to this movement.

In Birmingham it was decided to establish a completely centralised personnel department which would be given responsibility for implementing the recommendations of the Bains Report. A working party of councillors decided that, in the interests of a corporate approach, the newly established Personnel Committee should be the only employing committee and that teaching staff should also be brought under the auspices of the new department. This emphasis on complete centralisation was however opposed by the newly appointed Chief Personnel Officer. His main objection centred on the sheer size of the new Metropolitan District Council with 40,000 employees and 15,000 teachers. It was also noted that such a system of centralised personnel administration might be resented by departmental chief officers who could see the development as effectively compromising their authority. In fact, the Chief Personnel Officer took the view that the new department should be involved as little as possible in the purely administrative side of the personnel function. The department's chief responsibility was seen as the formulation and co-ordination of personnel policy for the authority as a whole and not the application of details of that policy within individual departments.

As a result of these arguments the plan for total centralisation was abandoned. Instead, a system was established whereby departmental personnel officers were to remain directly responsible to their appropriate chief officers. However, at the same time, these personnel officers were expected to maintain a close contact with the Central Personnel Department and have a responsibility to the Chief Personnel Officer for their contribution towards the implementation of overall personnel policy. It was also decided that teachers would be treated as a separate entity and a staffing branch was set up in the Education Department. This was given sole responsibility for the personnel requirements of teachers, lecturers and school ancillary staff.

The status of the personnel officer, as Bains emphasised, is important if he is to be accepted as a professional with a positive consultative role to play. In the larger departments in Birmingham there was little difficulty in justifying the appointment of personnel officers at a senior level, high enough at least to merit representation on departmental management teams. However, in the smaller departments where the establishment was sometimes below 300 the appointment of a personnel specialist at a senior level presented more of a problem. As a result the rather unsatisfactory practice was adopted of combining the personnel function with the senior administrative position Such subordination or dilution of the personnel role was obviously dangerous, but it was stressed at the time that such arrangements were of a purely temporary nature and represented a stopgap solution while a corps of qualified personnel officers was built up under a training plan in the Personnel Department itself.

Bains's observation on the lack of suitably trained and qualified personnel officers in local government was certainly applicable to Birmingham. While the new Personnel Department was able to recruit better qualified officers (largely on the strength of the well-publicised new image for personnel management in local government, heralded by the Bains Report), departmental personnel officers, with the exception of a few new senior appointments, were inherited almost totally *en bloc* and remained, therefore, establishments officers in new hats. Their new position, with a dual responsibility to their departments on the one hand and to the wider development of personnel management on the other, placed an even greater pressure on their abilities. In view of this situation it was decided that the main instrument of liaison, devised to keep all departmental personnel officers aware of central personnel policy, namely, the monthly meeting of personnel officers, should double as a training and information session. In this way it was hoped to compensate, in the short term, for any officer's lack of formal training while more detailed and sophisticated training courses were arranged.

In Birmingham the Central Personnel Department was divided up into six sections:

1   Recruitment and staff training
2   Manpower planning and Industrial relations
3   Work study
4   Establishments and O and M
5   Administration
6   Health and safety at work

As far as the overall role of the Department was concerned, it was generally agreed that its main task was to advise departmental chief officers on the effective and efficient utilisation of their manpower resources. Authority-wide statements of policy and practice were also considered to be part of the work of the Central Department although it was recognised that these had to be broadly stated in order to cater for the wide area across which they would be implemented. Actual implementation was left within the jurisdiction of the departmental chief officer, working, ideally, with his own personnel officer. A report by the Chief Personnel Officer to the Personnel Committee concerning the collection and use of manpower statistics for planning purposes provides an example of how this arrangement was supposed to operate in practice:

> Although the initiative for the collection of this manpower information has come from the Personnel Department . . . it should be emphasised that this information is also of use to departmental personnel sections. It is intended that summaries will be sent to departments with explanatory notes and that this will be followed by visits from members of my staff. In this way it is hoped that departments will begin to use the information themselves to initiate investigations into problem areas, calling on the staff of the Personnel Department as and when necessary for assistance. (A. J. Belcher, 'Report on manpower planning to the Personnel Committee', Birmingham MDC, March 1975)

The example used above is particularly significant since it is in this area of analysis and the compilation of manpower planning data that most progress has been made in Birmingham since the new Personnel Department was established. For example, the authority now makes use of monthly staff returns to analyse the long-term implications of identified trends; close attention is now given to collecting local, regional and national statistical data for the purpose of analysing the overall manpower situation and the use of this analysis to forecast supply difficulties; there are plans in hand for the computerisation of records. There has also been some progress in the area of personnel management which is concerned with the selection and development of individuals. Here the emphasis has been on the improvement and rationalisation of the authority's approach to recruitment and post-entry training at both junior and senior levels. Much of this has been done in conjunction with outside bodies such as the Local Government Training Board.

Significant as these developments are, it is evidence of progress in the broad area of human relations activities which is of prime interest in assessing the extent to which a fully developed personnel management function has been introduced. As we have seen, the term 'human relations activities' covers a wide field and, whereas progress can be seen to have been made in some aspects related to the area, other perhaps more important aspects have been neglected.

Progress has been particularly noticeable in the field of industrial relations where, for example, joint consultative committees for manual and non-manual staff have been established. The Personnel Department has also attacked energetically the task of implementing the provisions of the Health and Safety at Work legislation, preparing and undertaking safety inspection programmes, monitoring departmental safety records and reports and also advising on and participating in safety training generally. However, a serious failing is evident in the lack of attention given to some of the most important aspects of applied behavioural science. There is certainly nothing in Birmingham resembling a behavioural science unit for the investigation and monitoring of worker motivation, job enrichment possibilities, group conflict, and so on.

It was unfortunate that just as the seeds of a fully developed personnel management function had been sown the economic situation and a severe 'no growth' policy for local government acted to render its further development unlikely, at least in the short term. After all, the benefits to be gained from the application of many aspects of behavioural science are fairly long-term and intangible and have a less immediate return than, say, a more efficient industrial relations machinery or a more effective recruitment policy. In such a situation the greatest danger is the possibility of a reversion to the negative controlling role associated with the traditional establishments approach. A trend towards such a reversion was identified as early as 1975 and the concern over staff numbers in local government at that time unquestionably led to a resurgence of the establishment control factor in the job of the personnel officer.

In Birmingham the economic situation definitely had the effect of putting pressure on the Central Personnel Department to revert to the role of establishments control and operate as an instrument of constraint. This trend was seen by personnel specialists within the authority as detrimental to the Department's efforts to represent and develop the wider aspects of personnel management so that it could become an instrument of positive advantage to chief officers. Clearly, in a period of severe financial restraint and scarcity of resources local authorities will be mainly concerned with the essential activities which will ensure that local government continues to operate with the minimum interference to services. However, it was argued that if a local authority is to provide services in an efficient and effective way in future years then it is essential that the potential of its most expensive resource, its manpower, should be developed to the full. It was emphasised that more attention should be given to the medium-term development of the personnel function and that longer-term aims should not be forgotten under the inevitable pressures of short-term priorities.

The most obvious constraint on the development of the personnel management function in Birmingham (apart from the general resource situation) has been the lack of suitably qualified personnel officers, especially outside the Personnel Department. Often, departmental personnel officers, inherited from the establishments function and having little or no training in modern personnel techniques, were suddenly placed in the position of having to interpret and implement the policies of the Personnel Department. The Bains Report had pointed to the shortage of skilled personnel officers in local government generally and suggested the obvious solutions in training and recruitment. The relevance of this solution to Birmingham had been recognised by the Personnel Department from its inception. However, great difficulties seem to have been experienced in carrying out these recommendations. Attempts at recruitment have been for the most part unsuccessful. Applicants of the required calibre have not been forthcoming. Training has also been hindered by the fact that staffing levels have never been high enough to allow for officers to attend relevant courses.

Chief officers are likely to be too preoccupied with day-to-day administrative activities to be able to stand back and view the social system of their department or authority. However, it is clear that in Birmingham there is still a need for personnel officers who have been trained to perceive the ways in which individuals and groups interact within an organisation and who could then place this understanding and its practical implications at the disposal of those with specific service responsibilities.

The extension of such conclusions to local government in general is justified by the results of research carried out by the Institute of Local Government Studies (Greenwood *et al.*, 1977).

A survey of twenty-seven local authorities in the post-reorganisation period showed that in general 'the wide-ranging personnel function advocated by Bains has not been developed'. The questionable status of the personnel officer is reflected in the survey's observation that 'Personnel Officers are not normally full chief officers' and that, frequently, departmental officers are so low in rank (fourth tier or below) that they 'do not have the authority to deal with problems which arise'. The survey notes that since reorganisation the central concern of personnel management in the local authorities studied has been with industrial relations, organisation and methods, and work study (the two latter functions being in particularly great demand where authorities have been amalgamated and there has been a pressing need to standardise procedures, and so on). Other core functions, meaning those functions performed in most of the authorities covered in the survey, included establishment control (normally comprising staff administration and a watchdog function), recruitment and selection, and training (though it was noted that in very few authorities were there any specialist training staff). It is interesting to note that in many of the smaller authorities examined in the survey the personnel department was still concerned exclusively with traditional establishments operations. Nowhere in the description of personnel activities, even among those considered in the survey to be peripheral, is there mention of a conscious effort to establish an applied behavioural science capacity

It has been a central theme in the story of the development of personnel management that the personnel specialist should be recognised as an expert with a positive contribution to make to the process of policy formulation. However, the INLOGOV research showed that such a personnel involvement in the policy process has not been accepted by many authorities. The need for such involvement was certainly not considered to be a matter of any urgency and in some authorities was opposed altogether. The point was further emphasised by the lack of any direct personnel involvement with those bodies where policy-making might take place or at least be discussed, such as the management teams, the interdepartmental working groups and the central policy committees. The survey concludes that 'It would seem fair to say that personnel does not, generally, play any great part in the machinery and process of policy-making' (Greenwood *et al.*, 1977, p. 179).

The survey draws the following rather depressing conclusions. Personnel management does not play the sort of important central role envisaged by Bains before reorganisation. Personnel officers in local government tend to react to events rather than take any initiative. The personnel function is actually distrusted by many chief officers and is seen in a negative, rather obstructive light (they feel that personnel does not understand the professional needs and difficulties of the departments). Finally, the survey reiterates the point made earlier in this chapter that the development of a new and more creative personnel management function in local government has not been aided by the arrival of a period of economic crisis and severe financial restraint.

PART FOUR

THE DYNAMICS OF ORGANISATIONAL INNOVATION IN A LOCAL AUTHORITY – A CASE STUDY

THE DYNAMICS OF ORGANISATIONAL INNOVATION IN A LOCAL AUTHORITY – A CASE STUDY

THE OBJECTIVES OF THE STUDY

The interdependence which exists between the structural, procedural and cultural aspects of organisational design and functioning has already been emphasised at various points during the foregoing discussion of organisation theory and its application within local government. It is intended in this final section to reinforce this emphasis by reference to a case study of recent organisational innovation instigated by Birmingham Metropolitan District Council. The study is concerned in particular with offering an explanation, within a framework of organisation theory, for the rejection of those innovations and with the uncovering of any lessons which can be learnt about approaches to the introduction and assimilation of change in local authorities.

Most of the information upon which the case study is based was gained during a series of personal interviews with senior officers and councillors who had been directly involved in the design, instigation and later dismantling of the corporate system between 1974 and 1976.

Case studies of individual authorities inevitably present the problem of atypicality, especially when one attempts to incorporate the conclusions in a model of organisational behaviour applicable to local government generally. They present a particular problem when one is dealing with a large urban authority such as Birmingham, with its unique political history and administrative traditions. However, within the context of the present study the construction of such a general model can be defended, since the organisational characteristics that are salient to the analysis, those of structural and cultural differentiation, exist in all local authorities although in different degrees. Birmingham's size and the peculiar nature of its environmental setting merely mean that these features, and their effects, are likely to be more pronounced than in, for example, a smaller rural authority. In a sense this enhances the significance of the case study since Birmingham has proved to be a trend-setter.

It should be made clear from the outset that the study does not represent a defence of corporate management or matrix organisational design. The central concern is with approaches to organisational innovation within the cultural setting of a local authority. The exact form or direction of innovation is not important. For example, innovation in the direction of more formal, mechanistic structures within an organisation whose culture and value system identified more with an organic, flexible orientation would probably encounter similar problems to those identified in the case study of Birmingham in terms of resistance to change and cultural maladjustment. The essential purpose of the study is to demonstrate the need to match, as closely as possible, an organisation's culture with its structural and procedural arrangements.

BIRMINGHAM MDC – BACKGROUND AND ENVIRONMENTAL CONTEXT

The effect of reorganisation on the City of Birmingham and its surrounding area was substantial. The former County Borough ceased to exist and was replaced by the new Metropolitan District Council which represented a major second-tier authority within the new West Midlands Metropolitan County. The former County Borough's all-purpose status was eroded by the loss of responsibility for the police and fire services and the functions of strategic planning to the County Council. The activities of Birmingham's Water Department were integrated into the new Regional Water Authority and the Water Committee was disbanded. In addition, certain public health functions, such as the school health service, were lost to the reorganised National Health Service.

Despite this erosion of functions the new Birmingham District Council emerged as a large and important authority, charged with the provision of the most crucial services for a highly complex urban area. The complexity of the area was given an additional dimension with the absorption of the former Royal Borough of Sutton Coldfield which until 1974 had been an independent district council within the County of Warwickshire. The effects of this amalgamation were twofold. First, and most obviously, it greatly increased the geographical area to be covered by the new council. Secondly, and perhaps more significantly, it rendered the social and economic structure of the new council's environment more complicated. Sutton Coldfield was almost exclusively a suburban, non-industrial area with a predominantly middle-class electorate which had consistently returned a Conservative council. This contrasted sharply with Birmingham's industrial and more varied political tradition.

Thus an immediate result of reorganisation in Birmingham was a geographical widening of the authority's environmental area and an increase in its social and economic complexity. However, these changes represented only minor adjustments to an environment which had for a long period preceding reorganisation displayed a complexity and turbulence which had imposed a considerable strain on the authority's resources and planning capabilities.

Assessment of wealth, measured in terms of the rateable value per head of population, can be misleading when used as a guide to an authority's ability to cope with a wide range of complex problems. This is certainly the case in Birmingham which is, on the surface, a wealthy authority enjoying a high rateable value per capita. However, a large proportion of this rateable value is accounted for by industry and commerce which raises the ratio of rateable value to population. The important question is, does this rate income from industry and commerce offset the cost of meeting the demands of the population? It must be remembered that regional capital status brings costs as well as benefits. For example, it brings heavy demands for investment in infrastructure such as roads and cultural facilities.

From the point of view of particular services the authority had been experiencing the sort of demands commensurate with an area containing a population of some 1,080,000 (including a high immigrant population) and in which the demands of industrial development and modernisation exist side by side with the worsening problem of urban decay.

In the area of housing provision the authority had moved from a policy of redevelopment and slum clearance, which dominated the 1950s and 1960s, towards a more sophisticated policy of retention and improvement of dwellings. The pursuit of this policy had given rise to numerous problems. The city contained 75,000 older houses in need of repair and improvement, owned by a mixture of owner-occupiers, landlords and housing associations, as well as the local authority itself. All these owners of property had different problems, standards, needs and resources. Also, any programme for improvements required not only inputs from several external agencies, including the West Midlands County Council, but also the co-ordinated efforts of several departments. In Birmingham in 1975 there still existed an estimated deficit of some 17,300 dwellings and limited supplies of land suitable for new building within the Council's boundaries. Over 2,000 homeless families applied to the Council's Housing Department for assistance in 1973–4.

In the field of social services the opinion has been expressed that the potential demand from the elderly and chronically sick and disabled alone could account for the total budget of the social services department twice over.

'The interdependence of problems in Birmingham has been well illustrated by the reports produced as part of the recent Inner Area Study and the Community Development Project, both of which were sponsored jointly by Birmingham District Council and the Department of the Environment. Both investigations have shown how health, housing, employment and educational deprivation are coexistent in many inner areas and that any policies designed to tackle such problems must be community-oriented and framed in a comprehensive way, given the complex causal relationships which have been observed to exist between them.

There is, therefore, ample evidence to support the contention that the environmental context within which Birmingham District Council had to operate was at once expansive, complex and volatile. It displayed most of the characteristics associated with the most unstable of environmental contexts, described by Emery and Trist as a 'turbulent field type'. Birmingham's traditional structure and method of operation exhibited the mechanistic qualities described earlier as being potentially ineffective in such a situation. Therefore the validity of the reform objective, when seen as an exercise in matching organisational structure and working to environmental conditions, seemed proved.

The internal organisational structure of the old Birmingham County Borough was characterised by a high degree of differentiation. In Birmingham, as in most other local authorities, this was reflected in the multiplicity of committees, subcommittees and professional departments. In fact, the management structure in Birmingham prior to reform comprised up to thirty-one main committees, eighty-two subcommittees and twenty-nine separate departments. The authority had only limited formal integration machinery in the shape of a general purposes committee at member level and a town clerk's department at officer level, both of which exercised a totally informal, co-ordinative function based on the exercise of persuasion rather than formal authority.

STRUCTURAL AND PROCEDURAL INNOVATIONS

The structural and procedural innovations introduced in Birmingham had, on the surface at least, a commitment to the ideas and prescriptions contained in the various official reports and academic pronouncements which had appeared in the late 1960s and early 1970s. From the procedural viewpoint this meant the introduction of corporate planning as a means of meeting the requirements of a management task defined as one of relating the activities of the authority as a whole to the changing needs and problems generated by its turbulent environment. The adoption of a corporate approach to both planning and management meant the introduction of more organisational integration and less differentiation, both of which were to be achieved through appropriate structural innovation, largely following the pattern recommended in the Bains Report, though with some important differences.

The first major innovation concerning the authority's committee structure was actually introduced in 1972, when the incumbent leader of the Birmingham Council, Stanley Yapp (who in 1974 took over the leadership of the new West Midlands County Council), established a central Policy and Resources Committee. The Birmingham Policy and Resources Committee was a one-party committee with a membership approximating to that of the executive committee of the ruling Labour group. It did not have any other committee chairmen as ex-officio members but they were invited to attend meetings of the Committee when matters affecting their own committees were to be discussed. It was assumed that this arrangement would ensure satisfactory communications between the principal Committee and other committees. This was a somewhat different concept from that of the collective body of committee chairmen and other suitable members (including minority party representation) envisaged by Bains. Also, the Policy and Resources Committee in Birmingham was essentially a non-executive body, having no delegated powers. Thus all executive decisions had to pass through some other committee, either for delegated decision or for onward transmission to the Council. With this arrangement it was hoped that the opposition could not claim either that they were effectively excluded from discussion of major policy prior to full council session or that there was insufficient opportunity to refine policy at committee stage.

Another important departure from the letter of Bains concerned the status of the resource subcommittees with responsibility for land, finance, manpower and performance review. In Birmingham's plan these were given full committee status. The service committees could implement their approved policies and budgets under delegated powers but had to use the resource committees to procure land, personnel and finance in accordance with overall policy. Thus the resource committees had an important co-ordinative role. See Figure 9.

By 1974 a committee pattern broadly similar to that recommended by Bains had been introduced into the authority. Further innovations were introduced at officer level. The position of town clerk was abolished and Mr Francis Amos, a town planner by profession, was appointed as Birmingham's first Chief Executive.

COMMITTEE STRUCTURE 1974

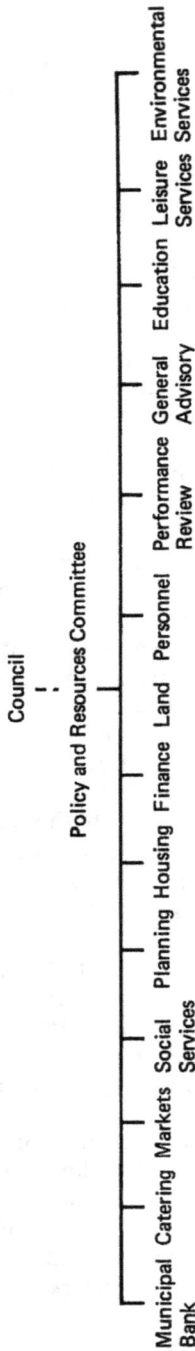

Council

Policy and Resources Committee

Municipal Bank | Catering | Markets | Social Services | Planning | Housing | Finance | Land | Personnel | Performance Review | General Advisory | Education | Leisure Services | Environmental Services

Subcommittees not shown

(i) Urban Renewal Committee (subcommittee of Environmental Services): has responsibility for co-ordination of city's urban renewal programme.

(ii) The subcommittees of the Education Committee.

(iii) The Youth and Community subcommittee of the Leisure Services Committee: concerned with all aspects of youth, voluntary and community development work.

Figure 9 Birmingham Metropolitan District Council: committee structure 1974-6

For the first time a principal officer had a general directing power over other chief officers. Amos was to chair a Principal Chief Officers' Management Team of seven officers, representing the major functional Departments of Social Services, Housing, Education, Environmental and Leisure Services and the Treasurer's and Planning Departments. The Management Team's terms of reference charged it with:

> advising the Policy and Resources Committee on the best ways to achieve its policy priorities . . . ensuring that the policies of different committees are complementary and consistent, and co-ordinating the implementation of programmes through departments. ('Corporate working in Birmingham', Report of the Chief Executive to the Management Team, February 1975)

Francis Amos emphasised the need for good communications within the authority if the Management Team was to be effective in discharging its functions:

> The team must . . . ensure that in advising the Policy and Resources Committee it must be fully conversant with the interests of those departments whose chief officers are not members of the Management Team. Conversely, it must be sure that when transmitting decisions outwards they are both realistic and intelligible. (F. J. C. Amos, 1974)

A monthly meeting of all chief officers was considered necessary to assist communication in this context.

A Central Intelligence Unit was established to assist the Chief Executive and the Management Team. This was originally envisaged as having an establishment of twenty-two but only sixteen staff were actually appointed.

Functional integration is basic to the achievement of a corporate approach but in Birmingham it was also seen as a means of improving administrative efficiency in a more tangible and immediate sense. Such increased administrative efficiency was to be achieved by, for example, bringing all financial staff in all departments under the overall control of the City Treasurer. The actual number of departments was reduced to twenty, this being achieved by a combination of amalgamation and the loss of functions such as police, fire, water and weights and measures to other authorities, under the general terms of reorganisation.

In this sphere of departmental structure there was another major departure from the Bains pattern. Even though the Council had appointed a Chief Executive with a Bains-style job description emphasising his central co-ordinating function, in Birmingham he was given substantial departmental responsibilities consisting of all the non-legal functions of the previous town clerk (a City Solicitor's Department was set up to perform the legal functions), plus research, corporate planning and performance review. This was completely at variance with the Bains recommendation that the chief executive be kept free of departmental responsibilities. See Figure 10.

In terms of managerial process the task was seen as one of designing machinery for the identification of policy issues, the formulation of alternative policies, evaluation, implementation and review.

A cyclical planning and budgetary process was proposed as the main vehicle for assessing the authority's achievements and for establishing policy priorities for tackling existing and future needs and problems. The cycle would begin in July with the presentation of a report on the general situation within the district to the Policy and Resources Committee. In October, after examining the mid-year estimates in conjunction with the July report, the Committee would declare its policy priorities. In December the Committee would examine programme statements and budget estimates prepared by other committees, in order to determine the extent to which they subscribed to the achievement of the overall policies and were mutually compatible. The Committee would then assess the apportionment of available resources as part of the process of fixing the rate.

This cyclical planning procedure was to be coupled with a modified budgetary process. This would abandon the traditional incremental approach, whereby budgetary allocations were determined annually on an 'adding to' basis through a crude bargaining mechanism, and would adopt instead a long-term planned approach, concentrating on the allocation of resources in accordance with a more consciously rational analysis of needs and problems.

The proposal for interdepartmental working and project groups, to be constituted as necessary on an *ad hoc* basis, was evidence of the acceptance in Birmingham of the need for flexible, transitory, horizontal organisational arrangements when tackling complex corporate problems. Special Issue Groups were to be set up where necessary to examine, in some depth, issues and problems which cut across programme areas which would themselves span departmental boundaries. Issues falling entirely within a given programme area would be tackled by Programme Area Groups with responsibility for assisting committees with an involvement in major programmes, such as that of urban renewal, to formulate and review policy and draw up programmes for action. Programme Area

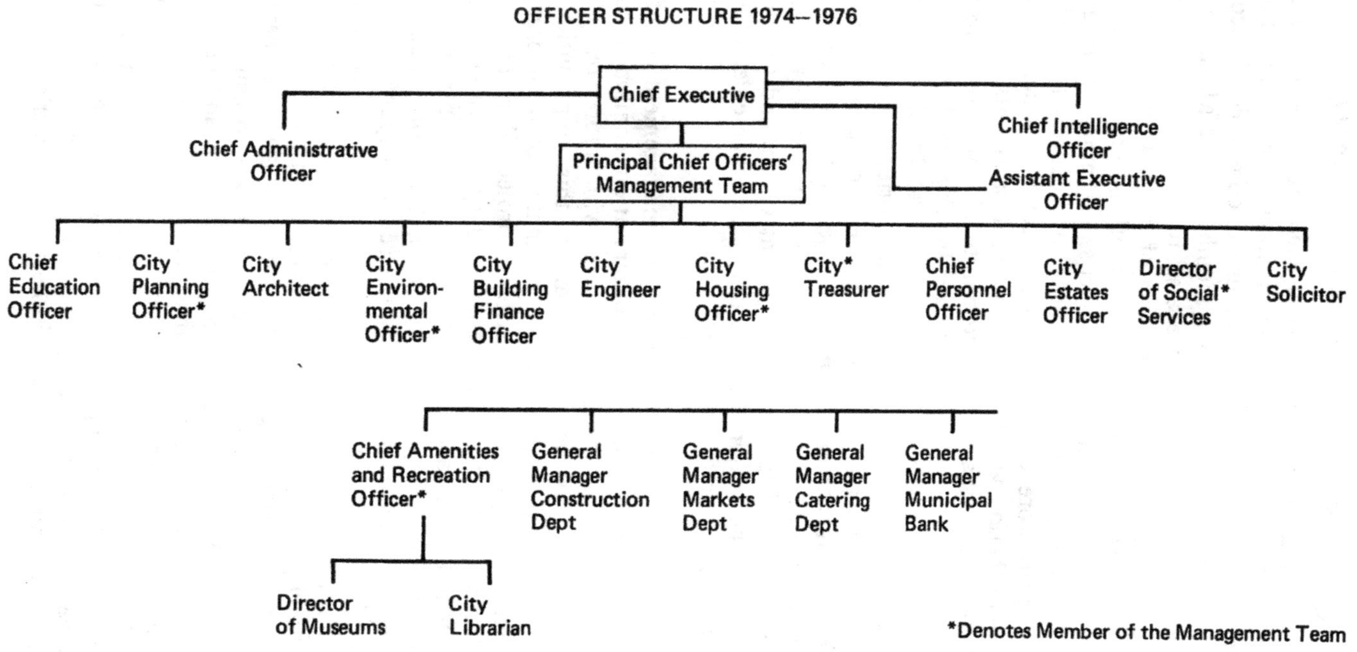

OFFICER STRUCTURE 1974—1976

Chief Executive

Principal Chief Officers' Management Team

Chief Administrative Officer

Chief Intelligence Officer
Assistant Executive Officer

Chief Education Officer

City Planning Officer*

City Architect

City Environ- mental Officer*

City Building Finance Officer

City Engineer

City Housing Officer*

City* Treasurer

Chief Personnel Officer

City Estates Officer

Director of Social* Services

City Solicitor

General Manager Construction Dept

General Manager Markets Dept

General Manager Catering Dept

General Manager Municipal Bank

Chief Amenities and Recreation Officer*

City Librarian

Director of Museums

*Denotes Member of the Management Team

Figure 10 Birmingham Metropolitan District Council: officer structure 1974–6

Groups were to consider the problems of each area as a whole at a level divorced from the more compartmentalised problems of one department. Five such groups were established, composed of second- and third-tier officers and chaired by a member of the Management Team. Project Control Groups were also to be set up when the need arose to oversee the implementation of major capital projects. These groups were to contain representatives of the relevant service departments, assisted by Architect's, Planning, Engineering and Treasurer's Departments as required. Interdepartmental Implementation Groups were considered to be necessary where a high degree of co-ordination was needed between departments.

Of the supporting apparatus of corporate planning perhaps the most important elements were the Central Intelligence Unit and the Corporate Planning Liaison Group. The Central Intelligence Unit had the function of co-ordinating the authority's research and information services and providing a nucleus of policy analysis services for the Management Team, the departments and the committees. The Corporate Planning Liaison Group had responsibility for the co-ordination of the new management system and contained representatives of the major departments, with other chief officers being co-opted as required. See Figure 11.

From this description it can be seen that the management structure adopted in Birmingham following reorganisation combined some elements of traditional vertical structure with more transitory horizontal elements. As was shown earlier, this combination of vertical and horizontal elements is called a matrix form of organisational design. In Birmingham a horizontal project element, represented by the various interdepartmental and special issue groups, interdepartmental teams and policy committees, was introduced to supplement, and work in conjunction with, the more traditional functional elements as represented by the service departments and committees. The matrix system was shown to be associated with the acquisition of the qualities of flexibility and adaptability and an enhancement of the organisation's problem-solving capacity. As an approach to management organisation, matrix design was demonstrated to be closely related to the organic model because of its emphasis on lateral structuring and communications and its use of heterogeneous groups to secure the diversity of inputs necessary for the diagnosis and treatment of complex problems (see Part One, Chapter 3). This structural design, when taken in conjunction with the proposed procedural changes aimed at improving the authority's planning capability, can be seen as part of a general attempt to impart organic characteristics to a hitherto mechanistic organisational setting.

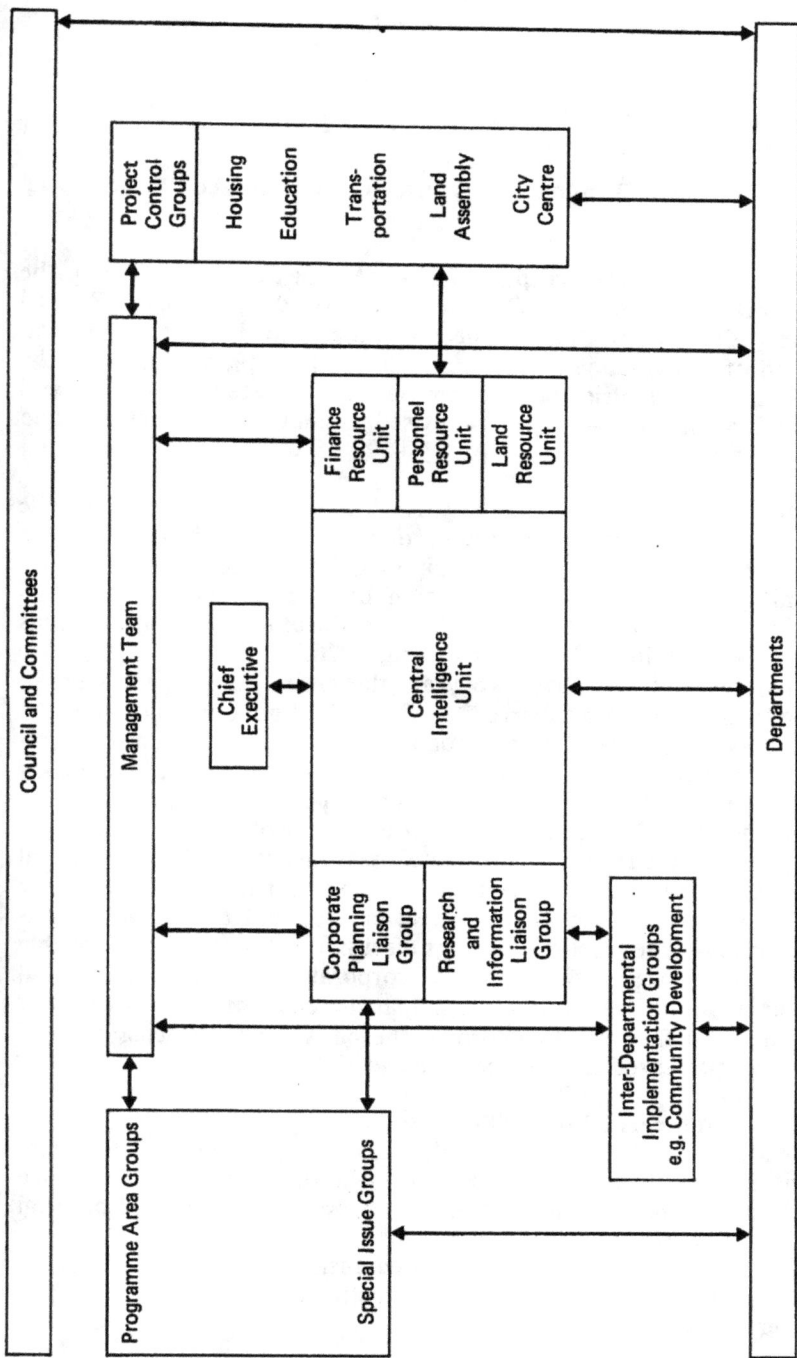

Figure 11 Proposed structure for corporate working in Birmingham

IMPLEMENTATION AND REJECTION – THE PHENOMENON OF
CULTURAL MALADJUSTMENT

On 6 July 1976 Birmingham District Council passed the following
resolution.

> That the system of corporate management adopted following the
> report of the Steering Committee approved by the City Council
> on 13th July 1973, has not been conducive to the best administra-
> tion of the Council's affairs and should be replaced and that the
> Finance and Priorities Committee be directed to devise and
> implement without delay a revised system of management and
> officer structure.

In the view of the new Conservative leader of the Council, Neville
Bosworth, the corporate system devised and established by the
Labour group under the leadership of Clive Wilkinson had been an
unmitigated failure. Its introduction had led to excessive centralisation, duplication of work, laborious documentation and serious
administrative inefficiency (Bosworth, 1976).

In something less than two years the entire corporate system in
Birmingham had been discredited. What had gone wrong? Had the
particular corporate system introduced in Birmingham some unforeseen inherent logistical weakness which made it unworkable? Or
were the reasons for the rejection of corporate management more
fundamental? Has the longstanding advocacy of corporate management been based on a fundamental misconception of the practical
management needs of local authorities like Birmingham? Or is the
fault to be found not in the approach itself but in the way it was
introduced? The research findings discussed below suggest a possible
explanation for the rejection of the corporate system in Birmingham,
an explanation set within the tripartite elemental framework of
organisation theory which formed the basis for the discussions and
analyses presented in the first three sections of this book.

The research carried out within the authority highlighted numerous
individual instances and general areas of organisational malfunction between 1974 and 1976. For the sake of analytical convenience
they can be grouped into two areas – operational detail and cultural
maladjustment.

In the first area must be included instances of excessive documentation and duplication of administrative effort. As one chief
officer noted:

The department was being drowned in a sea of paper – as was evidenced by the fact that almost overnight the volume of internal post exceeded the volume of external post, showing that more time and effort was being expended on talking amongst ourselves than on communicating with clients and carrying out what should have been our primary function . . . Now, before a report could be presented to members for decision, a preliminary report had to be submitted to the Management Team. Any subject which even marginally affected another department had to be subject to co-authorship by appropriate chief officers. Some reports, called joint reports, were prepared by several chief officers and were then presented to several committees.

Although such developments were serious and unquestionably represented a contributory factor in a reduction of operational efficiency within the authority, they could have been the subject of logistical solutions and in no way have undermined the theoretical legitimacy of the innovations introduced. As Clive Wilkinson pointed out:

Any system which attempts to analyse problems in greater depth and assess long-term implications is bound to generate more paper work . . . the trick is one of being selective in what one reads and in delegating sensibly the tasks of document preparation.

A much more fundamental and serious question is raised by those instances falling within the area of cultural maladjustment. This is because these are symptomatic of a basic lack of sympathy between the organisation's structural and procedural apparatus and its value system as manifested in the behavioural orientation of the organisation's human participants. Weakness or inadequacy in this area implies a basic failing in the whole approach to the introduction of organisational innovation and reform.

The results of the research carried out within the authority left little doubt that the majority of officers in Birmingham felt anxious and uncomfortable in a corporate or project setting. This was especially true of those with long experience of the traditional system and little or no experience of a corporate or directorate approach. Discomfort was in many cases accompanied by resentment at the way in which the new management system had been devised and introduced. It appeared to many that the new system had been imposed by so many new personalities with little or no appreciation of the facts of Birmingham's administrative life. Feelings of suspicion and resentment found a focal point in the person of the new Chief Executive who was himself aware of being cast in the role of a stranger from outside implementing a strange new system.

The corporate approach particularly attacks the departmental orientation of traditional local government management and its preoccupation with measuring the resource input associated with specific services rather than the effectiveness of their output. However, in both of these areas the new system in Birmingham failed to overcome the resistance of traditional values.

There was certainly a continuation of a departmental rather than a corporate orientation on the part of most chief officers. This manifested itself in the two extreme forms of either excessive conflict or, as was often the case during sessions of the Management Team, excessive silence. As Francis Amos commented: 'Generally the meetings got bogged down because officers went out of their way to avoid commenting on, or in any other way "trespassing" upon, another officer's departmental territory.' An alternative explanation for excessive silence during meetings of the Management Team was put forward by a team member who noted the presence of a general feeling that argument was pointless because 'the corporate planning corps would be sure to get their own way in the end'. The result was an outward display of corporate unity and common purpose but, underneath, the continuation of a traditional departmental orientation. This led to the emergence of what is probably the most damaging kind of conflict, that which is unspoken and atmospheric. Taking this into account it is not really surprising that the Management Team was subsequently open to the charge of not having accomplished anything constructive or having had any significant impact on the management of the authority (Bosworth, 1976, p. 7).

A similar situation existed in the authority's interdepartmental or project groups. The members of such bodies often saw their role as one of departmental guardians, there to see fair play and to ensure that when important decisions were being made the interests of their departments were adequately protected. Group discussions which should have focused primarily on the best interests of the authority as a whole often turned into bargaining sessions between departmental representatives, each intent on gaining as large a share as possible of resources being allocated.

Often direct contact with the corporate level caused a defensive reaction within departments. Requests from corporate level for even the most factual information were invariably treated with suspicion. A common response was the immediate interposition of the appropriate committee chairman as a barrier against suspected interference in departmental activities.

A further example of the reluctance of departments to adopt a corporate outlook and operate at an interdepartmental level was provided within the complex area of housing and urban renewal. In Birmingham, urban renewal was a comprehensive policy based in the Environmental Department, but with sections attached to other departments, including Housing. Urban Renewal Officers in the Housing Department expressed the view that they had never really been accepted, they had been conscious of considerable resentment and lack of co-operation. Failure to achieve co-operation was evidenced by the inability to establish similar areas as priority areas for both housing modernisation programmes and urban renewal strategy. Thus the Housing Department was concentrating on different areas from those identified by Urban Renewal Officers as areas requiring urgent attention. The Housing Department's modernisation programmes had been drawn up on a long-term basis and were being adhered to rigidly, despite the identification of new priorities by urban renewal specialists.

Illustrative of a continuing lack of interest in the assessment of the effectiveness of the output of services, and also of the apparent lack of appreciation of the objectives of corporate planning, was the fate of one department's planning procedure. In this department the initial response to the Conservatives' announcement of their intention to scrap corporate planning was, 'does that mean we don't have to fill in that big report any more?' The reference was to the departmental planning document which was designed to show details of the department's activities, past performance, future requirements, needs, objectives, and so on. The completion of these details was seen as an unnecessary and tiresome duty and the information provided was often inadequate. People rarely attempted to fill in objectives and restricted information to statistics which displayed a continuing preoccupation with the inputs associated with services rather than the environmental impact of service provision.

Closely associated with the fate of corporate management in Birmingham was the conflict of loyalties experienced by many of the officers interviewed. Such conflict was usually brought to a head by the demands made upon their time by the need to participate at corporate or project level. One chief officer described his reaction to such conflict of loyalties in the following terms:

> There came a time when one had to decide on priorities and, since I had been appointed to run this department and it would be my head on the block if the department became inefficient, I chose the department whenever possible. I did not see the point in exposing myself to such risks in order to be involved in planning the activities of other departments about whose affairs I knew precious little.

There is little doubt that the additional strains of participation at an interdepartmental level, pressure on time and extra documentation increased the feelings of anxiety and resentment among chief officers. Many felt that the new system presented a threat to professionalism and even personal security. A popular feeling was that corporate management represented an attack on the larger departments, an attempt to reduce them to the ranks, to be considered at the same level as minor departments and functions. To some extent such a view was understandable since, as Francis Amos commented:

> For the purposes of corporate management all departments were treated in exactly the same way. Thus the Chief Amenities Officer was given the same status as the Chief Education Officer and I think this was a bit of a shock for both of them. This probably added to the general feeling of apprehension, but recognising that all departments of the authority had a legitimate contribution to make in the corporate planning process is a long way from attacking the entrenched position of monolithic empire departments.

Feelings of resentment and anxiety were not confined to officers. Resentment was understandably pronounced among councillors belonging to the Conservative opposition who, they claimed, had been kept completely in the dark throughout the introduction of corporate management within the authority. More surprising, however, was the apparently schizophrenic attitude towards the new system adopted by many senior Labour councillors. Some committee chairmen who had not been privy to the deliberations of the small working party which had designed the system, and who were not members of the Policy and Resources Committee, tended to cling tenaciously to the more traditional departmental role, despite their support of the system's overall philosophy in full council.

The above reaction on the part of some councillors was sometimes the result of a feeling of being left out or excluded from the ranks of a corporate planning elite as represented by the oligarchic Policy and Resources Committee. This apparently elitist body of councillors had a parallel in the Management Team, the exclusive nature of which also proved a major source of resentment among chief officers, as one of them pointed out:

> There was very much a first- and second-class citizen syndrome concerning those who were members of the Team and those who were not. Moreover, those who were included were not always those who could make the best contribution in a particular situation – some important officers, for example, the City Engineer and the City Architect, were excluded.

Many chief officers who had served on the Management Team agreed that more flexible arrangements would have been preferable, for example, treating the Management Team as a small cabinet with the majority of chief officers serving on working groups related to particular programme areas.

The research revealed that a majority of the participants in Birmingham's corporate management system were not convinced of the need for change in the first place and remained sceptical and uncommitted to the system's basic principles. A recurring theme in the interviews conducted was the belief that the corporate system was in many ways divorced from the operational practicalities of local government administration. For example, the implication that there should be no special relationship between particular chief officers and the chairmen of particular committees was especially contentious:

> Such relationships which were often personal, informal and, in my opinion, very effective, have been a traditional strength of local government management. To suggest that such relationships should cease and that all chief officers be equally responsible to all councillors seemed very naive and to me demonstrated a basic failure to appreciate why local authorities like Birmingham have coped so well before. (A chief officer)

In Birmingham, feelings of anxiety and resentment were to a large extent caused by the imposition by a small group of enthusiasts of a system of organisation and management which involved senior officers and members in unfamiliar managerial situations and roles. Many of these roles were completely alien to the managerial environment and administrative culture with which the participants were familiar, in which they believed, and within which they had risen to senior level. The continued belief in the value of traditional structures and procedures and a cynical view of the innovations introduced was nurtured by poor communications and lack of consultation, a view which is readily conceded by the chief instigator of the new system:

> There should have been more consultation and exchange of information and ideas between us [the Labour group], senior officers and the main body of councillors. I think more effort should have been put into training both officers and councillors in the principles of corporate management and the purpose behind the changes they were experiencing. (Clive Wilkinson)

On the surface, the major emphasis in the Conservative group's critique of the corporate system in Birmingham (contained in councillor Bosworth's report of October 1976) is on time wasted and short-term financial cost. Corporate management was seen as involving highly paid officers in wasting time 'talking or listening to matters of which they had no knowledge or experience and frankly with which they were not particularly concerned'. The achievement of a co-ordinated system of working was seen as costing more than it was worth: 'it would not empty one more dustbin or build more houses.' However, the reassertion of more traditional organisational and administrative values is clearly evident in the justifications put forward for a complete reversion. As councillor Bosworth stated:

> I prefer independent-minded chairmen and chief officers . . . One accepts the occasional mistake and the odd failure of co-ordination, if members and officers are trying hard to achieve success in the field assigned to them . . . I like departments which are keen to get on with the job . . . and who resent interference from others . . . They are more likely to do something valuable other than sheltering behind joint committees and constantly deferring the need to take action.

On the theme of linking particular committees to particular departments Bosworth noted that:

> The close working relationship between the chairman of a committee and his chief officer . . . attacked as incompatible with the corporate concept, represented a partnership of immense value from which policy was often initiated.

Bosworth considered that the erosion of the powerful committees' ability to determine their own policy and control the administration of their own departments had gone too far and that the time had come to re-establish maximum independence for committees and chief officers.

In the period immediately following the May 1976 elections the Policy and Resources Committee was abolished and its duties were transferred to a Finance and Priorities Committee. The Chief Executive was instructed to cease calling meetings of the Management Team and to redeploy the staff then engaged on corporate planning and performance review. The Performance Review Committee itself was not reappointed, its unfinished work being passed to the Finance and Priorities Committee. The work of all project groups, working parties, and so on, was curtailed. The Land Committee was also terminated and its duties transferred to a Planning and Highways Committee which closely resembled the old Public Works Committee in terms of its functions. The Chief Executive, City Treasurer, City Solicitor and City Personnel Officer were to work together as a Chief Officers' Advisory Panel. This panel was to meet to discuss matters of mutual concern when this would further the interests of the Council. Such meetings were, however, to be held at irregular and infrequent intervals. The revised role of the Chief Executive was of particular significance in view of his previous position as the focal point of the corporate system. His new role was still seen in terms of overall co-ordination but on a macro, interauthority level rather than in an internal management setting. He was charged with responsibility for liaising between the District Council and other organisations and for ensuring that the work of the authority was co-ordinated with the work of neighbouring districts and with the county authority. In addition, he was to ensure that effective working relationships were developed with all private and public sector organisations whose activities might have implications for the City Council. (In June 1977 it was announced that the Chief Executive was to lose his employment altogether and that his duties, including that of overall co-ordination, were to be taken over by the City Treasurer).

In summary, the overriding principles of the new system in Birmingham included the following:

1 Departmental boundaries are sacrosanct in all but the most exceptional circumstances.
2 The primary responsibility of chief officers shall be to their committees and not to any general conception of 'the Authority'.
3 Interdepartmental, interdisciplinary communication shall be kept to a minimum.

All this amounted to a strong reassertion of the benefits of structural and functional differentiation associated with classical organisational design and the re-establishment of a procedural framework more in tune with the values and expectations of key personnel.

The final rejection of the corporate system in late 1976 followed a change in the political control of the Council. Thus one could explain its demise simply in terms of political expediency, as a predictable reaction by the incoming Conservative administration to a system of management about which they had not been consulted and in which they had been allowed no direct participation. Added to this is the inevitable association of particular approaches to management and particular political ideologies; for example, the association of centralised planning and corporate strategy with communalism and a socialist solution to environmental problems, compared with the Conservative belief in administrative competition and less centralised decision-making as the best way to achieve effective resource utilisation. However, in terms of organisation and administrative theory it can be held that the failure of organisational innovation in Birmingham was inevitable and indeed predictable because of the existence of a basic lack of correlation between the organisation's dominant culture and its procedural and structural machinery.

In the foregoing discussion organisational adaptation in Birmingham was associated with organisational innovation and reform in two areas. These were, first, the area of managerial process – through the adoption of corporate management and corporate planning and, secondly, the area of organisational structure – through the adoption of a matrix form. However, the case study shows that in Birmingham little attention was paid to the need to bring about an equivalent and complementary change in the authority's value system and hence its culture. The cultural element was defined earlier as encompassing the values, beliefs, prejudices, goals and expectations of the organisation's human members. Change in this area could have been generated initially through improved internal communications and consultation and a more comprehensive programme of training in the underlying theories and objectives of corporate management and the benefits and problems of operating matrix structures.

The cultural element is important since the success or failure of structural or procedural innovations in any organisation will be determined to a large extent by the degree of commitment experienced by the human participants. The Birmingham case study lends weight to the argument that the importance of cultural adjustment is magnified in organisations, such as local authorities which have particularly strong, well-established administrative values.

We have already seen that Argyris emphasised the need for structural and procedural changes to be accompanied by an 'appropriate influencing of values' (Argyris, 1962, p. 53). More recently he has pointed out that the importance of cultural adjustment is amplified when increased innovative capacity and organisational flexibility is sought through the adoption of a matrix design (Argyris, 1967). This is because matrix design tends to impose new and unfamiliar expectations with regard to perceptions of group identity and loyalty (as was the case with the relationships between chief officers and the Management Team) and new levels of challenge and responsibility (as reflected in the need to participate at corporate level). Clearly, the imposition of a matrix project dimension within an organisation which has hitherto only experienced a purely functional orientation will necessitate a considerable change in the behavioural orientation of incumbent managers and participants. Many managers will, during the course of such a system's operation, be removed from the familiar departmental environment where they are constantly reminded of sectional interests and are subject to goal displacement. Instead, they will be placed within an unfamiliar, less permanent, managerial setting involving equally unfamiliar interpersonal relationships and where the operational concern is less with service provision and more with interdepartmental, interdisciplinary analysis and problem-solving. Problems arise because the individual's orientation, the manager's everyday behaviour styles, will have been developed over time in a way which best equipped him to survive and succeed in the traditional organisation. However, as Argyris emphasises, the behaviour styles and values needed for the effective use of matrix organisation are different from those which would have been developed for the effective use of a traditional bureaucratic, mechanistic organisation.

Lawrence and Lorsch's extention of the concept of differentiation into the behavioural dimension (see Part One, Chapter 2) involved recognising the presence of differences in cognitive and emotional orientation on the part of members of different functional departments, brought about by excessive segmentation and functional specialisation. This feature relates strongly to the observed continuance of departmental chauvinism in Birmingham. The case study has shown that the strength of traditional values, the degree of entrenchment of the sectional, bureaucratic orientation proves to be a prime determinant of the potential effectiveness of attempts to introduce greater organisational integration.

In the sense of this discussion the fortunes of corporate planning in Birmingham were inextricably linked to the nature of the interpersonal demands inherent in its structural apparatus. With the introduction of the corporate planning system managerial process and organisational structure were fused together, but the effectiveness of this fusion was dependent upon the supportive or destructive response of the organisation's value system. In Birmingham the destructive nature of this response was evidenced through the reactions and behavioural inertia of many of the authority's key personnel. The evidence shows that the value system which had emerged over many years in Birmingham remained firmly entrenched after the introduction of the procedural and structural innovations. Thus the authority's culture continued to display the characteristics of one most conducive to the successful operation of a highly differentiated, bureaucratic organisation.

The basic lack of correlation between the authority's culture and its procedural and structural apparatus led to a reduction in operational efficiency. This provided evidence for those who distrusted the philosophy and theoretical legitimacy of the corporate system or who simply disliked the authoritarian way in which it had been introduced. Such evidence enabled them to attack the new system of management not on grounds of theoretical illegitimacy but on more practical operational grounds provided by inadequacies in the way in which the system had been introduced and in the whole approach adopted to organisational innovation and reform.

The case study of Birmingham reinforces the contention that any attempt to reform a hitherto static, mechanistic organisation and to create in its place a flexible, adaptive, organic entity must involve innovation in three areas:

1 The procedural – the actual philosophy and process of management adopted.
2 The structural – the structural mechanisms and devices which form the supportive framework within which the management process is to be carried out.
3 The cultural – the values, beliefs, goals and expectations held by the human members of the organisation.

In attempting to change the whole character of an organisation as well as its structures and functional procedures, these three elements must be fused together to form a comprehensive, fully integrated approach to organisational innovation and reform. For such reform to be effective it is imperative that the complex interrelationships and mutual dependence which exists between all three elements be clearly recognised. Preoccupation with only one or two elements to the exclusion or neglect of any other, can have the effect of nullifying the whole reforming effort. (See Figure 12.)

In Birmingham the structural and procedural elements were pushed ahead with little or no attention paid to the need to bring about an equivalent change in the organisation's value system and culture. Thus it can be argued that the rejection of corporate management and a more organic organisational framework was the result of a less than comprehensive and fully integrated approach to the management of change and organisational innovation.

What needs to be explored after the event are the possibilities of an alternative approach to organisational innovation in local government, given the particular strength of its administrative value systems.

Figure 12 'Cultural maladjustment' in organisational innovation and reform

Mechanistic Features

Predetermined hierarchy. Rigid, authoritarian structure. Functional structural differentiation.

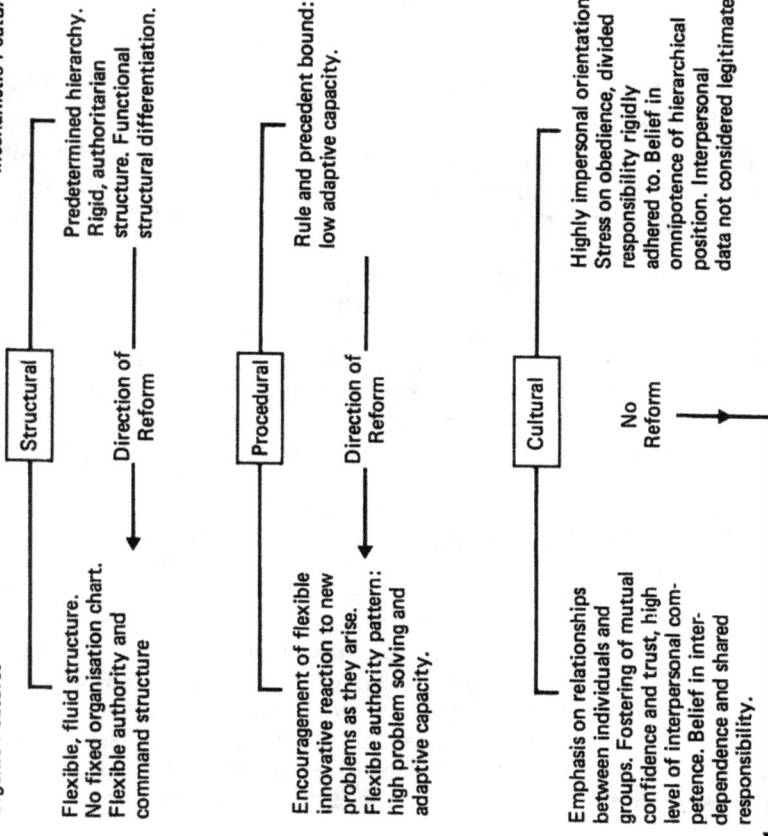

Rule and precedent bound: low adaptive capacity.

Highly impersonal orientation. Stress on obedience, divided responsibility rigidly adhered to. Belief in omnipotence of hierarchical position. Interpersonal data not considered legitimate.

Structural

Direction of Reform →

Procedural

Direction of Reform →

Cultural

No Reform →

Organic Features

Flexible, fluid structure. No fixed organisation chart. Flexible authority and command structure

Encouragement of flexible innovative reaction to new problems as they arise. Flexible authority pattern: high problem solving and adaptive capacity.

Emphasis on relationships between individuals and groups. Fostering of mutual confidence and trust, high level of interpersonal competence. Belief in interdependence and shared responsibility.

The Reformed Organisation

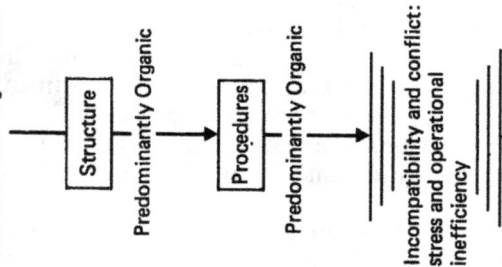

Structure — Predominantly Organic

Procedures — Predominantly Organic

Incompatibility and conflict: stress and operational inefficiency

Culture — Predominantly Mechanistic

OD AS AN ALTERNATIVE STRATEGY IN LOCAL GOVERNMENT – AN ASSESSMENT

The overall relevance of organisation development as an approach to the introduction of organisational innovation in local authorities becomes clear when one applies its main features to the Birmingham case study.

In the first instance, the introduction of the new managerial structures and processes was not planned in the sense of OD's planned process approach. In Birmingham most participants encountered a sudden and violent rejection of traditional roles, conventions and expectations. New committees and management groups appeared virtually overnight and were expected to begin striving towards the attainment of a new set of goals and objectives about which many participants remained ignorant or, at best, vague. Such a strategy, as Argyris has pointed out, can often have the effect of heightening the powers of resistance within the organisation, exacerbating resentment and feelings of hostility towards the innovations being introduced (Argyris, 1967, p. 35). The OD approach would have called for a more gradual adoption of the new system accompanied by a comprehensive, organisation-wide programme of training in the need for change and the ways in which the proposed structure and processes were conducive to increased organisational effectiveness. In addition, emphasis would have been placed on demonstrating the nature and value of the individual's contribution at all management levels throughout the organisation.

The fact that no change effort can succeed unless it has the sponsorship and commitment of top management was well illustrated by the case study of Birmingham. In the context of this study the term 'top management' must be taken as referring to chief officers and key personnel below them and not just to the political policy-making groups. Beckhard's reference to the need for knowledge and commitment in this connection is particularly significant. Knowledge and understanding of objectives and process is an essential prerequisite for personal commitment to any reform strategy. In Birmingham, lack of understanding, essentially the product of poor communication, was a barrier to such commitment particularly at the key middle management level of second- and third-tier officers, in which personnel experienced strong feelings of isolation, lack of direction and, in some instances, insecurity and outright intimidation.

It has been shown that the result of the structural and procedural innovations introduced in Birmingham was to impart organic organisational characteristics. To this extent a primary objective of OD was reflected in the introduction of corporate planning and matrix design. The change effort failed in several important areas where OD intervention would have had particular relevance. These were:

1 The area of group working and team development.
2 The area of intergroup conflict.
3 The area of process-monitoring, consultation, and general data feedback.
4 The area of education and training.

The effective use of teams and groups is essential if matrix design is to be successful. As was shown earlier, in the initial stages where interdisciplinary, interdepartmental teams are established a certain amount of inertia and conflict will exist. People will still tend to polarise issues, mistrust each other's motives and attempt to protect what they perceive to be their own function or area of responsibility. Certainly the evidence suggests that the extension of interpersonal, interdepartmental, and interprofessional conflict into management and project team situations proved an important barrier to the achievement of any real corporate identity in Birmingham. In this area the OD intervention techniques of T-group and confrontation sessions, as a means of exposing the causes of group and intergroup conflict, would have had direct relevance. The benefits of such exercises for Birmingham may have been considerable, given the often excessively competitive behaviour which existed between departments. In particular, the hostile attitude of departments towards the 'corporate planning corps', against whose policies all argument was considered useless, could have probably been mellowed considerably by the application of such blood-letting exercises. Although it is not suggested that the use of OD intervention in the areas of team building and the management of intergroup conflict would have completely neutralised the powerful centrifugal forces of departmentalism, there is little doubt that their application would have been beneficial, particularly at the level of the Management Team. As Francis Amos commented: 'Some sort of shock treatment was definitely needed to overcome the inertia of members. Perhaps a T-group session, properly conducted and supervised and held on neutral territory, would have led to the development of more constructive attitudes.'

Failure in the areas of data feedback and process consultation was evidenced by the fact that the instigators of the new system were quickly out of touch with its operation. The weakness of communication between chief officers and senior councillors meant that serious logistical problems were allowed to develop to the point where they threatened, and in fact damaged, operational efficiency. A well-organised monitoring and guidance programme may have facilitated essential adjustments to corporate management and planning procedures as the system became established.

Education and training rely upon good communication. It is not surprising, therefore, that in Birmingham many officers, and indeed many council members, remained vague and confused as to the methods and objectives of the reforms and managerial innovations which they were experiencing. It is in this area of educating and informing participants on the need for change and the methods for achieving change that OD intervention could perhaps have made its greatest contribution to the success of reform. The need to adjust cultural norms has been a central theme of this study. However, it is important to realise that well-established administrative and managerial values cannot be changed overnight in a once-and-for-all fashion. Rather, they must be worn down and eroded by an energetic programme of education and training. When changes in cultural norms are the result of such a strategy, as would be the case in a properly organised OD programme, then the changes subsequently introduced are more likely to survive the onslaught of initial logistical and operational problems.

Thus, in general terms, the approach of organisation development, when seen as an educational strategy which concentrates on the people variable, certainly has theoretical relevance to Birmingham's experiences. However, as was pointed out during the broader discussion of OD in Part Three, the approach should not be viewed as a panacea immediately applicable to all organisational problems. It was noted particularly that the practical applicability of OD is held to be dependent upon the state of cultural readiness within the organisation concerned. By this was meant the need for a certain minimum standard of receptiveness within the organisation and an acceptance of the basic values inherent within the OD approach: for example, the acceptance of interpersonal, emotional factors as legitimate data to be considered in the solution of managerial problems. The events and attitudes surrounding the rejection of corporate management and organic frameworks in Birmingham suggest that such a basic conflict between the values predominant within the organisation and those associated with OD would have existed. Thus, while OD would have continued to have had theoretical relevance as an aid to the attainment of the authority's reform objectives, in terms of practical application its techniques may have been rendered impotent by a general lack of sympathy on the part of participants.

It was also emphasised earlier that in organisations with particularly strong cultural traditions the role of change mediation is likely to be more effectively carried out by an internal change agent. In other words, the role needs to be adopted by someone who has, at one and the same time, an established identity within the organisation which will facilitate the speedy attainment of acceptance and credibility, and also a knowledge of the techniques and underlying principles of applied behavioural science. It was further argued that such a role could not at present be ascribed to internal personnel specialists in local authorities with appropriate training and experience. Lack of development in this area must represent a further qualification of the immediate applicability of OD as an alternative strategy for the introduction and assimilation of structural and procedural change in local authorities.

OVERVIEW AND CONCLUSIONS

This work has centred upon the analysis, within a conceptual framework of organisation theory, of recent managerial innovation in local government. This has been carried out by focusing on the three principal aspects of organisational design and functioning – the structural, the procedural and the cultural and, more importantly, on their mutual interdependence.

At the outset, the utility of classical prescriptions was measured against the practical operational demands made on local authorities as the full range of services and functions developed. The conclusion was reached that the preoccupation with classical, mechanistic design in local government was inevitable, given the close correlation which existed between the structural and procedural characteristics of bureaucracy and the needs of operational expediency and public accountability which local authorities had to meet. However, the ultimate consequence of exclusive reliance on classical design was shown to be a serious potentiality for conflict and imbalance between the authority and its environment, this because of the classical organisation's rigid, uncommunicative and insular character. The actual existence of such imbalance was presented as a principal reason underlying the need for reform in local government management.

The actual structural and procedural innovations prescribed were shown as attempting to impart organic characteristics to hitherto highly differentiated, mechanistic organisations, thereby increasing their capacity for sensitivity and responsiveness to environmental pressures for change and adaptation. The particular structural pattern prescribed was shown to follow a matrix design, which was identified with the organic qualities of flexibility and adaptability. The procedural changes introduced in the form of corporate management and planning systems such as PPBS were shown to reinforce this organic, environmental orientation by emphasising the need to relate the activities of an authority as a whole to environmental conditions both present and future.

Subsequent assessment and evaluation of the success of this reform strategy in local government generally was shown to be hampered by the great variation in commitment and approach observed to exist between authorities. However, it has been argued that, because all local authorities display basically similar structural and cultural characteristics, any assessment of the assimilation of the reform strategies which identifies problems that emanate from these basic features can be presented as having some general applicability and perhaps some prescriptive value.

In the assessment and evaluation of the adaptive response in Birmingham Metropolitan District Council, lack of innovation in the area of organisational culture has been presented as a serious omission, especially in view of the particular behavioural demands imposed by a matrix design with its unfamiliar project dimension and often alien managerial role expectations. The evidence has shown that the behavioural norms and cultural characteristics associated with the traditional bureaucratic organisation remained firmly entrenched after the introduction of the new structural and procedural patterns. The consequent lack of correlation between the actual behaviour, values and attitudes of participants and those prescribed by the new system (the state of cultural maladjustment) led to serious operational inefficiency. This provided evidence for those who distrusted the philosophy of the system, enabling them to attack it on more practical operational grounds. The conclusion was reached that, in Birmingham, the final rejection of corporate management was a direct result of operational inefficiencies which were, in turn, the result of basic inadequacies in the way in which the changes had been introduced. In particular, cultural maladjustment has been shown to be symptomatic of a less than comprehensive and fully integrated approach to the management of organisational innovation in terms of the tripartite elemental framework of organisational design and functioning presented at the outset.

Organisation development' has been introduced as a possible alternative approach to the management of organisational innovation which may have particular relevance for local government, given the special strength of its cultural values. Organisation development, as a strategy, was shown to take the cultural perspective as its starting point. The techniques associated with OD were shown to have a particular relevance to specific problems experienced by Birmingham District Council, especially in the areas of team building and conflict management. It was noted, however, that the practical applicability of OD is held to be dependent upon the state of cultural readiness within the particular organisation in question. The evidence suggests that Birmingham's administrative culture would have been in basic and fundamental conflict with the values associated with OD approaches. It must be concluded, therefore, that some form of preliminary training strategy would have been required with a minimum objective of convincing key participants (both members and officers) of the need for change and reform and of the value and relevance of an OD programme as a route to its achievement.

Finally, the functional role of change mediation and the concept of the change agent has been examined against the background of general developments in the field of local government personnel management. The potential overlap of expertise required by the modern personnel manager and an internal change agent was established. However, the limited development of the relevant areas of personnel management in local authorities generally, and in Birmingham in particular, led to the conclusion that the potential for such a specialised internal role is still lacking.

As a study in applied organisation theory the major conclusion reached in this survey of local government management is that when superimposing organic frameworks upon organisations which have previously displayed bureaucratic, mechanistic characteristics one must pay particular attention to the cultural aspect of organisational design and working. Whereas the need for structural and procedural changes is often fairly obvious, the need to innovate in the area of organisational culture is often less apparent but is none the less crucial. Organisational values are less tangible than structural and procedural features and are, therefore, less easy to subject to deliberate management and adjustment. However, it has been shown that procedures and strategies have been developed which, if properly utilised, can facilitate adjustment in this cultural area.

APPENDIX: TECHNIQUES FOR OPERATIONAL EFFICIENCY

Management systems like **PPBS** are designed primarily to ensure the organisation's long-term effectiveness. However, other management techniques or aids have been developed as a means of assisting in the attainment of day-to-day operational efficiency. Although a detailed examination of each of these management techniques has not been central to the development of the overall theme of this book it remains appropriate and useful to include the following notes on the central characteristics of some of the most widely used techniques and to describe briefly their practical application in local government.

NETWORK ANALYSIS

The technique of network analysis involves setting out in diagrammatic form all the separate events and activities which are integral to a complex project or task. The exercise has as its object the attainment of the most speedy and efficient completion of a project and the provision of a means of identifying potentially disruptive and expensive hold-ups and oversights.

The technique developed as a response to the need to manage increasingly large-scale and complex tasks in private industry, particularly in the United States, where du Ponts and the Rand Corporation first developed the technique for use in planning the construction of chemical plant. The same basic technique was used in the United Kingdom in the mid-1950s by the Central Electricity Generating Board in planning the maintenance of plant and was found to reduce the period for maintenance by some 40 per cent. Large savings were also recorded in the military field, where a similar technique, labelled Programme Evaluation and Review was applied by the United States Navy during the development of the Polaris missile programme. During the 1960s the technique developed rapidly and now forms the foundation of highly sophisticated management aids such as Resource Allocation in Multi-Project Scheduling (RAMPS) and Graphical Evaluation Review Technique (GERT).

Network analysis can be divided into three distinctive activities – planning, scheduling, and controlling.

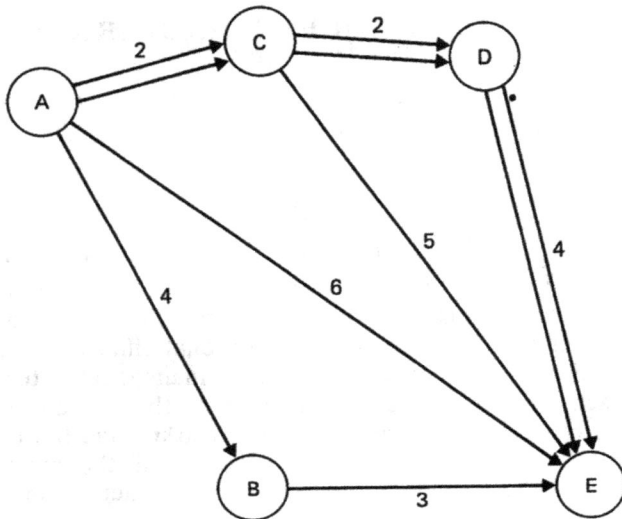

Figure 13   Network analysis – simple flow chart

The planning activity involves plotting the sequence and inter-relationships of the separate tasks or events involved in the project. This is achieved by the use of the characteristic flow charts associated with the technique. Figure 13 provides a simplified representation of such a flow chart. In this example, four tasks or events, A B C D, must be completed before the final goal of E can be achieved.

During the scheduling activity the estimated time taken for the completion of each task is inserted. Thus the time taken to move from stage A to stage C is estimated at two days and the time taken to move from stage A to stage B, four days, and so on. From this diagram a simple calculation shows the shortest time within which the entire project can be completed. This is shown as being eight days, calculated from the sequence A C D E. This sequence represents the critical path for the project. It is termed critical because, whereas delays on any other sequence can be absorbed by float time, that is, a margin of time to spare within the overall project time, any delay on the critical path will inevitably delay the whole project. It follows that if any overall tightening-up of the project schedule is desired then attention must be directed towards speeding up the events and tasks within the critical path sequence. Little would be gained, for instance, by concentrating on path A–E since this already has a float margin of two days. However, even a small increase in efficiency in the critical path sequence would be immediately reflected in the total project time.

The third activity, that of controlling, simply involves utilising the information contained in the flow chart. For example, for each task in the project it is possible to calculate the earliest and latest start times. In the example, the earliest time that task B can be started is 4 days, but the latest time at which B can start if the whole project is not to be delayed is 5 days, that is, 8 − 3, the critical project time less the time allowed to complete that last stage of B–E. Thus if task B has not been started after 5 days then project controllers know immediately that a potentially serious delay has occurred and that other activities feeding into the project may have to be rescheduled in order to prevent bottlenecks and even more serious delays.

The most obvious application of network analysis in local authorities lies in the area of building and other public works projects where a great deal of additional expenditure can accompany delays and the breakdown of schedules. However, the technique also has a contribution to make in the programming of long-term administrative procedures such as the preparation of annual departmental estimates. An account has been provided of such an application within an education department (Ray, 1977). The raw material for this exercise was a detailed diary of events leading up to the presentation of estimates to the Education Committee in the previous year. This information was analysed and fifty-eight distinct tasks were identified. The interrelationships between these key tasks were then demonstrated by the construction of a flow diagram. Although this particular network analysis project was never completed its inception did demonstrate some important points. For example, the very discipline of analysis and the construction of a flow chart brought considerable benefits:

> this was the first time that the intricate relationships between the various administrative tasks had been expressed clearly on one sheet of paper. At this point it was felt that even if the project went no further some useful improvements in communication had been achieved. (Ray, 1977)

Some important modifications were introduced in the administrative procedure of estimate preparation as a direct result of the completion of the initial planning phase of network analysis. Also, for the first time, the staff involved could see clearly where their contribution fitted into the overall framework and how seemingly trivial delays might prejudice the completion of the entire project.

ORGANISATION AND METHODS (O AND M)

Organisation and Methods is a generic term used to describe the group of investigatory techniques used in the systematic examination and study of work, particularly non-manual work, for the purpose of improving efficiency. Within local government the term generally refers to the study of administrative and clerical activities with a view to streamlining these wherever possible and obtaining real cost advantages by the eradication of waste or undue complexity.

·O and M in Britain had its origins in the Report of the Bradbury Committee on the Organisation and Staffing of Government Offices (Cd 62, 1919). As a result of this report a small Treasury Investigation Section was set up to promote the use of better office methods and equipment. However, it was not until the advent of the Second World War that a revival of interest in the simplification and streamlining of administrative procedures led to an enlargement of this unit and the first official usage of the term 'organisation and methods' to describe its work. By 1945 most government departments had their own O and M staff and by the early 1950s O and M had been adopted in the new nationalised industries and the hospital service and was being applied within larger concerns in the private sector.

A specific O and M assignment normally involves the following stages:

1 A preliminary survey; this is necessary for the O and M practitioner to gain an overall impression of existing organisation and procedures and to identify major problem areas. Usually this preliminary stage involves brief interviews with key personnel and the examination of such things as organisation charts, duty schedules, departmental records, and so on.
2 More detailed fact-finding; this is carried out by conducting more widespread and searching interviews with staff, observing work being carried out, measuring and assessing performance and examining relevant statistics and records. Interviews are usually structured around the questions, who? what? why? where? how? and when? This provides a more detailed picture of the duties, responsibilities and mode of work of individuals. It also provides an opportunity for recording participants' suggestions about how procedures, and particularly their own contribution, might be improved. In order to allow for the distortion or ambiguity which can accompany verbal communication, interviewing is supplemented by the physical

observation of important procedures so that the O and M practitioner can get an accurate idea of how the task is carried out, what it involves and how long it takes. Often this part of the fact-finding operation is completed by the O and M practitioner actually accompanying an operative during the period of a typical day. In this way procedural problems which even the operative concerned was unaware of may be identified. The actual measurement of administrative performance is fraught with difficulty. Sherman (1969) notes that one commonly cited distinction between work study and O and M is that 'Work Study men measure but O and M men do not'. There is some justification for making such a distinction. However, the committed O and M practitioner would not subscribe to the view that measurement is impossible when dealing with office work. Typically, the O and M practitioner measures in terms of broad yardsticks represented by target ratios between input, in terms of staff resources, and output, expressed in terms of a desired standard. Examples of such ratios would be 'pages per typist day' or 'rents collected per collector day'. The examination of current and historical statistics relating to particular aspects of administrative work can be useful as an aid to identifying trends, for example, in increasing workload, which may have particular significance when improvements in work methods are being considered. The inspection of records can tell the O and M investigator a great deal about a department's internal working arrangements and can be particularly helpful in identifying obvious instances of overdocumentation or unnecessary duplication.

3 Analysis and report; this final stage involves an analysis of the information gathered and the application of O and M expertise in the compilation of a report to management which may contain recommendations for improvements. In formulating recommendations for improvements. In formulating recommendations the O and M practitioner operating in the public sector must employ an additional facet of expertise. He must give due recognition to the presence of any political factors or legislative requirements which might govern the acceptability of specific plans for administrative reorganisation. Nor does the O and M involvement end with a scheme's acceptance and implementation. The O and M practitioner must monitor the assimilation of any changes introduced so that any problems can be identified and any necessary adjustments made.

In 1950 the Local Government Manpower Committee, a body set up in 1949 to examine the internal administrative procedures and organisation of local authorities, highlighted the benefits to be derived from the application of O and M techniques in local government. This had a particularly significant impact in Coventry where the Treasury O and M Division later assisted the Corporation in completing a comprehensive review of the organisation and administrative methods of the authority. An important outcome of this exercise was the setting-up of the Corporation's own O and M unit. At the same time the first joint O and M unit was set up by a number of London boroughs. This joint unit was to make great progress in developing the application of O and M in local government.

O and M has gradually achieved a wide acceptance in local government, and in most local authorities today, O and M, together with work study, forms the core of the management services function. The Bains study group noted the value of the independent advisory nature of O and M in local authorities and recommended in their report that the function should remain the responsibility of a specialist unit under the overall supervision of the head of administration. It was also emphasised in the Bains Report that O and M had an increasingly important role to play in keeping organisational structures and procedures under review and in ensuring that an authority's administrative machinery is kept in line with changing requirements and advances in administrative technology.

WORK STUDY

Work study involves 'a ruthlessly analytical and inquisitive approach to the use of manpower' (Currie, 1972). The basic aim of the application of the technique is to achieve greater productivity through greater efficiency. The quest for efficiency is also a central characteristic of O and M and indeed the two techniques share some common ground. For instance, both work study and O and M involve the study of work methods and work measurement, and both employ skilled and experienced investigators. However, the distinction between the two techniques lies in the type of work which is analysed and the precision of the measurement. O and M is applied primarily to non-manual work, particularly in offices, concentrating on clerical and administrative processes. Work study, on the other hand, is applied mainly to manual work or machine processes. Whereas the O and M investigator must be content with broad standards of measurement the work study specialist is concerned with a very much more precise analysis and measurement of physical operations both in terms of the method used and the time taken to carry out specific tasks.

The two main components of work study are method study and

work measurement. The two techniques are complementary, method study concentrating on the achievement of efficiency in movement and work measurement on the achievement of efficiency in the use of time.

The first task in the application of work study is to determine the most efficient method for doing the job under the circumstances which apply. A systematic approach to this problem is provided by method study, or motion study as it was originally called. This provides a means of improving the way a job is carried out by studying movement, the movement of the worker and the movement of materials. The objective in method study is to eliminate all unnecessary movement and to simplify as much as possible those movements which are essential. The technique was pioneered and developed by Frank B. Gilbreth (1868–1924) whose early interest in increasing efficiency in the building industry led him to develop certain 'general principles of motion economy'. Gilbreth himself defined motion study (1917) as 'a science which eliminates wastefulness resulting from unnecessary, ill-directed and inefficient motions'. The overall aim of method study is not, as is sometimes supposed, to make the worker work harder, but to enable the worker to use his energies more effectively, if anything lightening the burden, achieving greater production with the same or less effort.

When applied in practice, method study follows a similar sequence of stages as that followed in an O and M exercise. After management's selection of the job to be analysed all relevant data are marshalled and examined. The job is observed under normal operating conditions and notes made of any particularly laborious components or complex sequences of actions which might be lessened or simplified. A revised form of operation is then devised and presented both to management and employees (often with trade union involvement). After a trial period the revised operation is usually adopted permanently. The work study officer will keep the operation under revision for a period after formal adoption in order to diagnose and resolve any unforeseen problems which may arise.

The most commonly used approach to work measurement is that of time study. Time study is defined by the British Standards Institution (1969) as 'a Work Measurement technique for recording the times and rates of working for the various elements of a specified job, carried out under specified conditions, and for analysing the data so as to obtain the time necessary for carrying out the job at a defined level of performance.'

Time study contains the following elements or stages:

1 The content of the job is broken down into elements.
2 The time taken by the operator to perform each element is measured using a stop-watch.

3 The speed and effectiveness of the operator's rate of working is assessed against a predetermined standard rate of performance. This standard rating is defined by the British Standards Institution as 'the rate at which qualified workers will naturally work at a job provided they know and adhere to the specified method and provided they are motivated to apply themselves to their work. If the standard rating is maintained and the appropriate relaxation taken, a worker will achieve standard performance over the working day.'

4 The basic time for each element of the job is then calculated. By 'basic time' is meant the time for carrying out an element of work at standard rating. The calculation for basic time is:

$$\frac{\text{observed time} \times \text{observed rating}}{\text{standard rating}}$$

5 To this basic time is added an allowance for relaxation, that is, any rest necessary to maintain standards over a period. The exact amount of relaxation allowance will depend on the nature of the job. Allowances are usually obtained from established tables compiled to reflect the varying demands of different working conditions, for example, extra allowances for particularly unpleasant environmental conditions such as excessive heat, dust or noise; and also to reflect the physical energy output required to complete elements of the job, and so on. Clearly, the relaxation allowance for a heavy manual job carried out in unpleasant conditions, such as those experienced in a foundry, is likely to be much higher than that for a lighter, more sedentary job. The basic time for each element plus the relaxation allowance equals the work content of each element.

6 A further allowance is made for other contingencies such as machine malfunction or work interruptions from external sources.

7 The work content plus this contingency allowance gives the standard time for each element and, when totalled, the standard time for the job.

It is possible to speed up the process of timing the elements of a job by using synthetic times derived from past practical experience of timing similar tasks. Experienced work study sections will have usually built up synthetic tables covering recurrent elements found in jobs which are undertaken in their particular field of operation. Synthesis, as this practice is termed, can be defined as a work measurement technique for building up the time for a job, at a defined level of performance, by totalling elemental times obtained either from time studies on other jobs containing the elements or from synthetic tables derived from analysis of accumulated work management data.

Often, work study is introduced as a prelude to the introduction of incentive bonus schemes. With the introduction of such schemes both management and workforce can benefit from the establishment and formal recognition of a standard level of performance, since this can then be used to highlight additional effort, efficiency and productivity.

Work study in local government has a comparatively recent history, having been first introduced in the late 1950s when local authorities began to see the benefits to be derived from the introduction of incentive bonus schemes as a means of stemming a drift of manual labour to private industry. This was coupled with a need to utilise manpower as efficiently as possible in a time of general labour shortage.

In 1963 a conference entitled 'Work Study in Local Government' was organised by the National Joint Council for Local Authorities Services (Manual Workers). At this conference the development of work study as an aid to increased efficiency and productivity was supported by both the employers' and trades unions' side of the NJC. Papers were presented demonstrating the use of work study in the areas of highway maintenance, public cleansing, building, caretaking and cleaning, and in hospital work. An important outcome of the conference was the setting-up of a Local Government Work Study Group as a forum for the discussion of problems and a focus for the dissemination of expertise in the field.

As work study has gained more and more acceptance in local government the range of services to which it has been applied with good effect has widened to include refuse collection, cesspool and gully emptying, street lighting, demolition work, and so on. The Bains study group recommended that each authority should set up a small central unit to control the overall deployment of work study staff and to ensure that new techniques in the area are evaluated and staff trained in their use. Through such a central unit line managers would obtain the services of work study staff for their departments. Such a unit would also be responsible for undertaking any specific projects required by the chief executive or the management team.

OPERATIONAL RESEARCH

Operational Research (OR) has been defined as 'the application of scientific methods, techniques and tools, to problems involving the operations of a system, so as to provide those in control of the system with optimum solutions to the problems' (Churchman, Ackoff and Arnoff, 1957). It developed as an aid to management during the Second World War when the need to adopt scientific, interdisciplinary approaches to various problems of design and decision was most urgent. In terms of specific incident the birth of the technique can be traced to the efforts of Robert Watson-Watt and a small interdisciplinary team, comprising physicists, electricians, mathematicians, statisticians and engineers, to analyse and improve the introduction and operation of prototype radar equipment. It was Watson-Watt who labelled the activities of his team 'Operational Research'. The idea soon crossed the Atlantic and there, under the American title of 'Operations Research' the technique was applied in all branches of the armed forces. By the end of the war there were about one thousand OR scientists serving in the United States and just over two hundred in Britain.

The needs of reconstruction and rationalisation in British industry in the postwar period provided a fruitful field for the application of OR, especially in the new nationalised undertakings in the areas of coal, steel, gas, electricity, road haulage, railways and air transport. The emphasis was on the analysis of problems and systems by teams drawn from a range of disciplines and likely to bring a number of different perspectives and approaches to the search for solutions.

Operational research makes use of a number of analytical and diagnostic techniques and approaches most of which are highly specialised. Some of these techniques are discussed briefly below:

1 Mathematical statistics; used to calculate the probability of certain events occurring in given situations.
2 Linear programming; a mathematical technique useful in production planning and output scheduling, where decisions need to be made involving many interdependent variables. It is essentially a technique to aid the manager in his evaluation of multiple interdependencies, and provides a way of establishing the most effective mix of work and machines. In this way maximum output can be achieved at least cost in terms of time and money.
3 Queuing theory; this technique can be used to predict the functional efficiency of specific operational systems. It can relate the design of a system to the length and frequency of queues, whether these are queues of stocks of materials to be processed or customers waiting to be served. Queuing theory can be used to identify average waiting time, probability of delay, and so on. For example, the technique can provide simple formulae to predict how the average time spent queuing at a

supermarket would vary with the number of checkout counters operated.

4 Stock control; this is perhaps the most familiar application of OR and refers to the need to calculate, as accurately as possible, the size of stocks to be carried. By using this technique management can ensure that no type of stock is ever totally exhausted, thus holding up the entire production process. A certain safety margin of stockholding must be calculated, taking into account the trade off between the cost of tying up working capital in stock and the possible cost of an interruption in production. This minimum stock level is calculated, having due regard to variations in the rate of stock usage and stock delivery.

5 Computer simulation; most of the tools of OR mentioned so far employ fairly advanced mathematical models in the solution of problems. However, some situations may be so complex that they cannot be easily reduced to mathematical terms. For example, it may be very difficult to identify relevant variables and define the relationships which exist between them. Such information is essential if a useful mathematical model of a situation is to be constructed. In such situations computer simulation provides an alternative approach to the development of solutions. Ackoff and Sasieni define simulation in the following terms: 'Models represent reality, simulation imitates it. Simulation always involves the manipulation of a model; it is, in effect, a way of manipulating a model so that it yields a motion picture of reality.' (Ackoff and Sasieni, 1968)

Simulation uses logical models, normally represented by flow charts, in an attempt to copy the dynamics of a real situation. Such models, which are designed to include as much information as possible about a situation, are then transferred on to a computer. Once a model has been assembled and programmed certain hypothetical changes in the model's components can be introduced and the computer will simulate an approximation of how the real system would respond. Such exercises have a wide range of applications. They have been used for predicting the effect on a public transport system of linking buses to a central radio control (as conducted recently by the Leeds University Bus Operations Research Unit) and, on a somewhat larger scale, for predicting the effect on national economic growth and unemployment levels of a given average level of pay award.

The size and complexity of local government operations provides a fruitful field for the application of OR. However, the widespread use of the technique in local authorities has been a comparatively recent development. It was not until 1965 that the Local Government Operational Research Unit (LGORU) was established, under the auspices of the Royal Institute of Public Administration. This unit represents the only independent centre of OR in the country working exclusively for public authorities. The unit was set up to undertake studies by operational research methods to assist local authorities in their policy and management decisions and to co-operate with other research organisations in fields related to local government. In the true OR tradition the unit is staffed by experts from a wide range of disciplines, including mathematics, statistics, computer science, natural and social sciences and engineering. Members of staff specialise in particular areas of local government work, including education, housing, transport planning, vehicle management, social services and refuse collection and disposal.

In the years since the LGORU was established many local authorities have employed their own operational research experts who advise on specific problems. However, the LGORU still fulfils an important need. First, it provides a focal point for accumulated expertise and experience. Advice from the LGORU can help steer authorities away from blind alleys which may have been encountered elsewhere. Secondly, the LGORU can give long-term undivided attention to particularly complex projects. Such concentrated effort may be impossible for OR experts working within individual authorities since they usually have other duties to perform. Thirdly, by operating on a large scale the LGORU can afford to provide sophisticated and expensive support services, such as computing, and spread the cost over a number of projects and a wide range of work. Finally, the very independence of the LGORU brings important benefits. It is non-partisan and is therefore more likely to bring an objective, multi-perspective approach to problems than an internal OR unit, which would be more intimately involved. A detached stance can also aid the search for new and perhaps unconventional solutions. It is easier for an outside body to take the risk of proposing fairly radical and perhaps unpopular innovations.

Recent practical examples of the LGORU's work can be found in almost every area of local government operation. Particularly striking contributions are being made in the areas of transport planning and vehicle fleet management.

A study by the LGORU for the West Yorkshire County Council was recently carried out in Huddersfield during which the unit evolved a bus network that offered cost savings of around £300,000 a year while giving a level of service (measured by such things as passenger waiting and walking times) at least as good as the network then operating. This was accomplished by a series of highly detailed surveys and analyses of existing travel patterns and bus routes in the area. The same approach is being used in other authorities to evaluate a variety of mixed mode public transport schemes, such as park and ride, bus feeder to rail, and so on.

Vehicle management involves a number of related activities such as vehicle maintenance, vehicle purchase, stores control, accounts processing and labour management. However very few local authorities, most of which operate large vehicle fleets, have the kind of systematic reporting procedures necessary for effective transport management. A new study being undertaken by the LGORU aims at the development of more effective fleet management systems for local authorities. The objective is to devise standard procedures that convert data into regular brief reports that the transport manager has time to read and act upon, thus removing reliance on informal processes, partial systems and *ad hoc* investigations.

REFERENCES: APPENDIX

Ackoff, R. L., and Sasieni, M. W., *Fundamentals of Operations Research* (New York: Wiley, 1968).

Addison, M. E., *Essentials of Organisation and Methods* (London: Heinemann, 1971).

Barnetson, P., *Critical Path Planning* (London: Butterworth, 1970).

British Standards Institution, *Terms Used in Work Study and Organisation and Methods (O & M)*, BS 3138 (1969).

Churchman, C. W., Ackoff, R. L., and Arnoff, L. E., *Introduction to Operations Research* (New York: Wiley, 1957).

Currie, R. M., *Work Study* (rev. edn by J. E. Faraday (London: Pitman, 1972).

Gilbreth, F. B. and L. M., *Applied Motion Study* (New York: Sturgis & Walton, 1917).

Hull, J., *et al.*, *Model Building Techniques for Management* (Farnborough: Saxon House, 1976).

Littlechild, S. C. (ed.), *Operational Research for Managers* (Oxford: Philip Allan, 1977).

Randall, P. E., *Introduction to Work Study and Organisation and Methods* (London: Butterworth, 1969).

Ray, K. H., 'Practical experience with critical path analysis in the preparation of annual estimates', *Telescope*, February 1977, pp. 82–4.

Report of the Bradbury Committee, *The Organisation and Staffing of Government Offices*, Cd 62 (London: HMSO, 1919).

Sherman, T. P., *Organisation and Methods in Local Government* (Oxford: Pergamon, 1969).

BIBLIOGRAPHY

Arensberge, C., *Research in Industrial Human Relations* (New York: Harper, 1957).

Argyris, C., *Interpersonal Competence and Organisational Effectiveness* (Homewood, Illinois: Irwon, 1962).

Argyris, C., *Integrating an Individual and the Organisation* (New York: Wiley, 1964).

Argyris, C., 'Today's problems with tomorrow's organisations', *Journal of Management Studies* (February 1967).

Baker, R. J. S., 'Systems theory and local government', *Local Government Studies* (January 1975).

Beckhard, R., *Organisation Development: Strategies and Models* (Reading, Mass.: Addison-Wesley, 1969).

Bennis, W. G., *Organisation Development: Its Nature, Origins and Prospects* (Reading, Mass.: Addison-Wesley, 1969).

Berthalanffy, L., 'The theory of open systems in physics and biology', *Science*, vol. 3 (1950).

Berthalanffy, L., *General Systems Theory* (Harmondsworth: Penguin, 1968).

Blau, P. M., and Scott, W. R., *Formal Organisations – a Comparative Approach* (London: Routledge & Kegan Paul, 1963).

Bosworth, N., *A Revised System of Management and Officer Structure* (Birmingham: Birmingham MDC, October 1976).

Briggs, A., *History of Birmingham*, Vol. 2 (London: OUP, 1952).

Brown, R. G. S., *The Administrative Process in Britain* (London: Methuen, 1971).

Burns, T., and Stalker, G. M., *The Management of Innovation* (London: Tavistock, 1961).

Crichton, A., *Personnel Management in Context* (London: Batsford, 1968).

Crozier, M., *The Bureaucratic Phenomenon* (London: Tavistock, 1964).

Cuming, M. W., *The Theory and Practice of Personnel Management* (London: Heinemann, 1968).

Dror, Y., *Public Policymaking Re-Examined* (New York: Leonard Hill, 1968).

Dunsire, A., *Administration: The Word and the Science* (London: Robertson, 1973).

Emery, F. E., and Trist, E. L., 'The causal texture of organisational environments', *Human Relations*, vol. 18 (1965). Reprinted in F. E. Emery (ed.), *Systems Thinking* (Harmondsworth: Penguin, 1969).

Fayol, H., 'Administration industrielle et generale', *Bulletin de la Société de l'Industrie Minerale* (November 1916). English translation, *General and Industrial Management* (London: Pitman, 1971).

Fowler, A., *Personnel Management in Local Government* (London: Institute of Personnel Management, 1975).

French, W., *The Personnel Management Process* (Boston: Houghton Mifflin, 1970).

Garrett, J., *The Management of Government* (Harmondsworth: Pelican, 1972).

Gerth, H. H., and Wright-Mills, C., *From Max Weber – Essays in Sociology* (London: Routledge & Kegan Paul, 1967).

Greenwood, R., and Stewart, J. D., 'Corporate planning and management organisation', *Local Government Studies* (October 1972).

Greenwood, R. and Stewart, J. D., *Corporate Planning in English Local Government 1967–1972. An Analysis with Readings* (London: Charles Knight, 1974).

Greenwood, R., *et al.*, *The Organisation of Local Authorities in England and Wales: 1967–1975* (Birmingham: University of Birmingham, Institute of Local Government Studies, 1975).

Greenwood, R., *et al.*, *In Pursuit of Corporate Rationality: Organisational Developments in the Post-Reorganisation Period* (Birmingham: University of Birmingham, Institute of Local Government Studies, 1977).

Harrison, R., 'Understanding your organisation's character', *Harvard Business Review* (May–June 1972).

Heclo, H. H., 'The councillor's job', *Public Administration* (Summer 1969).

IMTA, *Programme Budgeting – the Approach* (London: Institute of Municipal Treasurers and Accountants, 1971).

IMTA, *Government and Programme Budgeting* (London: Institute of Municipal Treasurers and Accountants, 1973).

Institute of Personnel Management, in *Personnel Management*, March 1963.

Jones, G. N., *Planned Organisational Change – a Study in Change Dynamics* (London: Routledge & Kegan Paul, 1969).

Kingdon, D. R., *Matrix Organisation – Managing Information Technologies* (London: Tavistock, 1973).

LAMSAC, *A Review of the Theory of Planned Programme Budgeting* (London: Local Authorities Management Services Advisory Committee, 1972).

Lawrence, P. R., and Lorsch, J. W., *Organisation and Environment: Managing Differentiation and Integration* (Boston: Harvard University Press, 1967).

LGTB, *Personnel Management in the New Local Authorities* (London: Local Government Training Board, 1973).

Lindblom, C., 'The science of muddling through', *Public Administration Review* (Spring 1959). Reprinted in R. T. Golembiewski *et al.*, *Public Administration* (Chicago: Rand McNally, 1966).

Lupton, T., *Industrial Behaviour and Personnel Management* (London: Institute of Personnel Management, 1964).

Lyons, T. P., *The Personnel Function in a Changing Environment* (London: Times Management Library, 1971).

Mayo, E., *The Human Problems of an Industrial Civilization* (New York: Macmillan, 1933).

McGregor, D., *The Human Side of Enterprise* (New York: McGraw Hill, 1960).

McKinsey & Co., *A New Management System for the Liverpool Corporation* (London: McKinsey & Co., 1969).

Merton, R. K., 'Bureaucratic structure and personality', in R. Merton et al., *Reader in Bureaucracy* (Glencoe, Illinois: Free Press, 1952).

Mooney, J. D., *The Principles of Organisation* (London: Harper, 1954).

Mouzelis, N. P., *Organisation and Bureaucracy: An Analysis of Modern Theories* (London: Routledge & Kegan Paul, 1967).

Newton, K., *Second City Politics* (London: OUP, 1976).

Olsen, M. E., *The Process of Social Organisation* (London: Holt, Rinehart & Winston, 1970).

Parsons, T., *The Social System* (Glencoe, Illinois: Free Press, 1951).

Parsons, T., *Structure and Process in Modern Societies* (Glencoe, Illinois: Free Press, 1960).

Partin, J., *Current Perspectives in Organisation Development* (Reading, Mass.: Addison-Wesley, 1973).

Ray, K. H., 'Practical experience with critical path analysis in the preparation of annual estimates', *Telescope*, February 1977, pp. 82–4.

Report of the Bains Committee, *The New Local Authorities: Management and Structure* (London: HMSO, 1972).

Report of the Hadow Committee, *Report of the Departmental Committee on the Qualifications, Recruitment, Training and Promotion of Local Government Officers*, Ministry of Health, 1934.

Report of the Mallaby Committee, *The Staffing of Local Government* (London: HMSO, 1967).

Report of the Maud Committee, *The Management of Local Government* (London: HMSO, 1967).

Report of the Plowden Committee, *Children and their Primary Schools* (London: HMSO, 1967).

Report of the Royal Commission on Local Government in England (Chairman, Lord Redcliffe-Maud), Cmnd 4040, 3 Vols (London: HMSO, 1969).

Report of the Seebohm Committee, *Local Authority and Allied Social Services*, Cmnd 3703 (London: HMSO, 1968).

Roethlisberger, F. J., and Dickson, W. J., *Management and the Worker* (Cambridge, Mass.: Harvard University Press, 1939).

Schein, E. H., 'Organizational socialization and the profession of management', *Industrial Management Review*, no. 9 (1968).

Schein, E., *The Planning of Change* (New York: Holt, Rinehart & Winston, 1969).

Self, P., 'Nonsense on stilts: the futility of Roskill', *New Society* (2 July 1970).

Self, P., 'Elected representatives and management in local government', *Public Administration* (August 1971).

Self, P., *Administrative Theories and Politics* (London: Allen & Unwin, 1972).

Simon, H. A., *Administrative Behaviour* (New York: Macmillan, 1957).

Simon, H. A., and March, J. G., *Organisations* (New York: Wiley, 1958).

Simon, H. A., *New Science of Management Decision* (New York: Harper & Row, 1960).

Skitt, J. (ed.), *Practical Corporate Planning in Local Government* (London: Leonard Hill, 1975).

Steiner, G. A., 'The critical role of top management in long range planning', *Arizona Review*, no. 14 (1966).

Stewart, J. D., *Management in Local Government: A Viewpoint* (London: Charles Knight, 1971).

Stewart, J. D., *The Responsive Local Authority* (London: Charles Knight, 1974).

Thompson, V. A., 'Bureaucracy and innovation', *Administrative Science Quarterly*, vol. 10 (June 1965).

Urwick, L. F., *The Elements of Administration* (London: Pitman, 1943).

Urwick, Orr & Partners, in *New Patterns of Local Government Organisation*, INLOGOV Occasional Paper No. 5, Series A (Birmingham: University of Birmingham, Institute of Local Government Studies, 1971).

Warner, W. L., and Low, J. O., *The Social System of the Modern Factory* (New Haven, Conn.: Yale University Press, 1947).

Weber, M., *The Theory of Social and Economic Organisation*, translated by A. M. Henderson and T. Parsons (New York: Free Press, 1947).

Whitehead, A. N., *Process and Reality: An Essay in Cosmology* (London: CUP, 1929).

White Paper, *Local Government in England*, Cmnd 4584 (London: HMSO, 1971).

Whyte, W. F., *Patterns of Industrial Peace* (New York: Harper, 1951).

INDEX

For Product Safety Concerns and Information please contact our EU
representative GPSR@taylorandfrancis.com
Taylor & Francis Verlag GmbH, Kaufingerstraße 24, 80331 München, Germany

www.ingramcontent.com/pod-product-compliance
Lightning Source LLC
Chambersburg PA
CBHW061016280326
41935CB00009B/986